BREAKING THE SIMULATION

AN ANCIENT PATH BACK TO REALITY

W. PETER HOWELL

ISBN 979-8-9930934-0-6

Breaking the Simulation: An Ancient Path Back to Reality

This book is a work of historical, philosophical, and theological reflection intended for educational and inspirational purposes only. While care has been taken with historical sources, the author makes no claims of providing medical, psychological, financial, or legal advice. Readers are encouraged to engage critically and seek professional counsel where appropriate. While this book critiques digital technology, it necessarily exists within these systems to reach the maximum audience possible—an irony acknowledged and explored within the text.

Published by Ariadyne Press Inc.
Colorado Springs, Colorado, USA
ariadyne.com

Paperback Edition ISBN 979-8-9930934-0-6
Library of Congress Control Number: 2025946968

Cover design by Marko Ratko.

Publication Date: March 15, 2026

First Edition: 2026

THE
THRESHOLD

Table of Contents

Waking Up in the Wrong World viii

Part I — Inside The Simulation   1

Chapter 1 — Boot Sequence. 2
Chapter 2 — Eden: Before The Mirror. 13
Chapter 3 — The First Installation 24

Part II — Encoding The Simulation   35

Chapter 4 — The Serpent's Algorithm. 36
Chapter 5 — The Victim Virus 47
Chapter 6 — Babel: The Tower Protocol 57

Part III — Before The Simulation   71

Chapter 7 — Abraham: The First Exit 72
Chapter 8 — Egypt: The Worthlessness Factory. 83
Chapter 9 — The Wilderness: Receiving The Source Code 92
Chapter 10 — The Silence: Heaven Offline 104

Part IV — Beneath The Simulation   113

Chapter 11 — Greece: The New Mind. 114
Chapter 12 — The Anxiety Engine. 123
Chapter 13 — Rome: Terms And Conditions 132
Chapter 14 — Jesus: The System Crash 147

Part V — Within The Simulation   159

Chapter 15 — From Practice To Theology 160
Chapter 16 — The Sacred Machine 172
Chapter 17 — Reason: The New Mediator. 180
Chapter 18 — Velocity: The Economic Engine. 188
Chapter 19 — Debt: The Abstract Chain 196
Chapter 20 — Digital: The Pocket Pharoah .204
Chapter 21 — Artificial: The Borrowed Mind 216

Part VI — Through The Simulation   229

    Chapter 22 — Pattern Recognition.............................230
    Chapter 23 — The Fear Merchants.............................244
    Chapter 24 — Becoming Verb Again 258

Part VII — Beyond The Simulation   269

    Chapter 25 — Maximum Entropy 270
    Chapter 26 — The Profitable Division.........................284
    Chapter 27 — Emergency Override 297

Part VIII — Behind The Simulation   315

    Chapter 28 — What You See Now 316
    Chapter 29 — The Internal Work.............................322
    Chapter 30 — Staying Connected Across Difference.............339
    Chapter 31 — The Rhythm That Holds 350
    Chapter 32 — Practices That Work Alone (And Make You Findable) 357
    Chapter 33 — When Refuge Appears 367

Walking Home 377

Waking Up in the Wrong World

You wake up exhausted from sleep that didn't rest you.

Already behind before the day begins.
Already anxious about things that haven't happened.
Performing for an audience that might not exist.

This is how it starts. Every morning.

And you're not alone in this.
Look around—

We are more connected than any generation—
yet more isolated than ever.

We hold more tools to change our lives—
yet repeat the same cycles.

We have more knowledge than all history—
yet no foundation for wisdom.

These contradictions aren't accidents.

You feel it, don't you?

Like something is off.
Like you're playing a game where everyone knows the rules but you—
and no one admits it's a game.

Like you're performing in a play you never auditioned for,
reading lines you didn't write,
for an audience you can't see.

Everything feels slightly fake.
Slightly hollow.
Slightly wrong.

You can't point to what's wrong—only that something's missing.

Your relationships happen through glass.
Your work produces nothing you can touch.
Your food travels thousands of miles in darkness.
Your entertainment is other people's lives.
Your biggest fears are things that will probably never happen.
Your deepest anxieties are about numbers that have no substance—
scores, stats, balances, likes.

And beneath it all—
that persistent feeling,
like you're forgetting something essential.
Like everyone's pretending and you're the only one who notices.
Like the whole world is sleepwalking
and you're fighting not to join them.

You're not crazy.
You're awake.
Or at least, **starting to wake up.**

The Water You're Swimming In

Every morning you wake into a constructed reality.

Not the world as it is—
but the world as it's been framed for you.

Check your feed—
that's not news, it's narrative engineered for reaction.

Check social media—
that's not connection, it's performance designed to make you feel less.

Check your bank—
that's not wealth, it's numerical existence.

Check your dating apps—
that's not love, it's human shopping.

This false world—
I call it **the simulation.**

It's the interpretive layer between you and experience.
Every framework that explains what things mean.
Every system that tells you how life works.
Every voice that defines who you are and what you're worth.

All preventing direct encounter
with what actually **is.**

The simulation runs on fear.
It converts your uncertainty into lies that feel true:

- You're behind (but there's no race).
- You're insufficient (but there's no standard).
- They're dangerous (but they're also afraid).
- Time is running out (but for what?).

The fear feels real because everyone else is responding as if it is.

But it's just agreed-upon interpretation.
Profitable framing.
Inherited mis-seeing.

The prison isn't in your phone.
It's in how you've been taught to see.

The Ancient Pattern

This false world isn't new.
It's been building for thousands of years,
layer upon layer.

The technology changes.
The pattern doesn't.

Someone creates a false version of reality.
But it only runs if you feed it fear--
fear that drives specific behaviors,
behaviors that enrich its architects.

Pharaoh's Egypt did it with monuments.
Rome did it with spectacle.
The Algorithm does it with engagement.
Different technology. Same extraction.

Every empire has run this code.
Every system has used this pattern.
Right now, it's running through you.

That reach for your phone before your eyes opened?
That wasn't entirely your choice.

That anxiety about falling behind?
Someone authored it.

That fear about what "they" might do?
Someone's feeding on it.

That anger building inside you at the unfairness of it all?
That's not revolution—it's the simulation's end game.
The same pattern that gave you something to fear,
eventually harvests the anger.

But there's another path.

Older than the simulation is **the original code—**
the instructions that predate every empire.
The practices that keep humans **human.**

The Mirror, Not the Trap

One warning before we go further:
This book is a mirror, not a trap.

You can look away anytime.
But once you see the pattern,
you'll recognize it everywhere.

Once opened, this door doesn't close.
Once seen, this can't be unseen.

Still want to see?

Then let me show you the map.

Eight Ways of Seeing the Simulation

This isn't another book telling you to delete your apps,
think positive, or manifest abundance.

This isn't about optimization, transcendence,
or escaping the body.

It's about recognizing ancient patterns in modern clothing—
and finding others who see them too.

Part I: Inside the Simulation
The prison becomes recognizable — the morning anxiety, the performance
pressure, the sense that everyone else got a script that never arrived.

Part II: Encoding the Simulation
The story's installation becomes visible — how fear replicated itself through
family, culture, and education before anyone could speak.

Part III: Before the Simulation
A memory surfaces of what existed before the first lie — when humans knew
things directly, without interpretation, without anxiety, without performance.

Part IV: Beneath the Simulation
The buried layers appear — how Greece, Rome, and every system since built
architecture to hide what's true.

Part V: Within the Simulation
The performance layer becomes visible in real-time — the mask being created,
the image being maintained, the cost of keeping both running.

Part VI: Through the Simulation
The code becomes readable — the merchants recognizable, the patterns
identifiable, the difference between real and performed suddenly obvious.

Part VII: Beyond the Simulation
What happens when the mask cracks and fear has nowhere left to go — the rage, the pipeline, and the off-ramps that exist at every stage.

Part VIII: Behind the Simulation
What was always true comes back into view — the practices, the people, the presence that no system can simulate.

Not to escape reality—
you'll still live here,
pay rent,
deal with the same people.

But to see through the false layer
to what remains true.

To recognize the simulation for what it is:
a profitable story,
not an inevitable one.

Some Have Already Found the Way Out

You've probably met them—

That friend who deleted everything and seems... lighter.
That professor who laughs at what everyone else fears.
That neighbor who has people over every Friday night—actual people, actual food, actual laughter that carries through the walls.

They do know a secret.

And there are more of them than the simulation wants you to know.

They move differently through the world.
Less frantic.
More present.
Like they're not in the same race everyone else is running.

Because they're not.

They've found others—
practicing ancient rhythms in modern ruins,
keeping the thread alive,
walking each other home.

You can join them.
But first you need to see what they see.

What's Coming

Each page is another step out of the simulation
and back into what's real.

Some parts will feel like recognition—
"I knew something was wrong."

Some will feel like revelation—
"That's what's been happening to me."

Some will feel like relief—
"I'm not crazy. I'm not alone."

And some will feel like reckoning—
"I've been participating in my own imprisonment."

All of it is necessary.
All of it leads somewhere.

---

*Truth is what remains
when frameworks fall away.*

And it's been there all along—
waiting beneath the noise,
preserved by those who remember,
available to those who seek.

Ready?

Turn the page.

You're already further than most.

The exit has always been here.
Now you'll finally see it.

PART I
Inside The Simulation

Recognition:
The Prison Becomes Visible

Fear built the walls.
Not steel. Not stone. Framework.
The anxiety you wake up with is not
personal failure—it is the operating
system doing exactly what it was
designed to do.

Chapter 1

BOOT SEQUENCE

How the System Wakes Before You Do

LIGHT HUMS THROUGH glass.
The hand finds the phone before consciousness fully arrives.

The Morning Download

Still half-dreaming, the thumb already knows the pattern.
Email. News. Social. Messages. Weather. Email again.

The same loop performed thousands of mornings, checking for something unnamed.
The not-checking creates that specific chest-tightness, that particular breathing shallowness documented across millions of morning reports.

Before feet hit the floor, today's simulation has already booted up.
Not reality—but a constructed version of it.
Not events—but selected interpretations.
Not the world as it is—but as someone needs it to be seen.

The simulation doesn't download into your phone.
Your phone downloads you into the simulation.

The Day's Programming

"BREAKING: New Development You Should Know About"
"URGENT: Why This Matters Now"
"TRENDING: What Everyone's Talking About"

Each headline precisely engineered.
The words chosen by someone who understands exactly how attention works.
"Breaking" stops the scroll.
"Urgent" demands the click.
"Trending" ensures engagement.

Among infinite possible stories, these were selected for morning attention.
Not just reporting reality—constructing today's version of it.

The billboard promises "You deserve more."
The commuter's eyes scan, process, and move on.
Somewhere between retina and consciousness, a small dissatisfaction installs itself.
Not a lie — a frame.
Not false — just tilted toward a predetermined choice.

Stage 1: Afraid. The insufficiency registers before consciousness names it. Behind already. Missing something. Everyone else ahead.

The Social Simulation

The friend who posted from the gym.
Another announcement from that couple.
Someone's child did something remarkable.
A former colleague sharing good news.

These aren't false.
They're curated selections from infinite possible moments — the best angles of real lives.
But the nervous system doesn't process them as highlights;
it receives them as everyone else's every day.

Everyone else's highlight reel becomes your baseline.
Their performance becomes your reality.

Installation sequence begins:

- Comparison baseline established.
- Insufficiency detected.
- Urgency generated.
- Reaction harvested.

Time elapsed: 6 minutes.

The simulation installs today's parameters:
Behind. Late. Missing something essential that everyone else has figured out.

Stage 2: Vulnerable. The fear opens something. A gap where worth should be. The scrolling accelerates, searching for evidence of adequacy. Each image confirms the opposite. The vulnerability deepens—raw, unnamed, desperate for covering.

The Commute Programming

The podcast explains everything.
The audiobook has the answers.
The YouTube expert knows the secret.
They're all sharing something—wrapped in a particular frame of reality.

The world is changing (be afraid or excited).
Your generation faces unique challenges (special, doomed, or to blame).
This one approach changes everything (but first, accept the solution).

The simulation runs everywhere.

Every surface speaks.
Some messages inform.
Some inspire.
All create needs that didn't exist five seconds ago.

"Don't wait"—for what becomes irrelevant.
"Be your best self"—implying insufficiency of the current self.

The pattern reveals itself in repetition.
Same message, different fonts.

Same fear, different products.
Same insufficiency, different solutions.

The simulation isn't fake. It's edited.
Not completely false. Distorted.
Not conspiracy. Pattern.

The Workday Simulation

"How was your weekend?"
"Great! Really productive. You?"
"Good! So needed."

Both parties run identical code— the acceptable response, the approved character.
The real weekend—its actual texture of anxiety, emptiness, small joys—remains outside the simulation's parameters.

Stage 3: Masked. The curated self takes over. Smile at the right moments. Nod at appropriate intervals. Project confidence that doesn't exist. Everyone performing the character the simulation demands.

Everyone reading from similar scripts.
Not because anyone's forcing them, but because the vulnerability can't bear exposure.

The simulation runs on performed normalcy.
Everyone acting fine ensures no one is.

Lunch brings another wave of simulation updates.
Market movements. Political developments. Cultural discussions. Global events.
Each story processed through particular filters, emphasized certain ways, connected to specific concerns.

An event becomes:

- Catastrophe or correction.
- Victory or defeat.
- Beginning or end.
- Proof of opposite theories.

Depending on which simulation layer gets accessed.
The event itself—whatever actually occurred—disappears beneath interpretations.
Reality becomes what the loudest voice declares it to be.

The depletion accumulates through the day.
Each performance drains reserves.
Each comparison depletes worth.
Each update adds weight.

You were never meant to carry this alone—but the simulation ensures you do.

The Evening Loop

Home, but not present.
Back in the simulation.
The scroll resumes.

Everyone's evening looks intentional. Productive. Peaceful. Perfect.
The mind knows about curation. Understands filters. Recognizes performance.
But the simulation has installed something deeper—the feeling that everyone else has access to better code.

The apartment across the street glows with designer lighting.
A staged living room, visible through floor-to-ceiling windows.
Furniture that costs more than most annual salaries.
The space looks like a magazine spread for lives no one actually lives.

Maybe they're drowning in debt for that view.
Maybe they eat instant noodles to afford the rent.
Maybe the beautiful emptiness is exactly that—empty.
Maybe everyone's performing prosperity for everyone else.

Everyone performing ensures no one is living.

Even entertainment is simulation—
teaching what's normal, what's possible, what's acceptable.

Every show installing subtle updates about how reality works,
how relationships function,
what success looks like.

All shaping how experience gets processed,
how life gets interpreted,
how reality gets constructed.

The exhaustion isn't just physical.
It's the weight of maintaining the mask.
The cost of performed adequacy.
The price of pretending to be fine.

The Recognition

Somewhere in the cycle, maybe in that quiet moment before sleep, something
becomes clear:

This isn't living in reality.
This is living in a simulation of reality.

Layers of interpretation, frames of reference, selected perspectives—
all constructing a version of the world that feels real because everyone else
treats it as real.

This isn't conspiracy.
It's simpler:
Reality is too vast for direct experience.
So humans create compressed versions, simplified models, filtered selections.

These become the simulation—
the interpretation layer that stands between consciousness and direct
experience.

The prison has no walls because you are the walls.

Fear requires the simulation's framework.
Without the frame, fear has nowhere to live.

But once you see how it works, something else becomes possible.
Not immediate escape—but growing recognition.

The ability to see the mechanism—
this progression of afraid, vulnerable, masked that runs through everything.
The ability to notice its progression through your nervous system.
The ability to catch yourself between stages.

The Results Check

After a day in the simulation, the outcomes become measurable:

- More capable or more dependent?
- More connected or more isolated?
- More clear or more confused?
- More energized or more drained?
- More authentic or more performed?

The simulation always extracts more than it gives.
That's how it sustains itself—
through human depletion that feels like participation.

The depletion accumulates.
The insufficiency compounds.
The performance exhausts.
Until the mask fails—
as it always does.

When the mask fails, a choice point arrives.

One path: find refuge outside the simulation—others who see, practices that hold, truth that doesn't require performance.

The other path: return to masking. Find a different character to perform. Cover the vulnerability again. Let the fear and vulnerability fester beneath new pretense.

Each time the mask fails, the opportunity repeats.
Each time you return to masking, the wound deepens.

Eventually, if no refuge is found—if the cycle repeats enough times—the human breaks.
Not the mask.
The person beneath it.

When humans break—when all hope of resolution is lost—the simulation offers solutions that ensure you never leave: medication without community, distraction without resolution, numbing without healing.

But every mask failure is an invitation.
A chance to stop performing.
A chance to seek what's real.
A chance to find others carrying the same unbearable weight.

The Architects

Who builds these simulation layers?
Anyone with something to gain from reactions:

Those who need:

- Attention for revenue.
- Data for prediction.
- Engagement for growth.
- Purchase for profit.
- Compliance for control.

Your loneliness has shareholders.
Your anxiety has architects.
Your insufficiency has investors.

The simulation runs through everyone—including those trying to help.
No one stands outside it completely.
Everyone participates, consciously or not.

But some are learning to see it.
Some are finding each other.
Some are remembering what came before the simulation.
Some are practicing what remains true beneath it.

The Choice Point

Right now, reading this, a choice presents itself.

Dismiss this as overthinking.
Return to the simulation without question.
Accept its parameters as reality.
Hope the anxiety it generates will somehow resolve.

Or begin to notice.
Watch the pattern run through your morning.
Feel the stages progress through your body.
Afraid when the news loads.
Vulnerable when the comparison hits.
Masked when the performance begins.

The simulation isn't technology or media—those are just delivery systems.
The simulation is accepting constructed reality as unconstructed reality.
Mistaking someone's version for the only version.

Tomorrow, The Simulation Continues

The simulation continues either way.

But once you see the pattern, you can't unsee it.
Once you spot the frame, the edges become visible.
Once you feel the stages, you notice them in others.

Tomorrow morning, the hand will still reach for the phone.
The simulation will still boot up.
But something will be different:

That moment between afraid and vulnerable—you'll notice it.
That shift from vulnerable to masked—you'll feel it happen.
That exhaustion from maintaining performance—you'll recognize its source.

And in that recognition—that tiny gap between simulation and reality—lives
possibility.
Not instant freedom, but growing awareness.
The ability to see its parameters.

To notice its effects.
To choose more consciously which interpretations to accept.

Some depend on the simulation for survival—
for work, for connection, for managing impossible circumstances.
The goal isn't to drop everything immediately.
It's to clearly see what's happening.

Recognition is the first medicine.

When the morning download begins,
when the frames start installing themselves,
a different question might arise:

Not "How do I escape?"
But "Who else sees this?"

Not "How do I win?"
But "Who can I walk with?"

Not "How do I become sufficient?"
But "Who told me I wasn't?"

The first path leads deeper into anxiety, comparison, performance.
The second leads to something else—not escape, but companionship.

The simulation doesn't imprison you.
It convinces you that walls mean safety—
that dependence is weakness,
that vulnerability must be hidden.

So the walls go up.
Not because you're broken,
but because the lie made finitude feel like failure.

But the walls were never the problem.
They become prisons when they stay sealed.

When you remember you built the walls,

you remember you can cut openings.
You can make doors.

And when enough people make doors,
walls become homes you can invite others into.
Prisons become gathering places.

Simulations become stories.
And stories can be rewritten.

That's the paradox. And the possibility.

Not individual escape—but collective recognition.
Not personal optimization—but shared awakening.
Not better performance—but dropped masks.

The simulation fears:

- Humans remembering they need each other.
- Humans discovering they're all afraid.
- Humans realizing they're all performing.
- Humans finding each other beneath their masks.

Tomorrow, the pattern runs again.
But now you know the stages.
Now you can watch them progress.
Now you can recognize others caught in the same cycle.
Now you can remember what the simulation makes you forget:

No one was meant to carry this alone.
Everyone is performing the same exhausting show.
Behind every mask is another human, afraid and tired.

Some patterns only end one way. Unless they're interrupted.

The exit isn't up or out.
It's through—together.

Chapter 2

EDEN: BEFORE THE MIRROR

When Seeing Was Still Being

IMAGINE EXPERIENCING REALITY without interpretation.
Morning arrives.
Not anxiety about the day, but day itself.
Light comes—not as an alarm that declares time is passing, but as daylight.
Birds sing—not as a soundtrack driving productivity, but as melody.
Hunger rises—not as a scheduled interruption, but as the body saying *"food would be good now."*

No layer between consciousness and what is.
No framework explaining what things mean.
No commentary track running over direct experience.
Just the thing itself, met directly, known immediately.

This was **Eden**—
reality before the simulation,
before mediation,
before anyone figured out how to insert interpretation between humans and their actual lives.

Before the sale, there was no one selling.
Before the frame, nothing needed framing

The Infrastructure of Direct Knowing

Eden wasn't paradise because nothing bad happened.
It was paradise because nothing stood between consciousness and reality.
No interpretive layer.
No explanatory framework.
No one selling their version of what experience means.

Consider what this made possible:

The Creator Without Mediation

They walked with God in the cool of the evening.
Not metaphorically — actually.
The Creator of reality was as present as trees,
as tangible as earth,
as directly encountered as any other aspect of existence.

No priest interpreting God's words.
No prophet explaining God's will.
No system claiming exclusive access.
No expert mediating divine intention.

Just direct encounter.
God spoke; they heard.
They spoke; God heard.
Simple as breathing.

The modern believer processes God through layers—
what the preacher said about what the commentary said
about what the translation said about what the prophet said God said.
Each layer adding interpretation, possibility for error, opportunity for control.

But in the garden, God's voice needed no translation.
Like recognizing your mother's voice in darkness—immediate, unmistakable, unmediated.

When you know the Author directly,
you don't need interpreters.

Work Without Meaning-Making

They were placed in the garden to tend and keep it.
Not to "find their purpose" or "manifest their destiny."
The work was obvious—this tree needs pruning, that soil needs water.
The work was its own meaning.

No career anxiety.
No ladder to climb.
No success to achieve.
They didn't "have jobs"—they worked.
They weren't "gardeners"—they gardened.
Verbs, not nouns. Direct action, not interpreted identity.

The morning's work revealed itself:
stems bent under fruit weight, soil cracked from heat, new growth tangling old.
Response arose naturally.
Hands moved to support, water, untangle.
No decision.
No evaluation.
Just obvious response to visible need.

The modern simulation requires layers of meaning on top of work.
What does your job say about you?
Where does it rank?
What does it lead to?

But in Eden, work was just work — direct participation in ongoing creation.
No interpretation needed.

They didn't work to become.
They worked because work needed doing.

Bodies Without Commentary

They were naked and felt no shame.
Not because they had "body positivity" or "self-acceptance."

Those concepts require first having body negativity, self-rejection—problems that didn't exist.

Bodies just moved through the garden.
Skin registered sun, shade, breeze.
Muscles engaged with soil, branches, water.
No mirror to check appearance.
No standard to measure against.
No audience to generate performance for.

A modern human spends seventeen minutes examining reflection, adjusting, comparing to impossible standards.
But they had no reflection except in still water—fleeting, functional, forgotten.

Shame requires an audience.
Without an audience, there's just skin.

Relationship Without Definition

"This is now bone of my bones and flesh of my flesh."

Not "this is my wife" (noun).
Not "we are married" (state).

Just recognition—this one is like me, from me, with me.
Direct knowing without categorization.

They moved through the garden together the way rivers flow—
sometimes converging, sometimes parallel, always part of the same watershed.

No discussion of "relationship status."
No negotiation of boundaries.
No working on their connection.

Modern couples spend hours defining what they are, processing what they mean, analyzing their dynamic.
But they just were. Together.

Simple as two trees growing near each other, roots naturally intertwining, no contract needed.

Before relationship was a category,
there was just relating.

The Absence of Framework

Without simulation, entire categories of modern anxiety couldn't exist.

No Success / Failure Binary
The trees either bore fruit or didn't.
But this wasn't success or failure—just what happened.
Some seeds grew, others didn't.
Not victory or defeat—just gardening.
No framework overlaying meaning onto simple outcomes.

A tree that didn't fruit wasn't "failing."
It was young, or resting, or dying back to make room.
Each state equally real, equally acceptable, equally part of garden's rhythm.

No Time Anxiety
Day followed night.
Seasons changed.
But no clock counted productivity.
No calendar created deadlines.
No age brought crisis.

Time passed but didn't threaten.
It simply was—like air or light—a medium moved through, not interpreted against.

They knew time by shadow length, stomach emptiness, air temperature.
Body time. Garden time. Not mechanical time that cuts reality into anxiety-producing segments.

Without clocks, time doesn't threaten.
It just passes.

No Identity Performance
Ask them "who are you?" and they couldn't answer in modern terms.
No titles, no roles, no brands, no profiles.
They would have to answer with actions—"I tend this garden. I walk with God."

All verbs. All direct. No identity layer to maintain.

The modern human maintains about seven different versions of self—professional, social, family, public, private, online, offline.

They maintained none.
They just were.

No Comparison Framework
They were the only humans.
No one else's garden to envy.
No one else's relationship to judge.
No one else's work to feel insufficient about.

Comparison requires alternatives viewed through evaluative framework.
They had neither alternatives nor framework.

Comparison requires others.
Without others, there's just being.

Why Fear Couldn't Take Root

Fear needs framework.
It needs interpretation.
It needs simulation.

To fear losing something, you must first interpret it as possessable.
But they didn't "have" the garden—they were in it.
They didn't "own" anything—they used things.
They didn't "possess" each other—they were with each other.

To fear death, you must first have framework for ending.
But nothing in their experience had ended.
Everything cycled—day to night to day, season to season, seed to tree to seed.

Death wasn't in their interpretive framework because death wasn't in their experience.

Without the lens that converts uncertainty into fear,
there was only response to what is.

Pain, yes—thorns still pricked.
Caution, yes—cliffs still dropped.
But not chronic dread.
Not imagined catastrophe.
Not fear of what might happen.

In Eden, terror had no foothold.
Not because nothing could harm,
but because nothing stood between reality and response.

The Pure Verb State

They lived as pure verbs:

- Not "I am hungry" but feeling hungry.
- Not "I am working" but work happens.
- Not "I am happy" but joy happens.
- Not "I am afraid" but... no fear at all.

Fear required framework they didn't have.

Modern language forces noun-state: "I am an anxious person."
As if anxiety is identity rather than weather passing through consciousness.
They had no such construction.
Everything was movement, action, happening.

Nouns trap. Verbs flow.
They flowed.

The Last Day of Direct Reality

Picture the last morning before the simulation booted up.

Eyes open to a brightening sky.
No thought about what day means, what needs accomplishing, or what others are doing.
Just light arriving, consciousness rising to meet it.

Body rises because sleeping is complete, not because schedule demands it.
Feet find earth still cool from the night.
Skin registers air movement.
Stomach notes emptiness.
Simple data — no interpretation.

Movement toward fruit trees happens naturally, like water finding lowest ground.
Fruit gets picked, eaten.
Sweetness happens.
Satisfaction happens.

Work reveals itself through garden's need:
Wilted leaves say "water here."
Tangled growth says "untangle here."
Heavy branches say "support here."

Response arises without decision.
Hands move to meet need.

God arrives for evening walk.
Not appointment. Not obligation.
Just the rhythm they've always known.
Conversation without agenda.
Presence without interpretation.
Questions without hidden meanings.

Night comes. Sleep comes.
No processing the day — because the day needs no processing.
No planning for tomorrow — because tomorrow needs no planning.
Just consciousness releasing into rest, trusting rhythm to continue.

This is **reality without simulation** — direct, immediate, uninterpreted.

No layer between experience and experiencer.
No framework making meaning.
No shame about being finite, so no fear.

What Makes This Paradise Vulnerable

For simulation to install, certain conditions must arise:

Distance from Source
As long as God walks with them daily,
no one else can interpret God's words.
Direct encounter needs no mediation.
But if that direct connection were questioned...

Doubt About Reality
Direct experience is self-validating.
But doubt—just a sliver—makes interpretation seem necessary.
And whoever provides the interpretation controls the reality.

Comparison Standard
Without something to measure against, evaluation is impossible.
But introduce an ideal, a standard, a "you could be more"—
and suddenly what is becomes insufficient.

The Paradise That Remains

This is what existed before frameworks:

- Morning without anxiety.
- Work without identity.
- Bodies without shame.
- Time without threat.
- Relationship without definition.
- God without mediation.

Not perfection—just reality encountered directly.
Not absence of challenge—just absence of interpretation.
Not eternal ease—just present presence.

The garden remains.
Not lost—just buried.
Not destroyed—just covered.
Layer by layer by layer of interpretation.

Every human since has been born into layers of simulation—inheriting frameworks, living in interpretation, experiencing reality through someone else's lens.

Searching for something they can't name:
Direct experience.
Immediate knowing.
The presence that was there before the first framework.

Simpler than language can hold: it's just real meeting real.

No layer between.
No one selling anything.
No fear that won't resolve.

Tomorrow, everything changes.
A question will be asked that creates distance between knower and known.
A lie will be offered that reframes finitude as failure—then sells the fix.
A doubt will be planted that makes interpretation seem necessary.

But tonight, pause.
Before you learn how the simulation started,
remember what existed before it:

Direct knowing.
Immediate presence.
Reality without seller.

It's still there.
Under everything.
Waiting.

Not in the past—that's just a story.
But right now.
Under the frameworks.
Beneath the fear.

Behind the sale.

Real.
Direct.
Here.

Chapter 3

THE FIRST INSTALLATION

How Framework Replaced Reality

THE SERPENT WAS already coiled around the forbidden tree when they arrived.

Not invading—dwelling.

Not trespassing—belonging.

Scripture calls it *arum*—shrewd, crafty, able to see angles others miss.

Not necessarily evil.

Just operating from different code.

Like the algorithm that knows which ad will make you click.

Like the voice that finds the gap in every confidence.

It understood something crucial:

You can't create fear where finitude is accepted as part of design.

But you can reframe limitation as deprivation.

You can turn boundaries into grievances.

You can make "I cannot" feel like "I am being denied."

The serpent didn't find someone broken.

It found someone contemplating their limitations—

and convinced her that this was a problem to be solved.

The serpent didn't sell fruit.
It sold framework.

The Target Assessment

In Eden, experience was direct.
Sensation passed through consciousness like weather—arising, felt, gone.

Hunger was just hunger—not I might starve.
Tiredness was just tiredness—not I'm falling behind.

No fear—because fear requires a story.
And in a garden of infinite yes, there was only one no.
Not prohibition as punishment,
but boundary as invitation.

Then came the first fracture.

Eve approached the tree alone.
Adam elsewhere, tending the garden.
No shared perception. No confirmation.

She stood before the only boundary in abundance—
and the mind began to reach.

Why this tree? Why this limit? Why would God withhold this?

Boundaries create curiosity.
Restriction implies importance.
The forbidden suggests the valuable.

The serpent recognized the moment:
She wasn't just seeing the tree anymore—
she was thinking about the tree.

The gap between experience and interpretation had opened.
Once story begins, fear, desire, and doubt have somewhere to live.

Target acquired.

Installing the False Frame

---

*"Did God really say you shall not eat from
any tree in the garden?"*

The serpent knew what God had said.
Accuracy wasn't the point—installation was.

First: exaggeration, to force correction.
By overstating, it made Eve articulate the rule herself,
focusing on lack instead of abundance.

Eve answered:
*"We may eat fruit from the trees in the garden,
but God did say, 'You must not eat from the tree in the middle,
and you must not touch it, or you will die.'"*

She added what God never said—don't touch.
The simulation was already working.

Then came contradiction: *"You will **not** surely die."*

The serpent wasn't selling fruit—
it was installing a framework where God couldn't be trusted,
while offering a solution to perceived limitation.

The Fear Behind the Framework

*"For God knows that when you eat it your eyes will be opened,
and you will be like gods, knowing good and evil."*

The message beneath the words:

- God is withholding.
- You are incomplete.
- You're being controlled.
- Reality has hidden layers.

The deepest reframe:
Your natural limitation isn't design—it's deprivation.

Your dependence isn't invitation—it's deficiency.
What if the God who walks with you is threatened by you?

If you can't trust the Author of reality,
how can you trust reality itself?

*The serpent didn't create doubt about a rule.
It created doubt about reality itself.*

And with that doubt came fear—
not from nothing,
but from her natural uncertainty now reframed as shameful lack.

The Vulnerability Creation

Before the serpent's framework:

- Complete — finite, dependent, bounded.
- Sufficient — every tree but one.
- Trusting — God walks with us.

After the installation:

- Incomplete — eyes not yet open.
- Lacking — missing knowledge.
- Suspicious — Creator hides truth.

The vulnerability was always real—
humans are finite by design.
What the serpent generated was the shame about it,
and the lie that eating would resolve it.

But once that shame is installed, it feels more real than reality.

Every simulation works this way:
Exploit existing uncertainty →
Reframe it as shameful insufficiency →
Use the shame as proof the framework is true →
Offer the framework's solution as cure.

The Action Compulsion

"When the woman saw that the fruit of the tree was good for food and pleasing to the eyes, and also desirable for gaining wisdom, she took some and ate it."

But she was seeing through the serpent's framework now.
The tree hadn't changed.
Her eyes were interpreting through newly installed lenses.

She took.
She ate.
She gave to Adam.
He ate.

No recorded discussion.
The framework was that compelling.

The New False Reality

"Then the eyes of both of them were opened, and they realized they were naked;"

Their eyes opened not to godhood but to frameworks of evaluation.

The serpent promised resolution—"you will be like gods."
But the fear didn't resolve.
It multiplied.

Now they feared God.
Feared each other's gaze.
Feared their own bodies.

The false certainty had failed—
and left them more afraid than before.

Nakedness wasn't new—the framework that made nakedness shameful was.

The transformation from verb to noun:

- Before: They simply WERE.
- After: They were NAKED (category).
- After: They were AFRAID (state).
- After: They were HIDDEN (position).

They sewed fig leaves—the first masks.
Not because bodies had become shameful,
but because the framework made them see bodies as shameful.

God's Response

"Where are you?"
Not location—recognition.
Where has the framework taken you?

"I heard you in the garden and I was afraid because I was naked; so I hid."

There it is—the complete simulation installed:

Afraid → natural uncertainty reframed as shameful lack.
Naked → the shame exposes wounds.
Hidden → fig leaves cover what now feels unbearable.

The pattern installed:
Natural uncertainty encounters false frame.
False frame converts uncertainty into fear.
Fear exposes vulnerability.
Vulnerability demands performance.
Performance exhausts.
And the exhausted mind reaches for the nearest framework.
The cycle feeds itself.

The Cascade Effect

"Who told you that you were naked?"

God's question cuts through everything.
Who installed this framework?

Who made you see through these categories?
Who taught you to interpret rather than experience?

Adam: *"The woman you put here with me—she gave me fruit from the tree, and I ate it."*
Not just blaming Eve — blaming God for creating Eve.

Eve: *"The serpent deceived me, and I ate."*
True, but incomplete.
She accepted the framework.

The simulation makes everyone else the enemy.

Isolation ensures the narrative's continuation.
Because once trust dies, verification dies.
And when no one trusts, conspiracy reigns.

That's where we live now.

Truth fragments into tribes.
Every voice becomes its own authority.
Every algorithm its own prophet.

*When everyone becomes their own source,
no one can find the Source.*

The Medicine in the Expulsion

God's response looked like punishment but was actually prescription.

"By the sweat of your brow you will eat your bread."

This wasn't cruelty—it was mercy.

Inside Eden with the framework running,
they had infinite time to dwell on what they'd lost.
No urgency to move from thought to action.
No necessity to pull from interpretation to participation.

An idle mind dwells on the framework's lies:
What you don't have, who has more, how you've failed, why you're not enough.

But a mind engaged in necessary work has no space for the serpent's whispers.
When your hands are in soil, when sweat stings your eyes—
the framework can't run. You're too present. Too real.

The simulation thrives on abstraction.
Work demands presence.

God knew: Better to struggle with real thorns than to rot in interpreted paradise.

"Cursed is the ground because of you."

The ground's resistance wasn't punishment—it was occupation.
Something real to push against.

When you're fighting thorns, you're not thinking about being "like gods."
When exhausted from labor, you sleep without the framework's commentary.

Physical necessity interrupts philosophical anxiety.
Survival silences simulation.

This is why "an idle mind is the devil's playground" rings true.
Not because rest is evil,
but because unoccupied consciousness fills itself with the framework's narratives.

The Permanent Installation

Once installed, the simulation becomes self-validating.

Now that they saw themselves as naked—they were naked categorically.
The framework created the reality it described.
The simulation became true by being believed.

They couldn't unsee their nakedness.
Couldn't unfear the presence.
Couldn't unhide from the categories.

The simulation doesn't imprison you.
It convinces you to imprison yourself.

What the Serpent Achieved

With one conversation, the serpent had:

- Transformed verbs into nouns.
- Replaced direct experience with mediated framework.
- Showed how to fill uncertainty with fear-generating stories.
- Converted natural finitude into extractable anxiety.
- Installed a permanent loop.
- Established an economy of insufficiency.
- Made humans marketable to fear.

The serpent discovered:

You don't need to change reality if you can change how uncertainty is interpreted. You don't need actual danger if you can fill the contemplative gap with threatening narratives. You don't need real insufficiency if the story makes finitude feel unbearable.

The Recognition

Right now, inherited frameworks operate between consciousness and direct experience —
layers of interpretation converting natural uncertainty into manufactured fear.

"You're behind" (but behind on what?)
"You're failing" (but at whose game?)
"You're not enough" (but by whose measure?)

These aren't observations—they're installations.

*Fear doesn't rise from facts—
it rises from the story attached to facts.*

The serpent still speaks:

- "Are you sure you're seeing clearly?"
- "Shouldn't you be further along by now?"
- "What are you missing?"

Every notification is the tree.
Every ad is the serpent.
Every voice that reframes your finitude as failure is installing framework.

Tomorrow's Acceleration

Tomorrow, the simulation learns to replicate itself.
What began as doubt in a garden becomes architecture for civilizations.

But tonight, notice your frameworks.
Notice interpretation versus experience.
Notice stories attached to facts versus facts themselves.

The cure was always hidden in what looked like curse:
Sweat defeats speculation.
Soil silences simulation.
Necessary work quiets unnecessary fear.

The serpent thrives in abstraction.
Reality lives in dirt under fingernails.

Tomorrow, the simulation accelerates—
training its citizens in the serpent's method.
But tonight, before the next installation,
your hands remember what your head forgot.

Dirt doesn't lie.
Sweat doesn't simulate.
And the body still knows the way back.

PART II

Encoding The Simulation

Genesis: How Fear Learned to Replicate

Fear didn't begin with you. It migrated—from body to story to system. You were born into the middle of transmission. Not your fault. But now in your hands.

Chapter 4

THE SERPENT'S ALGORITHM

The Pattern That Rewrites Reality

THE SERPENT DIDN'T just deceive once.
It demonstrated a method—
a reproducible formula for making humans participate in their own imprisonment.

Every empire since has been the serpent's student:
perfecting the technique, accelerating the delivery,
but never changing the fundamental code.

The method works because it doesn't attack—it recruits.
Doesn't imprison—it conditions.
Doesn't force—it exhausts into compliance.

Watch how it works.
Not in ancient gardens but in this morning's feed.
Not through talking snakes but through glowing screens.
The tongue is different.
The technique is identical.

The Disconnection Protocol

The simulation's primary requirement: participants must react, not evaluate.

Critical thought introduces fatal latency—
the moment of testing between stimulus and response.
The moment where someone might weigh a claim against known reality:
"Wait, who benefits from my fear?"
The moment where evidence challenges the desired conclusion.
The moment that could break the entire program.

So the method eliminates evaluation.

Before the notification arrives, the nervous system is already primed.
Yesterday's scroll set today's baseline anxiety.
Last night's news created this morning's ambient dread.
The body carries fear it can't name,
ready to react to whatever framework explains the feeling.

Then the headline appears:
"BREAKING: New Threat You Should Fear"

No evaluation, just immediate response.
The prepared nervous system floods with recognition:
"Yes, this explains what I was already feeling."

The framework doesn't create fear—
it finds the uncertainty already running, gives it shape, points it at targets.

The genius isn't making people afraid.
It's keeping them uncertain,
then offering fear that feels like an answer.
And an answer — even a terrifying one —
feels better than not knowing.

Journalists must be free to follow evidence rather than support desired conclusions.
Citizens must be capable of testing claims against experience.
But the simulation ensures neither happens—

by keeping everyone too reactive to evaluate,
too exhausted to compare,
too overwhelmed to test.

Strategic Exhaustion

A mind inside the simulation isn't stupid—it's busy.
Overwhelmed with information.
Drowning in urgency.
Responding to notifications.
Processing contradictions.
Managing performances.

Every input demands response.
Every story requires position.
Every post needs reaction.

The mind that might have tested claims is too tired to think.
The attention that might have compared narratives to reality is scattered across
a hundred small emergencies.

This isn't accidental.
Exhaustion is the goal.

An exhausted mind can't evaluate frameworks,
can't test narratives against experience,
Can't compare stories to known facts,
can't ask who profits.
It can only react to what's presented—
following the path of least resistance,
which the simulation has carefully prepared.

When everything is urgent, nothing is examined.
When every headline is breaking, no pattern is tested.
When every question is dangerous, no evidence surfaces.

The result isn't ignorance but strategic depletion—
minds too tired to evaluate, too overwhelmed to compare, too busy to test.

From Thinking to Echoing

The exhausted mind stops evaluating claims.
It begins transmitting pre-approved packets—outrage, fear, approval—
but not analysis. Not questions. Not comparison to reality.

Watch the transformation:

Week 1-4: Reality Questioning
The installation begins with doubt about what you've always known.
"Everything you've been told is a lie."
"You're one of the few who can see."
"Wake up before it's too late."

This phase creates special status through paranoia—
the dopamine hit of special knowledge mixed with the cortisol spike of urgent
threat.

Week 5-8: Pattern Provision
Once reality is questioned, alternative patterns are provided.
"Here's what's really happening."
"Connect these dots."
"This explains everything."

Complex reality becomes simple conspiracy.
Overwhelming uncertainty becomes clear pattern.
The exhausted mind embraces the relief of explanation,
over the discomfort of testing claims against evidence.

Week 9-12: Identity Formation
Once patterns are accepted, identity crystallizes around them.
"You're part of something bigger."
"We see what others don't."
"You're the resistance."

The isolated finds belonging through opposition.
Meaningless suffering gains purpose through struggle.
Worthlessness becomes chosenness.

Evaluation becomes echoing.
The participant transmits the simulation's signals,
defending frameworks that imprison them,
recruiting others into the same conditioning.

The Psychology of Comforting Certainty

Critical thought is uncomfortable.
It demands living in tension, holding paradoxes, testing claims against incomplete evidence.
It requires comparison, evaluation, the admission of partial ignorance.

The simulation removes that discomfort
by offering ready-made worldviews with heroes, villains, and scripts.
Every complex issue becomes simple binary.
Every nuanced situation becomes clear choice.
Every difficult question has an obvious answer—
no testing required.

Thinking critically makes you lonely.
You can't echo with the group.
Echoing passionately makes you belong.
You're synchronized with others.

Most choose belonging over accuracy.
Choose certainty over truth.
Choose the simulation's comfort over reality's complexity.

This is why ideological movements, regardless of content, are fragile.
Their unity depends not on reasoned agreement
but on synchronized outrage.

The moment someone stops to evaluate a claim,
to test it against known evidence,
to compare it with direct experience—
they threaten the entire synchronization.

The simulation doesn't fear disagreement.
It fears the moment before agreement—
the moment of evaluation.

Historical Repetition

In Eden, the serpent's method was personal—one conversation, one installation.
But the method proved scalable.

Egypt industrialized it:
massive architecture declaring Pharaoh's divinity,
daily rituals reinforcing servitude,
exhaustion through labor preventing evaluation.

Babylon unified it:
one language, one tower, one story reaching heaven—
the first universal framework, complete synchronization.

Greece abstracted it:
philosopher-kings who knew better,
abstract ideals no one could match,
the body as prison for the soul.

Rome legalized it:
classifications that created reality,
frameworks with force of law.

The Church institutionalized it:
interpretive authority replacing direct experience,
priests mediating between human and divine,
rituals exhausting simple presence.

Velocity economized it:
perpetual insufficiency driving consumption,
exhaustion through productivity,
belonging through brands.

Now algorithms personalize it:
customized frameworks for each nervous system,
personalized exhaustion protocols,
individual isolation within apparent connection.

Same serpent's method.
Different technology.
Faster delivery.

The Modern Acceleration

The smartphone executes the serpent's method more efficiently than any previous technology.

6:00 AM - Installation begins before consciousness fully arrives.
6:15 AM - Reality questioning through curated news.
6:30 AM - Pattern provision through synchronized narratives.
7:00 AM - Identity formation through social positioning.
7:30 AM - Exhaustion through information overload.
8:00 AM - Isolation within apparent connection.
8:30 AM - Dependent on frameworks for navigation.

In thirty minutes, the method accomplishes what once took weeks.
The conditioning that required physical temples now happens through portable screens.
The exhaustion that demanded manual labor now occurs through mental processing.

The serpent's tongue became electric.
The method's delivery became instant.
The conditioning became environmental.

The Antidote Hidden in Plain Sight

But the method has one vulnerability: it requires continuous input.
The conditioning needs constant reinforcement.
The exhaustion must be maintained.
The simulation requires daily installation.

Which means the antidote is simple: **evaluation**.

Not meditation. Not mindfulness.
Not some app selling you peace-as-product.
Just the actual testing of claims against reality—

the moment between stimulus and response where you ask:
What do I actually know?
What am I being told?
Who benefits if I believe this?

The thumb hovers over the headline.
Three seconds of comparison:
Does this match my direct experience?
Does the evidence support this conclusion?
Or am I being fed the conclusion first?

That's it.
That's the revolution.
Three seconds of evaluation—
the smallest test that breaks the largest machine.

This is what **Sabbath** was always meant to be:
not religious obligation but humanity's systematic return to direct experience.
Regular interruption of mediated reality.
Scheduled reconnection with what's real.
One day in seven where frameworks couldn't install,
exhaustion couldn't accumulate,
because hands were in bread-dough,
bodies were at table,
faces were unscreened,
presence replaced performance.

**Every empire outlawed or corrupted Sabbath
because every empire knew:**
direct experience breaks mediated control.
Rested minds evaluate claims.
Present bodies know what's real.

Recognizing Your Conditioning

The signs are consistent across all applications of the method:

The uncanny valley feeling—
The smile on a coworker's Zoom square freezes a half-second too long.
The influencer's laugh sounds practiced.

Everything seems slightly off, performative, not quite real.
This is your nervous system recognizing the gap between reality and framework.

The perpetual insufficiency—
You close the laptop after midnight, the task complete, yet your hand still twitches toward the phone.
The next notification promises the satisfaction that never arrives.
This is the framework preventing completion cycles.

The synchronized outrage—
Thousands chant the same slogan, comment the same insult, post the same flame emoji.
Different faces, identical rhythm.
This is the echo replacing evaluation.

The exhaustion without accomplishment—
Tabs open like windows in a collapsing tower.
Coffee grows cold beside unread messages.
You've scrolled the world and gone nowhere.
This is strategic depletion working.

The isolation despite connection—
Your feed floods with smiling faces; your apartment stays silent.
Hundreds of contacts but no one to call.
Thousands of followers but no one who knows you.
Infinite connection. Perfect isolation.

The reactivity without reflection—
The headline triggers rage before you finish reading.
The post demands sharing before you verify.
The narrative feels true before you test it.
This is conditioning replacing judgment.

These aren't personal failings.
They're evidence of conditioning — proof the method is running.
Signs you're inside the simulation.

What Cain Shows Us

Tomorrow's chapter reveals what happens when the method runs without interruption—
when an entire generation becomes perfectly conditioned.
When no one evaluates.
When everyone echoes.
When all accept the framework as reality.

Violence isn't the breakdown of the system—
it's the system's culmination.

The exhausted mind, the isolated individual, the synchronized outrage,
the manufactured insufficiency—
they all lead to the same place.

The place where Cain arrives,
holding a rock, looking at his brother,
running the serpent's code,
no longer able to test the narrative against reality.

But tonight, before tomorrow's violence,
notice your conditioning.
Notice the exhaustion.
Notice the echo.
Notice the framework installing between you and direct experience.

*The serpent's method only works on those
who don't know it's running.*

Now you know.

*Evaluation between feeling and conclusion—that's where
freedom lives. Testing between stimulus and response—
that's where recognition happens. Direct experience
between updates—that's where reality exists.*

The simulation feeds on your need for certainty.
Reality waits in your willingness to test.

Tomorrow, the method produces murder.
Tonight, you can still evaluate.

Chapter 5

THE VICTIM VIRUS

When Isolation Became Inevitable

CAIN BROUGHT AN offering. Abel brought one too. God looked on Abel's with favor. On Cain's, not so much.

The text doesn't explain why.

Cain was left with uncertainty: Why wasn't mine accepted? What does this mean about me?

The questions weren't wrong. They were human—finite beings trying to understand infinite responses.

The uncertainty was natural. Built into the design.

What happened next wasn't.

The Narrative Choice

Cain could have asked God directly. Could have examined his own heart. Could have sought understanding.

He didn't.

Instead, he looked at Abel and constructed a story: Abel is the problem. God prefers him. I am rejected. This is unfair.

Not "What did I miss?" but "I was wronged."

The victim narrative wrote itself faster than the question could form.

The Intervention Offered

God saw what was forming:

> *"Why are you angry? Why is your face downcast? If you do what is right, will you not be accepted? But if you do not do what is right, sin is crouching at your door; it desires to have you, but you must rule over it."*

An intervention. An off-ramp.

But that would mean releasing the narrative. Admitting uncertainty again. Returning to the vulnerable position of not knowing.

Cain chose certainty. Even false certainty. Especially false certainty.
He doubled down instead of testing.
And that choice made what happened next inevitable.

The Pattern That Doesn't Resolve

Cain killed Abel in the field.
After Abel lay still in the dirt, Cain didn't feel better. He felt worse.
Now he feared God's response. Feared being found. Feared every face he'd encounter.

The violence hadn't closed the wound. It had torn it wider.

God's question came: "Where is your brother?"
Cain's answer: "Am I my brother's keeper?"

The first person to claim victimhood while standing over a body.

The First City

"Cain was building a city, and he named it after his son Enoch."

The first walls. The first structure built from fear instead of need.

The city lacked elders to test narratives, shared stories about handling insufficiency, places to go when victim stories form.

Just isolation formalized into architecture.

Cain's children absorbed the pattern: When insufficient, blame someone. When wronged, isolate. When rage builds, strike.

The pattern replicates through observation, not teaching.

The Violence Algorithm

Cain's city wasn't just the first urban center. It was the first reproducible template for escaping reality through violence.

The pattern was elegant in its simplicity:

1. Create false narrative about being wronged.
2. Let fear ferment into rage.
3. Eliminate the comparison that exposes your insufficiency.
4. Build alternative reality where your narrative is true.
5. Teach your children the pattern.

Within seven generations, Lamech would boast:

> *"I killed a man for wounding me, a young man for injuring me. If Cain is avenged seven times, then Lamech seventy-seven times."*

Not just escalation—multiplication. Each generation computing the violence algorithm with greater efficiency. Each iteration requiring less provocation. Each cycle normalizing what the previous cycle saw as extreme.

Violence doesn't just spread. It multiplies. Each wound creates a wounder.

The Multiplication Pattern

Watch how quickly the threshold drops.

Cain killed Abel over divine preference—cosmic wound, fundamental rejection. Lamech killed for a wound—physical injury, but not life-threatening.

The degradation accelerates:

- Generation 1: Kill for ultimate rejection.
- Generation 2: Kill for physical wound.
- Generation 3: Kill for verbal wound.
- Generation 4: Kill for imagined wound.
- Generation 5: Kill for potential wound.
- Generation 6: Kill for feeling wound might be possible.
- Generation 7: Kill because killing is what we do.

Each murder created another person convinced of their own victimhood, where violence was justified, where their false narrative was true.

Each victim created more victims. Exponential multiplication of private realities.
Every killer thinks they're the victim. Every violence believes it's justice.

The Boundary Dissolution

The violence wasn't just horizontal—human to human. It began breaking fundamental boundaries.

Genesis emphasized at creation: "according to their kinds." Each species distinct. Each boundary sacred. Each category maintaining its integrity.

The text strains to describe what happened next:

"The Nephilim were on the earth in those days—and also afterward—when the sons of God went to the daughters of humans and had children by them."

Beneath the mythology was something real: boundaries that should never be crossed were being eliminated.

The same impulse that crossed the line from anger to murder would cross every line it encountered.

If you can kill your brother, why not mate with what isn't human? If you can destroy human life, why not corrupt life itself? If boundaries don't matter for violence, why should they matter for anything?

Violence doesn't respect boundaries. It dissolves them—first moral, then physical, then genetic.

By Noah's Time

The assessment came:

"The LORD saw how great the wickedness of the human race had become on the earth, and that every inclination of the thoughts of the human heart was only evil all the time."

Not some thoughts. Every inclination. Not sometimes. All the time.
The violence algorithm had become the only program running.
This wasn't just moral crisis. It was existential threat. A species at risk—not from predator but from itself.

A few more generations and no humans would remain—just violent hybrids running murder algorithms in bodies no longer quite human.

God's Diagnosis

"The LORD regretted that he had made human beings on the earth, and his heart was deeply troubled."

Not the regret of mistake—grief of necessity. The surgeon amputating to save the patient. The parent quarantining the infected child.

God wasn't angry. He was watching humanity delete itself.

The Flood as Mercy

The flood wasn't punishment. It was preservation.

Like radiation therapy—destroying the infected to save the organism. Like fever—burning out infection before it claims the host. Like amputation—losing the limb to save the life.

God wasn't destroying humanity. He was saving it.

The eight people on the ark weren't lucky survivors—they were the genetic preserve, the seed stock for replanting the species.

"Noah was a righteous man, blameless among the people of his time."

But the Hebrew adds something crucial: *tamim* in his *toledot*—perfect in his generations.

Not just morally perfect but generationally perfect—genetically uncorrupted, still fully human, still bearing the divine image intact.

The flood had to happen when it did. Wait another generation and even Noah's line might be compromised. Wait two generations and no pure human DNA would remain.

The flood wasn't too late. It was almost too late.

What the Water Washed

Every private reality where violence was justified dissolved. Every simulation where "I am the victim" sank beneath the waters.

The flood eliminated:

- Genetic corruption.
- Hybrid offspring of violated boundaries.
- Structures built on pure violence.
- Accumulated private simulations of seven generations.

But water can't wash consciousness. Noah and his family still carried the original programming—the violence potential, the ability to create false narratives.

The hardware was preserved. The corrupted files were deleted. But the virus remained in the operating system itself.

Water can wash away bodies. It can't wash away patterns.

After the Flood

When Noah stepped out of the ark, he stepped into a world washed clean of everything except what most needed washing—the pattern generator in human consciousness.

His first act was sacrifice—smoke rising, aroma pleasing, connection restored. His second act revealed what the flood couldn't wash away.

"Noah, a man of the soil, proceeded to plant a vineyard. When he drank some of its wine, he became drunk and lay uncovered inside his tent."

Look at the sequence: Survival. Gratitude. Self-destruction.

He'd watched the world drown. Heard humanity's screams stop. Floated above the corpses of everyone he'd ever known.

Now, in the silence of the new world, the weight of being chosen became unbearable.
Why him? Why did he live when millions died? What made him worthy of survival?
The same questions every survivor asks. The same weight that drives veterans to bottles, survivors to guilt, souls to numbness.

Wine promised an answer. Or at least promised to stop the question.

He drank until he couldn't feel it anymore. Woke naked on the tent floor, the question still there, the weight still crushing.

The pattern survived even the survivor. Even after the reset. Even in the world washed clean.

God's Second Assessment

> *"Never again will I curse the ground because of humans, even though every inclination of the human heart is evil from childhood."*

From childhood.
Not born that way. Learned that way.

Children absorb how their parents respond to uncertainty. They inherit patterns through observation, not instruction. They become what they see, not what they're told.

The flood saved the species. It couldn't save humans from themselves.

What Changed

But something would emerge after the flood that didn't exist before. Slowly. Imperfectly. Places to go.

Kingdoms formed—not perfect, but loud enough to stop a blade mid-swing. Cities grew—not just walls, but elders at gates telling stories of another way. Laws emerged—lines everyone agreed not to cross. Refuge cities appeared— actual doorsteps where someone running could stop, breathe, and be safe.

The key difference: collective response instead of individual isolation.

Violence still emerged. The pattern still spread. People still convinced themselves they were victims.
But now, when someone's hand moved toward the blade, there was a doorstep to run to first.
Post-flood violence never reached pre-flood levels again.

Not because humans changed. Because refuge existed.

The Modern Parallel

The friend who can't stop talking about being wronged. The online community united by shared grievance. The algorithm feeding stories of threats. The movement organized around victimhood.

Everyone running a version of the same pattern: "I was wronged. They're the threat. My response is justified."

The pattern spreads fastest in isolation: No community to test the narrative against. No shared reality to compare stories with. Everyone their own source of truth.

Then everyone becomes their own victim. Everyone's violence becomes self-defense.

The Condition We're Rebuilding

Isolation despite connection. Ten thousand feeds. Ten thousand separate universes. Everyone seeing different enemies.

Everyone in their own algorithm-personalized feed. Everyone isolated in their own version of being wronged. Everyone convinced their rage is justified. Nowhere to go for a different pattern.

The pre-flood condition wasn't primitive. It was sophisticated isolation. We're just recreating it with better technology.

Isolated humans without collective refuge always arrive at the same endpoint.

The Question

The flood couldn't wash away the pattern.
But collective refuge can contain it.

Not perfectly. Not permanently. But enough.

Enough to interrupt the cycle. Enough to teach a different response. Enough to remember: you were never meant to carry uncertainty alone.

The pattern exists in everyone.

The question is: Do you have collective refuge to interrupt it?
Or are you alone with your narrative, isolated with your rage, running Cain's pattern, with nowhere to go?

Tomorrow

Tomorrow, Babel attempts to solve isolation through universal simulation—one narrative, one tower, one reality everyone must agree to.

Trading individual isolation for collective delusion.

The tower rises tomorrow.
Tonight, find refuge.
Or become another brick.

Chapter 6

BABEL: THE TOWER PROTOCOL

One Language, One Reality, No Escape

THEY GATHERED IN Shinar's plain, every single one of them.
Not some families.
Not one tribe.
Everyone.

Their grandparents had floated above corpses.
Heard the world's screaming stop.
Watched mountains disappear under water.

Eight people survived in a wooden box.
Eight people to repopulate everything.

The story was impossible, but it was true.
And everyone carried it.

Now God had given a command:
"Be fruitful and multiply and fill the earth."

Fill the earth.
Spread out.
Scatter.

The survivors heard something else:
"Go out there. Alone. Vulnerable. Where I can kill you again."

The Gap Opens

Natural questions arose:
Why did God save us?
What does He want from us?
Why destroy everyone, then tell us to spread out?

The questions weren't wrong.
They were human—finite beings trying to understand infinite actions.

But the questions didn't lead to seeking.
They led to contemplation.
And contemplation opened a gap.

In that gap, uncertainty settled:

Why scatter?
What happens if we're separated?
Will we survive alone?
Can we trust this command?

Not fear yet.
Just the natural state of finite beings facing infinite possibility.
The questions without answers.
The uncertainty without framework.

This is where humans always live—in the space between what they know and
what they cannot know.

Uncertainty isn't the problem.
It's the design.

The First Focus Group

"Come, let us build ourselves a city, with a tower that reaches to the heavens, so that we may make a name for ourselves; otherwise we will be scattered over the face of the whole earth."

Not "let me build" or "some should build."
Always **"us."**
Always **"we."**

The first manufactured consensus—
everyone agreeing to the same story
before anyone asked if the story was true.

Nimrod didn't find a fearful crowd.
He found an uncertain one.

People with questions but no answers.
People facing the unknown without framework.
People living in the natural state of finite beings in infinite reality.

And into that uncertainty, he inserted a narrative.

They gathered in Shinar's plain like iron filings around a magnet.
Not drawn by beauty or bounty, but by its **blankness.**
A plain has no features to create division.
No mountains to separate.
No valleys to distinguish.
Just endless sameness—
perfect for creating a single, shared reality
where everyone would see the same thing
because there was nothing else to see.

Nimrod's pitch was simple:

"Remember the flood?"

The crowd stiffened.
Of course they remembered.
The screams.
The silence.
The eight people.

"God promised no more water," Nimrod said.
"But promises end. Waters rise.
And what lives in the places He wants to scatter us—
the things that survived the deep?"

The questions they'd been asking—now spoken aloud.
Their uncertainty—now given voice.

"And He wants us to scatter. Separate. Spread out across the earth."

A pause.

"Alone, we're nothing. Scattered, we're vulnerable.
What if scattering is the setup?
What if He's separating us to destroy us one by one?"

There it was—the narrative.
The framework imposed on uncertainty.
The story that converts questions into answers,
ambiguity into certainty,
wondering into knowing.

The uncertainty they'd felt transformed instantly.
No longer "Will we be okay scattered?"
Now: "Scattering = death."

"But together—together we can build something even God can't destroy.
Stay together or die alone."

The narrative generated the fear.
The fear gathered the crowd.
The crowd validated the narrative.

Uncertainty became fear the moment someone provided the framework.

The Consensus Manufacturing Process

The flood survivors all carried different versions of the trauma—
different nightmares,
different private questions,
different uncertainties about why they survived.

Chaos.
Everyone running their own version of "why me and not them?"

But what if everyone agreed to the same story?
What if all private uncertainties merged into one shared narrative?
What if the natural ambiguity of finite beings could be collectivized into synchronized certainty?

The formula was simple:

1. Identify shared uncertainty (what does God want from us?).
2. Provide narrative framework (scattering = death).
3. Generate shared fear (we're vulnerable alone).
4. Propose shared solution (build beyond God's reach).
5. Demand shared participation (everyone must build).
6. Promise shared identity (we'll make a name).

Everyone who accepted the narrative converted their uncertainty into fear.
Everyone who participated made the simulation more real.

The narrative wasn't truth.
It was framework imposed on uncertainty.

And framework—any framework—feels better than ambiguity.
Even when the framework is false.

Uncertainty is natural.
Narrative generates fear.
Fear builds towers.

Consensus isn't truth.
It's agreed-upon fiction.

The Brick Program

"Come, let us make bricks and bake them thoroughly."

Not gather stones—**make bricks.**
The difference is everything.

Stones are found— each unique, each requiring placement.
Bricks are manufactured— each identical, requiring only stacking.

But they weren't just making bricks.
They were **becoming** them.

The transformation happens in stages:

- Day 1: Making bricks feels productive.
- Week 1: Making bricks feels normal.
- Month 1: Not making bricks feels wrong.
- Year 1: Identity becomes brick-maker.
- Year 5: Identity becomes brick.

When humans become bricks, certain things become impossible:

- You can't question the building— you're part of it.
- You can't leave the structure— you'd create a hole.
- You can't be different— you won't fit.
- You can't stop building— that's what bricks do.

What began as individual fear became collectivized agreement—
an entire people seeing through the same frame,
building the same defense, running the same program.

First you make the brick.
Then the brick makes you.

The Name Machine

"Let us make a name for ourselves."

Not *names*—**name**. Singular.
One identity for all.
One story.
One simulation running in every consciousness.

This wasn't just branding.
It was **reality replacement.**
Instead of discovering who they were through living,
they would be told who they were through belonging.

Identity wouldn't emerge from experience.
It would be **assigned by system.**

The pattern operates everywhere:

- "We are Americans" — not people living in America.
- "We are Christians" — not people following Christ.
- "We are professionals" — not people working.
- "We are users" — not people using.

The collective noun overwrites the personal verb.

You don't have a name.
The name has you.

The Language Monopoly

"The whole world had one language and
a common speech."

One language doesn't just mean one way to communicate—
it means one way to **think**.

One set of categories.
One framework for reality.

One simulation everyone must run.

Different languages allow different realities.
Spanish has "ser" and "estar"—two ways to be.
Hebrew thinks in verbs.
English thinks in nouns.

But one language creates one possibility.
One way to be human.

Modern platforms achieve this without eliminating languages.
Everyone uses the same emoji vocabulary.
Everyone speaks in the same metrics—likes, followers, views.

The universal language isn't English or Mandarin.
It's platform syntax.

One language, one reality.
Many languages, many realities.
No language, actual reality.

The Height Delusion

"A tower that reaches to the heavens."

Not to meet God—to become **unreachable** by God.
Not to transcend earth—to escape it.
Not to achieve heaven—to engineer immunity from judgment.

Each floor up was another layer of abstraction.
Another degree of separation from ground-truth reality.

From the ground: humans are individuals.
From floor 50: humans are units.
From the top: humans are mass.

Every floor up is a floor away.
The higher they climbed,

the smaller humans looked.
Until they stopped looking like humans at all.

The Fear Foundation

Beneath the entire project was the narrative-generated terror:
"Otherwise we will be scattered over the face of the whole earth."

The narrative had converted uncertainty into specific fears:
Scattering means loss of consensus. Loss of collective defense. Loss of identity.
Loss of control.

The tower wasn't built from confidence.
It was built from manufactured fear.

Every brick mortared with terror that didn't exist until someone provided
the framework. Every floor built on dread that wasn't natural until someone
named it.

They weren't building despite fear.
They were building because narrative generated fear.
And fear demands action.

The higher the tower, the more real the narrative.
The more real the narrative, the deeper the fear.

God's Reality Check

"But the LORD came down to see the city and the t
ower the people were building."

The irony cuts deep.
They were building to heaven,
but God must come **down** to see it.

Their consensus reality is so small
that Reality itself must stoop to notice.

"If as one people speaking the same language they have begun to do this, then nothing they plan to do will be impossible for them."

This wasn't compliment.
It was **diagnosis.**

Unified in simulation.
Standardized in thought.
Driven by narrative-generated fear.

Humanity could achieve anything—
including total disconnection from reality,
permanent residence in simulation,
final forgetfulness of what humans actually are.

They could build a false reality so complete
that true reality would be forgotten.

Unity isn't always strength.
Sometimes it's psychosis.

The Confusion Gift

"Come, let us go down and confuse their language."

God didn't destroy the tower.
Didn't kill the builders.
Didn't flood the plain.
He redirected the steering.

The people didn't stop understanding each other.
They stopped moving in the same direction.
One group looked at the tower and saw safety.
Another looked and saw prison.
Another looked and saw nothing worth building at all.

The simulation fractured.

Not into chaos — into difference.
The monopoly on reality broke.
The singular framework became plural.

This wasn't punishment—it was **prevention.**

Confusion was cure.
Diversity of direction was deliverance.
Scattering was the exit Nimrod had made them fear.

The Scattering Gift

They scattered, carrying fragments of the broken simulation.
Each group developing its own framework, its own tower.

But now there were options.
Alternatives.
Other ways to be human.

Someone raised in one simulation could meet another and realize:
both are constructions,
neither is ultimate reality.

Many lies reveal the lie.
One lie becomes the truth.

The Pattern Continues

The ancient dream returns through new architecture.
One language—Internet.
One platform—Global.
One simulation—Digital.

The new tower isn't physical—it's virtual. The new bricks aren't clay—they're data.

Everyone seeing through the same feeds. Everyone thinking in the same metrics. Everyone responding to the same triggers.

The platform is Shinar's plain—flat, featureless, same everywhere.
The algorithm is Nimrod—finding uncertainty and providing narrative.

The formula still works:
Identify shared uncertainty ("What's happening?").
Provide narrative framework ("They're coming for you").
Generate shared fear (real, visceral, urgent).
Demand shared participation ("Share this").

Natural uncertainty about complex reality converts to manufactured fear through simple narrative.

The platform doesn't find fearful people.
It finds uncertain people and makes them fearful.

Babel didn't fail.
It just went digital.

The Builders Who Refuse

But some remember they're not bricks.
Some refuse the uniformity.
Some keep their own language,
their own sightline to reality.

They're not trying to destroy the tower — that's not how towers fall.
They're just refusing to be part of it.
Refusing to accept the narrative.
Refusing to convert uncertainty into manufactured fear.

They remember what Babel forgot:
plural sight is sanity.
Different ways of seeing prevent any one way from becoming total.

The cure for one big lie
is many small truths.

The Crack in the Code

Somewhere in Shinar, while everyone else mixed mortar and stacked bricks, one builder paused.

A question before the next command. A memory of sky beyond scaffold. The recognition: This is consensus, not reality. This is narrative, not truth. This is fear we built from uncertainty we could have carried.

The pause lasted only a moment. Then the builder reached for the next brick. But something had shifted.

Every consensus begins to crumble the moment one person sees it as consensus.
Before freedom, remembering.
Before escape, awareness.

The builder kept working. But the pause had happened.
And somewhere in the scaffold, another builder felt the same hesitation.

The tower kept rising.
So did the recognition.

The Pattern Made Visible

From Cain to Babel, the progression is complete:

Uncertainty is natural.
Narrative converts it to fear.
Fear collectivizes into system.
System becomes reality.

Until someone sees it as system.

Nimrod weaponized uncertainty. Provided narrative. Generated fear.
Manufactured consensus. Created the template every empire would follow.

But he also revealed the mechanism.

The tower still stands. The algorithm still runs. The platform still promises safety through consensus.

But someone in every generation pauses. Questions. Remembers.
Because before tower, before brick, before narrative—there was uncertainty without fear.

The pattern is visible now.

Not as history—as present.
Not as metaphor—as mechanics.

The simulation runs everywhere until someone sees it running.

Then the code cracks.
The question forms.
Someone is about to remember.

PART III

Before The Simulation

Memory: When Humans Knew Directly

There was a time when nothing stood between experience and awareness. The ancient practices come from there—rhythms meant to keep humans whole before we forgot how to be human.

Chapter 7

ABRAHAM: THE FIRST EXIT

Leaving the Known for the Real

BEFORE THE DUST of Babel settled, another city was already rising— Ur of the Chaldeans.

Not chaos this time, but perfect order.
Not rebellion against heaven, but a system that claimed to manage it.

Ur was where humanity perfected the god machine.

The God Machine

Not like Babel's crude attempt to storm heaven— Ur had systematized it.

The great ziggurat rose in calculated steps, each level representing divine administration. At the top, Nanna the moon god managed time itself. Below him, subsidiary deities ran their departments: Inanna for fertility and war, Utu for justice, Enki for wisdom.

Every aspect of existence had an assigned divine administrator.
Every human need had a corresponding transaction portal.

The gods weren't beings to know, but systems to navigate. Input offering, receive blessing. Insert prayer, obtain result.

The gods weren't worshipped.
They were operated.

The Idol Factory

Abraham's father Terah ran a successful business: manufacturing gods.

Not metaphorically— literally. His workshop produced deities on demand. Pocket idols for protection. Household gods for blessing. Corporate deities for success.

The process was standardized:

- Client describes need.
- Appropriate deity selected.
- Idol crafted to specifications.
- Ritual activation performed.
- God delivered, payment received.

His son Abram grew up watching humans purchase their own creators— people bowing to what their neighbors had carved, the devout worshiping what last week had been a tree.

The contradiction was so obvious no one saw it.
Like fish not noticing water.
Like users not seeing the platform.

The simulation was total.

First you make the god.
Then the god makes you.

The Day Reality Broke Through

The tradition preserves the moment in story:

Terah left young Abram to manage the idol shop. Customers came wanting to buy. To each, Abram asked the same question:

"How old are you?"
"Fifty," one said. "Sixty," said another.
"Woe to a sixty-year-old who wants to bow to something made yesterday."

One by one, they left. Embarrassed. Unable to answer.

Then a woman came carrying a plate of fine flour.
"Offer this before them," she said.

Abram took a stick, smashed every idol except the largest, and placed the stick in its hand.
When Terah returned to the wreckage, Abram explained:

"A woman brought an offering. I set it before them. Each one said, 'I will eat first.' They fought — and the biggest one took the stick and destroyed the others."

"Why are you mocking me?" Terah shouted. "Do they know anything? They're clay and wood!"
"Don't your ears hear what your mouth is saying?"

The silence that followed was the sound of simulation cracking.
The system you serve cannot save you — because you created it.

Every system runs on collective amnesia.
Remembering who built it breaks the spell.

The Voice Outside the Program

It was to this man—who had already seen through the simulation—that the Voice came.

"Lekh lekha."

Not detailed instructions. Just: Leave.

But the leaving was layered:

- "Leave your land"—the physical matrix, the geography of programming.
- "Leave your birthplace"—the cultural coding, the inherited assumptions.
- "Leave your father's house"—the generational patterns, the family system.

Each harder than the last.

"To the land that I will show you."

Future tense. Not the map before the journey— vision during the walk.

There are no words for what Abraham heard. Not thunder—though the body registered it like thunder. Not command—though every cell understood: move. The Voice didn't argue with the ziggurat's gods or provide a better system. It simply called from somewhere outside the machinery.

Abraham had spent his life surrounded by gods who required transaction. The Voice required nothing. Offered no deal. Promised only: "I will show you."

The gods gave instructions.
The Voice gave invitation.

The simulation shows everything first.
Reality reveals itself through walking.

The Mechanics of Leaving

Abraham was seventy-five— the age when patterns harden, when simulation's hold is strongest.

But he left.

Took his wife Sarai, his nephew Lot, his possessions, his people—walked away from civilization's peak.

From indoor plumbing to tents.
From predictable irrigation to unpredictable rain.
From systematic theology to mysterious Voice.

What Abraham didn't do reveals the pattern:

He didn't destroy Ur.
He didn't debate Ur.
He didn't create anti-Ur.

He simply walked away.

No manifesto. No movement. Just one family exiting the machine.

You can't destroy the simulation—it's too big.
You can't debate it—it doesn't listen.
You can only leave.

Escape isn't revolution.
It's exodus.

The Tent Principle

Abraham lived in tents the rest of his life.

Kings offered him land—he refused.
Cities offered him citizenship—he remained alien.
Success brought wealth—he kept it mobile.

The tent was theological: God moves, so Abraham moved. The divine wasn't housed in temples but encountered in journey. Not accessed through system but met in wilderness.

The tent was practical: No maintenance required. No mortgage to pay. No permanence to defend. When the Voice said "move," Abraham could move.

The tent was prophetic: Declaring that the simulation's permanent structures were actually temporary, while his temporary structures pointed to something permanent beyond any system.

Abraham woke to the sun rising, as had become his custom in the decades since leaving Ur. Not to ceremony. Not to ritual. Just to be in the presence of the One who had called him out. Some mornings the Voice spoke. Some mornings it didn't. But even the mornings of silence were different from Ur's noise. In Ur, divine encounter had been scheduled, systematic, transactional. Here, outside the machine, Abraham simply waited. And the waiting itself became the encounter.

This was what humans had lost. This was what the ziggurat had replaced.

Permanence is the simulation's promise.
Movement is reality's nature.

The Altar Alternative

Everywhere Abraham camped, he built an altar— never a temple.

Temples house gods; altars mark encounters.
Temples require priests; altars are personal.
Temples systematize; altars remember.
Temples are permanent; altars can be left behind.

Each altar said: "Here heaven touched earth. Here the Voice spoke. Here reality broke through."

But Abraham didn't stay. Didn't monetize. Didn't organize.

Mark the encounter, don't manage it.
Build the altar, don't become its priest.

The Egyptian Test

Famine came— the first test of exit.

When you've left the system, where do you turn when resources fail?

Abraham went to Egypt—the prototype of every future slavery. At the border, fear replaced faith. He told Sarah to lie about their marriage. Pharaoh took her into his house. Abraham grew rich from the deception.

Plagues fell. Truth emerged. Pharaoh rebuked him: "Why didn't you tell me she was your wife?"

The simulation's king displayed more integrity than the man who walked with God.
When you re-enter the system after leaving, you play by worse rules than those who never left.

The exit isn't a one-time event. It's a daily choice.

The Separation

The land couldn't support Abraham and Lot together. Their herdsmen quarreled.

Abraham offered peace: "If you go left, I'll go right. If you go right, I'll go left."

Lot looked toward the Jordan Valley—lush, well-watered, gleaming like Egypt. The cities of the plain promised everything Ur once did.

Lot chose what looked like abundance.
Abraham took the harder hills.

They separated—geographically and philosophically.
Lot moved toward the machine's comfort.
Abraham stayed in the wilderness's clarity.

Comfort is the simulation's reward—
freedom its cost.

The Rescue

War came to the plains— four kings against five. Lot, now living inside Sodom's walls, was captured.

Abraham armed 318 men—those born in his household, trained outside empire's logic. They attacked at night. Rescued everyone.

The pattern proved itself: Someone can leave the system and still have power. Someone can refuse the simulation and still help those trapped inside.

Exit doesn't mean abandonment.
It means freedom to help without joining.

The Sodom Refusal

After the victory, the king of Sodom offered reward.

Abraham raised his hand in refusal:

"I have sworn to the LORD, God Most High, Creator of heaven and earth, that I will accept nothing belonging to you, not even a thread or the strap of a sandal, so that you will never be able to say, 'I made Abram rich.'"

Advanced exit strategy: Refuse the simulation's rewards even when earned.

The simulation's gifts become debts.
Its rewards become recruitment.
Even thread becomes chain.

The Lot Reflection

Lot left Ur but never left the simulation.

He followed Abraham's body out while his heart remained inside. He pitched tents outside Sodom but moved them incrementally closer. Eventually he sat in the gates as a respected citizen.

His wife looked back—not in disbelief, but in longing.

Leaving without detachment is relocation, not exit.

Lot's story is the tragedy of partial exodus—the man who almost left, who followed the call without hearing it.

The simulation doesn't need walls when desire is enough.

The Terrible Teaching

Abraham taught his children about the Voice, about the exit, about reality beyond simulation.

But children who grow up in tents dream of palaces.
Children who inherit freedom fantasize about security.

Isaac dug wells. Jacob negotiated. Joseph optimized Egypt.

The children of exit entered empire.
The descendants of the tent-dweller built pyramids.

Exit isn't inheritable.

Parents can teach that freedom exists. But they cannot transfer the encounter itself. Cannot give their children freedom—only the memory that freedom exists.

The Pattern Established

Abraham established the pattern every exit must follow:

- Recognition: See through the simulation.
- Call: Hear the voice outside the program.
- Exit: Leave completely—land, birthplace, father's house.
- Tents: Refuse permanent installation.
- Altars: Mark encounters without systematizing.
- Refusal: Decline the simulation's rewards.
- Teaching: Pass on the memory that exit is possible.

But he also revealed the warning: Re-entry tempts when resources fail. Your children might choose chains. Exit must be chosen in each generation.

The memory of the tent survived.
So did the dream of the palace.

The Individual Paradox

Abraham proved individual exit possible—one person can leave, can hear, can walk away from the machine and survive.

But he revealed the paradox: Individual exit isn't enough.

His descendants would rebuild the system he escaped. Would enter Egypt. Would forget the Voice.
The simulation doesn't need to prevent individual exits. It just waits. Welcomes the next generation.

Individual exit threatens nothing. The system absorbs the children.

What Abraham Remembered

There was a time before the god machine. When humans walked with God in the cool of the day. When the Voice spoke directly. When relationship required no priest, no temple, no offering except presence.

Abraham remembered what others forgot: The divine isn't a system to operate but a Person to walk with.
Every morning, outside his tent, Abraham remembered.

The ziggurat still stood in Ur. The god machine still hummed. But somewhere in the wilderness, one family woke to a different reality.

The simulation continued. But outside its borders, a testimony stood.

Exit was possible. The altars proved it.

The Longing

Abraham's story isn't just history. It's memory.

Memory of what humans were before the simulation. What direct encounter felt like before it became religious transaction.

The story preserves the possibility that relationship doesn't require system. That exodus is possible even when it looks impossible.

But it also preserves the warning: The next generation forgets. Empire rebuilds itself in every human heart that chooses framework over encounter.

Abraham's descendants will enter Egypt. Moses will have to lead millions out. Because the simulation learned:
Let individuals leave. Keep their children. Make their grandchildren slaves.

The tent stands in the wilderness.
The ziggurat rises in every city.
The pattern repeats.

And somewhere, always, someone hears their name called from outside the machine. Someone remembers that reality exists beyond the simulation.

Someone refuses the gods they manufactured and waits for the Voice that speaks from everywhere and nowhere, requiring nothing but presence, offering nothing but "I will show you."

The altars remain.
The memory persists.
The call continues.

And those who have ears to hear—
hear.

Chapter 8

EGYPT: THE WORTHLESSNESS FACTORY

When Production Replaced Presence

"LOOK, THE PEOPLE of the children of Israel are more and mightier than we. Come, let us deal shrewdly with them, lest they multiply, and it happen, in the event of war, that they also join our enemies and fight against us."

This was Pharaoh's pitch to Egypt.
Not facts—narrative.
Not reality—simulation.

The Israelites weren't "more and mightier." They were shepherds living in Goshen—no army, no weapons, no threat. Just living, working, multiplying. Being human.

But Pharaoh needed them to be dangerous.

Because if they were a threat, they could be treated as one. If they were dangerous, they could be controlled. If they were enemies-in-waiting, they could be crushed.

The narrative didn't need proof. It just needed Pharaoh.

How Salvation Became Slavery

Four hundred years earlier, Joseph had saved Egypt from famine. His interpretation of Pharaoh's dreams, his plan to store grain during seven years of plenty—this preserved life when famine struck. The text is clear: Joseph's wisdom saved Egypt and the surrounding nations from starvation.

But what happened during the famine? Genesis records the transaction, though not who designed the system or how much autonomy Joseph actually had. Pharaoh was still absolute ruler. Joseph was still, fundamentally, a Hebrew administrator risen from slavery. The decisions were Pharaoh's. The power was Pharaoh's.

What we know is the pattern that emerged:

Year One of the famine:
"Give us grain," the Egyptians begged.
Joseph opened the storehouses. "That will be all your money."
They paid. Survival first. Worry about cost later.

Year Two:
"The money is gone," they returned. "But we still need food."
Joseph nodded. "Bring your livestock. Your cattle, sheep, horses, donkeys."
They brought them. Empty barns beat empty stomachs.

Year Three:
"The animals are gone," they came again. "Our children are starving."
"Then give me your land," Joseph said. "Deed it to Pharaoh."
They signed. Land means nothing to the dead.

Year Four:
"We have nothing left," they said. "Nothing but ourselves and our families."
"Then give me yourselves," Joseph replied. "Sell yourselves to Pharaoh. He'll give you seed to plant, food to eat. You'll work his land as his property."

They agreed. What choice remained?

Four years. Four steps. From citizen to property. From free to owned. All through the generous hand of salvation.

The system was elegant. Efficient. Perfectly legal. Everyone signed willingly. Everyone chose slavery. Because the alternative was death, and between death and bondage, the human body always chooses to live.

The empire learned: You don't need to force people into chains. Make them choose the chains. Make the chains feel like rescue.

The Double Simulation

Three generations later, Pharaoh's fear narrative installed a second layer.

For Egyptians, the story ran:
"These Hebrews are multiplying too fast. They'll overwhelm us. In war, they'll join our enemies. We must control them for our own survival."

The shepherds became a demographic threat. The vulnerable became dangerous. The powerless became the enemy. The Egyptians, despite their armies, their monuments, their absolute power, began to fear.

And fear, once established, justifies anything.

For Hebrews, a different narrative installed:
"You exist to build our monuments. Your value is your labor. Your worth is your output. You are alive because we allow it."

Day by day, brick by brick, the message repeated: *You are less. You are worth less. You are other.*

Two populations. Two simulations. Perfectly interlocked.

The Egyptians' fear justified dehumanization. The dehumanization produced the very resentment Egyptians feared. Each belief validated the other. The machine fed itself.

Neither population saw reality. Both lived in the narrative. Both became less than human—the Egyptians through fear, the Hebrews through worthlessness.

The oppressor's fear creates the oppressed. The oppressed's acceptance validates the oppressor. Both live in simulation. Neither in reality.

Manufacturing Worthlessness: The Generational Program

The transformation was methodical. Systematic. And faster than anyone wants to believe.

Generation 1: Guest Status
Different but present. Separate but tolerated. The children of Israel dwelt in Goshen. Not quite Egyptian. Not quite foreign. In between.

Generation 2-3: Useful Status
Strong backs noticed. Clever hands employed. Work offered. Integration through labor.
Voluntary... at first.

Generation 4-5: Essential Status
The building projects require Hebrew labor. Egypt's glory rises on Hebrew sweat.
"Without us, you'd be nothing."

Generation 6-7: Property Status
No longer workers. No longer even servants. Tools. Resources. Human machinery. Pharaoh's calculations count them like livestock, inventory them like grain.

Seven generations. Just over two centuries. That's all it took.

Freedom is never more than one generation away from extinction. Not because people choose slavery — but because children can't remember what they never experienced.

Slavery doesn't happen suddenly. It happens slowly—then completely—then seems eternal.

The Daily Curriculum

Every morning, Hebrew children woke to the same lesson:

Fathers in the brick pits before dawn. Mothers preparing the cucumbers, onions, fish that Egypt provided—adequate food for productive workers. Siblings nursing whip-marks that wouldn't be called injuries. Bodies fed. Spirits crushed. Just the cost of existence. Just the price of permission to breathe.

The food was sufficient. The labor was endless. This was the genius: Egypt kept Hebrew bodies strong enough to work while breaking Hebrew souls completely. Fed workers don't starve. Dehumanized workers don't revolt.

They saw Egyptian children walking to school while Hebrew children trudged to mud. Egyptian temples gleaming while Hebrew prayers echoed off slave-quarter walls. Egyptian families gathering for meals while Hebrew families collapsed from exhaustion.

The daily lesson required no words: *They matter. We don't. This is the natural order of things.*

But deeper than circumstance, the worthlessness became identity.

The Look—eyes sliding past, or inspecting, but never quite seeing. The way Egyptians gazed through Hebrew bodies searching for defects, counting productivity, measuring output. Never meeting eyes. Never acknowledging presence.

The Voice—tone used for animals, for broken tools, for things that serve. Commands without courtesy. Orders without acknowledgment. The sound of speaking to something that breathes but doesn't quite count as human.

The Space—markets where Hebrew bodies moved like furniture. Conversations that paused when they approached, resumed when they passed. The constant message of rooms rearranging themselves: *You are here, but you are not present.*

Every interaction declared: You are not like us. You are not fully human. You exist for us.

The deepest slavery convinces the slave they were born for chains.

How Worthlessness Runs in Families

By generation ten, Hebrew parents taught worthlessness as survival strategy:

"Keep your head down." "Work harder—maybe they won't hurt us today." "Don't dream of more." "We're lucky they let us live."

Not cruelty. Mercy. Preparing children for the only world that existed. Teaching them to expect what was inevitable, to want what was permitted, to measure themselves by the metrics that mattered.

Worth became what Egypt assigned. Value became what Egypt allowed. Meaning became what Egypt defined.

Parents passed down worthlessness like inheritance. Like legacy. Like love. Because believing worthlessness hurts less than believing worth and being proven wrong daily.

Hope is torture when you're property. Better to expect nothing. Then the whip is just Tuesday. The exhaustion is just existence.

The Pharaoh Who Knew Not Joseph

"Then a new king, to whom Joseph meant nothing, came to power in Egypt."

Not forgot—*unknew*. Chose not to know. Because remembering Joseph meant admitting Hebrews had saved Egypt. Meant acknowledging Hebrew brilliance, Hebrew value, Hebrew indispensability.

Easier to delete the history. Easier to rewrite until they've always been nothing.

This is how worthlessness embeds at the structural level: Erase all evidence of worth. Delete contributions from the record. Remove names from monuments. Revise history until the present seems inevitable.

The archive itself becomes weapon.
Control the past, control the present.
Control the story, control the reality.

Language as Cage

The simulation embedded even in speech:

Egyptians had *names*. Hebrews had *numbers*.
Egyptians had *homes*. Hebrews had *quarters*.
Egyptians *died*. Hebrews were *lost*.
Egyptians *ate*. Hebrews were *fed*.
Egyptians *lived*. Hebrews were *kept*.

When you control language, you control thought. When worthlessness becomes vocabulary, worth becomes unspeakable.

Silence isn't absence of speech. It's absence of permitted meaning.

The Midwives' Crack

When exploitation plateaued, Pharaoh escalated: "Kill the Hebrew boys at birth. Keep only the girls."
But Shiphrah and Puah, the Hebrew midwives, "feared God and did not do what the king of Egypt commanded."

The first crack in the simulation. Two women declaring: Human life has worth that empire cannot revoke.

They used Egypt's prejudice to protect life—"Hebrew women are so vigorous, they give birth before we arrive." Weaponized stereotype to preserve humanity.

Sometimes worth is not argued but enacted.

Moses: Between Simulations

Moses lived between both frameworks—Hebrew by birth, Egyptian by adoption. He saw Hebrew suffering with Egyptian eyes. Egyptian privilege with Hebrew conscience.

The worthlessness narrative couldn't install completely. He existed as a contradiction.

When he saw an Egyptian beating a Hebrew, the simulations collided:

Egypt's narrative: *This is order.*
Hebrew narrative: *This is destiny.*
Moses saw: *This is wrong.*

He killed the Egyptian—not just the man, but the logic.
The next day, Hebrews mocked him: "Who made you ruler? Will you kill us too?"

Too Egyptian for Hebrews. Too Hebrew for Egyptians. He fled to Midian. Forty years in wilderness. Forty years to deprogram. Forty years to discover worth that required neither oppressor nor victim to validate.

The Pattern's Echo

The architecture Egypt perfected echoes through every empire that followed:

The hand that reaches for the phone before consciousness fully arrives—checking metrics, measuring worth, calculating productivity. The shame of rest. The guilt of presence. The anxiety of never enough.

"I didn't accomplish anything today" becoming "I am worthless today." "I'm not contributing" becoming "I don't deserve to exist." Weekend guilt. Vacation anxiety. Burnout as virtue. Exhaustion as credential.

Working sick because "that's what you do." Missing life for a job that won't remember the sacrifice. Accepting impossible conditions. Internalizing systemic failure: "If I just worked harder..." "If I were better..." "Maybe I don't deserve more..."

Modern Egypt doesn't need whips. It has performance reviews. It doesn't need chains. It has debt, rent, healthcare tied to employment. It doesn't need taskmasters. It has internalized worthlessness becoming its own overseer.

The bricks still get made. The quotas still get met. The system still runs. But now the slave has become the slavemaster, and the imprisonment has become invisible.

Tomorrow's Burning

Tomorrow, a bush burns without being consumed. Tomorrow, Worth Itself speaks to a murderer in exile. Tomorrow, the God who sees says "I have seen their misery." Tomorrow, liberation begins.

But tonight, hundreds of years of programming runs its course. Tonight, Hebrew children learn they matter less. Tonight, Egyptian children learn to stop seeing. Tonight, the simulation perfects itself, generation by generation, until both populations forget what reality looked like.

The worthlessness factory operates at full capacity. The metrics update. The quotas increase. The machine hums.

And somewhere in Midian, a shepherd who fled both simulations tends someone else's sheep, waiting for the Voice that will call him back to challenge the oldest lie empire ever told:

That some humans are worth less than others. That worth must be earned. That value requires permission.

Tomorrow, that lie begins to burn.

Chapter 9

The Wilderness: Receiving The Source Code

Downloading Reality's Original Instructions

A BUSH BURNED without being consumed.

Moses—murderer in exile, shepherd of someone else's sheep—stopped to look. Forty years since he fled Egypt. Forty years herding in wilderness. Forty years outside both Egyptian privilege and Hebrew slavery. Forty years of unlearning.

Then the Voice:
"I am the God of your father, the God of Abraham, Isaac, and Jacob."

And immediately after:
"I have seen the misery of my people in Egypt. I have heard them crying out. I am concerned about their suffering. So I have come down to rescue them."

The Creator of reality had been watching. Listening. Attentive.

The worthlessness program was exposed as incomplete. They mattered. They'd always mattered. Someone had been keeping track all along.

"So now, go. I am sending you to Pharaoh to bring my people the Israelites out of Egypt."

Sending a stuttering shepherd. A failed prince. A successful fugitive. Not because Moses was worthy—but because worth isn't the point.

The Voice doesn't call the qualified. It qualifies the called.

Moses argued. Of course he argued.
"Who am I to go to Pharaoh?"
"They won't believe me."
"I can't speak well."
"Please send someone else."

Every excuse rooted in worthlessness programming. *Who am I?* (Nobody important.) *They won't believe me.* (My voice doesn't matter.) *I can't speak.* (I'm inadequate.) *Send someone else.* (Anyone would be better.)

But God's response bypassed the worth question entirely:
"I will be with you."

Not "You're worthy." Not "You're capable." Just "I will be with you."

Liberation doesn't depend on worth. It depends on presence.

The Return: When Liberation Enters Simulation

Moses returned to Egypt carrying only a staff and a promise. No army. No strategy. No leverage. Just an eighty-year-old shepherd with a stutter telling the most powerful man on earth to release his entire workforce.

The absurdity was the point.

If Moses had returned powerful, Egypt could credit strength. If wealthy, economics. If armed, force. But he returned with nothing except presence—so when liberation came, no one could mistake its source.

"Let my people go" wasn't negotiation. It was reality informing simulation that the game was over. Truth telling lies their time was up. Worth declaring worthlessness void.

Ten Demolitions of False Worth

What followed wasn't random destruction but systematic demolition of Egypt's worth framework. Each plague targeted a specific Egyptian god, proving the system's impotence:

Blood: Hapi controlled the Nile's flooding — Egypt's source of life. The Nile became death. The god of abundance couldn't keep water as water.

Frogs: Heqet, the frog goddess, guaranteed fertility. Her sacred creatures became infestation. What Egypt worshipped, Egypt couldn't escape.

Gnats: Geb protected the earth itself. The ground Egypt claimed to own turned against Egyptian skin. Their magicians tried to replicate it and failed — "This is the finger of God."

Flies: Khepri, the scarab god, sanctified the swarm. Only Goshen — where slaves lived — remained untouched. The worthless had peace while the worthy suffered.

Livestock: Hathor, the cow goddess, protected Egypt's herds. Egypt's wealth died in fields while Hebrew livestock lived. The goddess of abundance couldn't save a single animal.

Boils: Isis promised healing. Egyptian bodies — including the priests' — corrupted with sores. The healers couldn't heal themselves, couldn't even enter temples to pray for relief.

Hail: Nut, goddess of the sky, was supposed to shelter Egypt. Instead, fire fell with ice. The sky attacked what it was built to protect.

Locusts: Renenutet guarded the harvest. Years of stored wealth consumed in hours. The goddess of nourishment watched Egypt starve.

Darkness: Ra, the sun god, supreme deity of Egypt — extinguished for three days. Darkness so thick it could be felt. Slaves had light in their quarters while Pharaoh sat blind.

Firstborn: Pharaoh himself was considered a living god — his heir the continuation of divine rule. The future of Egypt's godline died in every household. Every Hebrew household lived.

Each plague inverted hierarchy. The system that defines value cannot protect those it values most.

The Night Everything Reversed

Passover night rewrote the simulation.

Slaves gave orders to masters: "Mark your doors with blood if you want to live."
The powerless held power. Hebrew blood became salvation. Egyptian blood meant nothing.
The worthless became essential: "Take our gold, our silver, just leave!"

Pharaoh, who said "Who is the LORD?" now screamed "Go, worship the LORD!"

But the deepest reversal was internal: For one night, they acted like free people. Ate with shoes on—ready to leave. Packed belongings—claiming ownership. Made choices—exercising agency.

After centuries of worthlessness, they did something worthy. After lifetimes of slavery, they exercised freedom.

Freedom begins with one free act.

A million slaves walked out of Egypt in broad daylight. Not revolt—release. Not rebellion—reversal.

The Sea, The Death, The Terror

But Pharaoh changed his mind.

The same Pharaoh who screamed "Go!" looked at his empty construction sites, his unfinished monuments, his silent brick fields — and sent his army to drag them back.

Six hundred chariots. The finest in the world. Thundering south across the desert.
The Israelites looked up and saw dust on the horizon.
They looked ahead and saw the Red Sea.
They looked around and saw desert on both sides.
No escape. No weapons. No army. Just a million former slaves with nowhere to go.

The programming surfaced instantly:

"Was it because there were no graves in Egypt that you brought us to the desert to die? It would have been better for us to serve the Egyptians than to die in the desert!"

Centuries of programming in one sentence. They would rather return to slavery than face uncertainty. They couldn't imagine a third option: living free.

The sea split. They walked through on dry ground. Pharaoh's army followed — and the waters returned.

They stood on the far side, completely free. No army chasing. No Pharaoh commanding. No taskmasters driving. No quotas. No bricks.

And they had absolutely no idea what to do next.
They were free bodies carrying enslaved minds.
They had escaped Egypt, but Egypt hadn't escaped them.

When God Offered Direct Access

At Sinai, the mountain burned with Divine fire. Smoke billowing. Thunder pounding. Lightning cracking. Reality itself vibrating with divine frequency.

Then the Voice. Not internal. Not mystical. Actual sound waves from actual God to actual humans.

One million people—former slaves, children, foreigners—heard the exact same words at the exact same time. Direct download. No priests needed. No interpretation required. No mediation necessary.

A five-year-old heard what Moses heard. A foreigner heard what Aaron heard. A nursing mother heard what elders heard.

No hierarchy. No mediation. Only encounter.

"I am the LORD your God, who brought you out of Egypt, out of the land of slavery."

First words: identity and liberation. *I exist. You're free. Now learn to stay that way.*

The Choice That Changed Everything

The people couldn't handle direct encounter.

"Speak to us yourself and we will listen," they begged Moses. "But do not have God speak to us or we will die."

This moment—more than the golden calf, more than the complaints—appears to change everything.

They asked for mediation instead of direct connection. They requested distance from the Source. They were afraid of direct encounter, vulnerable before unmediated divinity, desperate for a buffer between themselves and Reality.

They had just watched God destroy Egypt's mediators—every priest, magician, and god-king proven false. Now God offered what no nation had ever had: direct access. Unmediated truth. Clear instruction from the Source.

And they said: "No thanks. You do it for us."

In that moment, they created space for every religious system that would follow. Every priest claiming exclusive access. Every institution positioning itself between humans and truth. Every hierarchy built on mediated encounter.

They chose simulation over reality.
But God gave them the Torah anyway.

Freedom Technology: The Antivirus Code

Torah—not "law" but instruction. From *yarah*: to point toward a target, to show direction. Not telling them what they couldn't do. Telling them what would keep them free.

Sabbath: Every seventh day, the entire machine stops. Master and servant, citizen and stranger, human and animal—all cease. The hands stop forming. The feet stop carrying. For one day every week, no one produces. In that cessation, the body learns: worth precedes output. Value predates productivity. The simulation cannot run.

This interrupts Narrative: The weekly break from productivity framework. The counter-story that worth ≠ output. Every seven days, narrative immunity builds.

Jubilee: Every fiftieth year, complete economic reset. All debts cancelled. All slaves freed. All land returned. Accumulation reversed. Inequality demolished before permanence installs. No permanent underclass possible. The economic simulation reboots to factory settings.

This interrupts Fear at the source: Prevents worthlessness accumulation. Breaks debt cycles. Makes economic anxiety temporary, not existential.

Gleaning: Leave the field edges unharvested. Don't maximize extraction. Let abundance leak. The corners belong to others by design. Structured sharing proves there's enough for everyone when hoarding stops.

This interrupts Fear: Material proof that scarcity is choice, not reality. Abundance demonstrated, not promised.

Testimony: Truth-telling required. False witness prohibited. Reality over fiction. The community cannot function on consensus lies.

This interrupts Narrative: Communal reality-checking. Truth verification. Prevents false framework installation through collective agreement on facts.

Festivals: Passover remembers liberation. Sukkot practices impermanence. Shavuot celebrates direct encounter. Yom Kippur resets accumulated corruption. Regular scheduled maintenance. Systematic debugging sessions.

This interrupts Isolation: Mandatory gathering. Can't fully withdraw when weekly Sabbath presence is expected. Physical proximity creates intervention opportunities.

Every instruction either forces vulnerability (confession), interrupts fear (Sabbath rest), or removes masks (direct access). The entire system targets the simulation's installation process.

Instructions that disable empire's operating system.

Forty Days Without Moses

Forty days Moses stayed on the mountain receiving instructions. Forty days the people waited below. Forty days without the only person who spoke to God directly.
Then panic.

"Come, make us gods who will go before us. As for this fellow Moses who brought us up out of Egypt, we don't know what has happened to him."

Read carefully: they didn't say "make us new gods." They said "make us gods who will go before us" — who will lead us forward. Moses was gone. Maybe dead. The God who rescued them was invisible, untouchable, on a mountain wrapped in fire and thunder.

They hadn't abandoned their God. They'd lost their mediator and couldn't bear the silence.
Aaron collected their gold and fashioned a calf — a bull. Not random. But not what most people assume either.

Look at what the plagues had just demolished: the Nile god, the frog goddess, the earth god, the sky goddess, the sun god. Every major Egyptian deity exposed as powerless. But the bull — associated with strength, with the power that drives forward — wasn't on the list.

Perhaps they chose the one symbol that hadn't been defeated. Perhaps they weren't building an Egyptian god at all. Perhaps they were trying to create a visible image of the invisible God who had shown such strength — the God who overpowered everything Egypt worshipped.

"These are your gods, Israel, who brought you up out of Egypt!"

They attributed the exodus to the image. They credited the rescue to something they could see, touch, carry. Not because they were faithless — but because the uncertainty of an invisible God, a missing leader, and an unknown future was more than they could bear.

This is what fear does. It doesn't make you worship foreign gods. It makes you try to shrink the real God down to something manageable. Something visible. Something you control.

The golden calf wasn't betrayal. It was desperation. The same desperation that makes people today reduce the infinite to a system, a formula, a framework they can hold.

Moses descended to find them dancing — not around Egypt's god, but around their own attempt to make the invisible visible. He smashed the tablets. Not anger — accuracy. They weren't ready for direct instructions. They still wanted mediation. Still needed something between themselves and the overwhelming reality of unmediated encounter.

The simulation survives inside. Not because people are faithless — but because freedom without structure feels like falling. And falling people grab whatever's closest.

The Wilderness Generation

For forty years, they wandered. Not punishment—reprogramming.

Every morning, bread with the dew. Manna—just enough for the day. When they hoarded, it rotted—teaching trust. When they rested on Sabbath, it lasted—teaching rhythm. Even decay obeyed the freedom code.

Their clothes never wore out. Their feet never swelled.
Physics itself paused to make a point: *Reality provides. Simulation depletes.*

But the older generation couldn't fully adapt. Their bodies still flinched at Egyptian memories. Their minds still calculated worth by output. Their hearts still measured safety by brick quotas met.

Too infected to be healed. Too programmed to be reformatted.

One by one, they died in the wilderness. Not all at once, but over forty years, the Egypt-programmed generation stopped breathing. They had seen miracles. Heard God directly. Tasted manna. Walked through parted seas. But their neural pathways had been carved by hundreds of years of slavery.

The kindest mercy was letting them carry their programming to the grave.

The New Generation

But their children—born in wilderness, raised on manna, educated by miracles—grew up with different programming.

They didn't remember Egypt. They remembered provision.
They didn't fear scarcity. They expected abundance.
They didn't need taskmasters. They had direct instructions.
They didn't measure worth by productivity. They measured it by presence.

A baby born in year one of the exodus turned forty as the wilderness ended. That baby had never made a brick. Never heard a whip crack. Never felt worthlessness install through daily degradation.

That baby learned that food falls from sky. That water comes from rocks. That worth is inherent. That God speaks directly. That Sabbath comes weekly. That community matters more than output.

That baby entered the promised land with a clean operating system.

The Threshold

On the edge of the Jordan River, one generation buried, another one ready, Moses gave final instructions:

"See, I set before you today life and prosperity, death and destruction. Choose life."

Not complicated theology. Not elaborate rituals. Just: *Choose life.*

Choose practices over performance.

Choose community over isolation.
Choose truth over narrative.
Choose presence over mediation.
Choose freedom's vulnerability over slavery's certainty.

Then Moses died. The mediator removed. The voice between God and people — silenced. Even Moses couldn't enter — the generation that would live the instructions needed no one standing between them and direct encounter.

Joshua led them across the Jordan. A new generation. A free generation. A wilderness-formed, manna-fed, Torah-taught people who had never known anything except God's direct provision.

For one generation—unevenly, imperfectly—they lived closer to the design.

They practiced Sabbath. Celebrated Jubilee. Left gleanings. Told truth. Gathered regularly. Maintained the instructions that kept them free.

For a time, Torah constrained corruption faster than it could consolidate. Instructions followed without institution. Practices performed without mediation.

For one generation, humans lived free.

Then they requested a king.
Then they built a temple.
Then they created hierarchies.
Then they forgot what wilderness taught.
Then the silence began.

But that's the next chapter's story. Tonight, at the threshold between Egypt's death and promise's life, one generation proved it was possible.

Freedom is possible.
Direct encounter is possible.
Community without coercion is possible.
Life outside simulation is possible.

The instructions work.
The practices preserve—when practiced

The code runs clean.

One generation proved it.
Which means another generation can too.

Chapter 10

THE SILENCE: HEAVEN OFFLINE

Four Hundred Years Without a Word

MALACHI STOOD IN the rebuilt Temple, watching priests go through motions.

Sacrifices performed. Incense rising. Prayers recited. Everything functioning. Nothing connecting.

"When you bring blind animals for sacrifice, is that not wrong? When you sacrifice lame or diseased animals, is that not wrong?"

The priests shrugged. The system ran. Whether God noticed seemed irrelevant.

Malachi's final message: "See, I will send the prophet Elijah before that great and dreadful day of the LORD comes."

Then silence. No prophet. No voice. No recognized presence.
For the next four hundred and fifty years, heaven would feel absolutely still.

When heaven stops speaking, humans can't stop explaining.

The Unbearable Void

Silence is unbearable—especially divine silence.

When heaven goes quiet, humans either manufacture noise or assume no one listens. Both happened.

The Temple continued its rhythm: morning sacrifice, evening sacrifice, Sabbaths, festivals, endless repetition. Form without presence. Words without response. Faith without encounter.

At first, they waited. Surely another prophet would come. A month. A year. A decade. Nothing.

Then they wondered: Had they sinned too greatly? They doubled their efforts—more rules, more precision, more performance. Still nothing.

The silence wasn't lack of sound. It was absence of presence. The glory once filling the Temple—gone.

Four generations passed. Then ten. Then fifteen. Children heard stories of prophets as myths of a time when God supposedly spoke.

When heaven won't answer, humans find interpretive voices to fill the void.

The Persian Whisper

Exile to Babylon exposed Israel to Persia. When Cyrus freed them, they returned with Zoroaster's ideas in the air around them.

Two cosmic powers locked in eternal combat: Ahura Mazda—light, truth, order. Angra Mainyu—darkness, lies, chaos.

Not Hebrew thinking. Genesis told of one Creator calling everything good.

But silence made dualism feel logical. Why suffering? Cosmic war. Why injustice? Temporary defeat. Why silence? God busy fighting elsewhere.

The infection was subtle. They didn't adopt Persian religion—they absorbed its framework.

Before: satan = the adversary, a role in God's court.
After: The Satan = cosmic enemy, god's rival.

Before: death = Sheol for all.
After: heaven or hell, sorted eternally.

Before: angels = messengers.
After: armies with hierarchies.

Before: history = God's story with His people.
After: cosmic battlefield of light versus darkness.

Dualism doesn't need two gods. It only needs two categories. The mind supplies the rest.

When the Unseen Turned Hostile

When the Voice withdrew, the unseen grew crowded. Fear fills every gap presence leaves.

In the Persian years, evil stopped being action—it became entity.

The Hebrew *satan*—"adversary," a function in God's court—mutated into Satan: independent, powerful, recruiting. Sin wasn't separation—it was invasion. Evil wasn't choice—it was possession. Suffering wasn't consequence—it was attack.

By the second century BCE, Jewish texts spawned hierarchies of harm: Belial commanding legions, demons named and ranked like Roman battalions. The Book of Enoch mapped the demonic: fallen angels breeding with women, creating Nephilim, corrupting creation at the genetic level.

Evil stopped being primarily a verb. It became a noun.

Before the Persian years, *satan* had a function. The word meant the one who tests, who presses, who asks the question you'd rather not answer. Not an enemy. A stress-test. The fault line that revealed whether your foundation was real. When that function mutated into a being, something quietly disappeared: **the obligation to examine yourself**. You didn't have to face the question anymore. You just had to survive the attacker.

Evil as entity invites battle. Evil as action demands repentance.

Rabbis developed defensive theology—not from paranoia, but from precaution: *mezuzot* on doorposts (spiritual force fields), *tefillin* as armor (binding protective words to the body), *mikvah* baths (washing off invisible attackers). Every prayer became a ward.

The world that once pulsed with It is good now required constant vigilance. Eden's open garden became a fortified city. Walking with God became warfare for God.

The silence had done its work: Direct encounter now felt too dangerous to risk. Better to fight demons than face God. Better to blame possession than acknowledge choice. Better to perfect the fortress than venture into garden.

The War Scroll Vision

The Essenes carried dualism to its extreme. In Qumran's caves they wrote: "The War of the Sons of Light Against the Sons of Darkness."

They divided humanity: Sons of Light—the elect, the pure, the remnant. Sons of Darkness—the deceived, the corrupted, the damned.

No middle ground. No redemption.

They trained for purity like soldiers for battle—awaiting trumpet calls from heaven.

The problem with cosmic warfare: everyone thinks they're the light.

The Angels Multiply

Prophets gone, angels expanded to fill the gap. Once rare messengers—now entire bureaucracies of heaven.

Every star had an angel. Every nation a prince. Every person a guardian.
The Book of Enoch detailed the hierarchy: seven archangels, angels of thunder, dew, wind, and fire.
Heaven became corporate. God the distant CEO. Angels middle management.

Once God walked in gardens. Now requests processed through channels.

Distance became doctrine.

The Mathematic of Purity

Without the Voice declaring "clean" or "unclean," humans made formulas.

The Pharisees turned purity into math. Thirty-nine categories of Sabbath work, each with subcategories, exceptions, clauses. One command—"remember the Sabbath"—became a flowchart needing experts.

If Torah said, "don't boil a kid in its mother's milk," they separated meat from dairy entirely—different dishes, sinks, hours.

Not from legalism, but longing. If perfection could break the silence, they would code perfection through precision.

When God can't be heard, everything else gets measured.

The Apocalyptic Imagination

The silence birthed a new genre: apocalypse—"unveiling."

If God wouldn't speak plainly, maybe He spoke in symbols. Beasts, horns, numbers, visions. History as code. Reality as cipher.

Time divided in two: This Age—evil reigns. The Age to Come—God intervenes.

Present pain explained by future hope.

But it also makes the present feel unchangeable—why fix what God will soon destroy?

The simulation loves apocalypse. It keeps people waiting instead of acting, dreaming of tomorrow instead of changing today.

The Splintering

By Rome's conquest (63 BCE), Judaism had fractured:

Pharisees—Obedience will end silence.
Sadducees—System must survive.
Essenes—Purity through separation.
Zealots—Freedom through violence.

Each offered explanation. Each claimed authority. Each built its own simulation.

Brother against brother over calendars. Fights over purity laws. Violence over vowels.

When God goes silent, human voices compete to fill the void.

The Simple Ones

But among the working poor—the *anawim*—something gentler survived.

They didn't systematize the silence. They endured it.

Lighting Sabbath candles because light felt like promise. Sharing bread because eating together kept them human. Telling old stories because memory was presence enough.

No cosmic maps. No purity flowcharts. Just daily bread, weekly rest, seasonal hope.

They couldn't explain why God was silent. They couldn't build theories about cosmic warfare or philosophical frameworks about the divided self.

They simply kept the practices alive. Kept the table set. Kept the lights burning.

Not because they understood. Because practice doesn't require explanation to remain practice.

The sophisticated built towers of interpretation. The simple just kept walking.

The Infection Complete

Four centuries of silence prepared the soil.

Persia had divided reality in two—light versus darkness. Evil became entity instead of action. Angels and demons filled the imagination. The unseen became battlefield. Existence became warfare.

But a deeper infection approached from the West.

Greece would offer something subtler—not cosmic war, but total comprehension. Where Persia split the universe, Greece would split the self. Where Persia made heaven and hell, Greece would make mind and matter.

Silence had made humanity desperate for meaning. Persia supplied drama. Greece would supply certainty.

Philosophy would replace prophecy. Logic would substitute for revelation. The mind would become the temple. Thought would become the god.

The void demanded filling. Greece had perfected its product. And the market—souls starved for sound—was ready.

The Approaching Dissection

The Greek infection would prove more subtle and more complete than Persian dualism.

Where Persia externalized evil, Greece would internalize it—making body the prison, desire the demon, humanity itself the problem.

Between Persian cosmic warfare and Greek philosophical categories, the simple invitation "Where are you?" would be buried under centuries of interpretation.

When the Voice finally returned—speaking through a carpenter from Nazareth—almost no one would recognize it as presence rather than threat.

They would be too busy fighting cosmic battles and solving philosophical problems to hear someone say: "The kingdom of God is within you." "Your sins are forgiven." "Follow me."

Simple words. Direct presence. No demons to battle. No philosophy to master. Just an invitation to walk again.

But by then, the infections would run too deep. They would turn even him into cosmic warrior and philosophical problem.

The simulation had learned to absorb its own cure.

The Pattern

Every generation finds new demons when heaven feels silent and meaning must be supplied elsewhere. The names change, the frameworks don't.

When heaven falls silent, humans imagine hell everywhere. When presence withdraws, paranoia fills the vacuum. When God feels absent, everything else feels dangerous.

But danger was never out there. It was always in the choice—to extract rather than generate, to fear rather than love, to categorize rather than connect.

No demons required. Just humans choosing simulation over reality, one terrified interpretation at a time.

The Anticipation

For four centuries, the silence held. Empires rose. Philosophers reasoned. Prophets did not speak.
The systems multiplied, but no one spoke with authority. The words became many; the presence, none.
Humanity waited—not knowing for what, only that the noise wasn't enough.

They built temples of logic, theories of truth, laws of order.

But somewhere beneath all the systems, a question still echoed through the silence:

"Where are you?"

And the world, still hiding, did not yet know how to answer.

PART IV

Beneath The Simulation

*Empire: The Weight
That Crushes Truth*

The simulation runs on nouns. Reality runs on verbs. Empire buried presence beneath abstraction, being beneath performance—and the weight you feel is not life. It's empire.

Chapter 11

GREECE: THE NEW MIND

When Thinking Replaced Listening

WHEN THE VOICE grew quiet, the world began to think in its place.

Not the wondering thought that asks, "Who are You?" but the self-enclosed kind that asks, "Who am I, without You?"

Into that silence came architects of intellect—men who believed reason could rebuild what revelation had withdrawn.

Where prophets once listened, philosophers analyzed. Where Presence once spoke, logic now lectured. The sacred conversation became a monologue about the self.

At first, it felt like progress. Equations where once there were mysteries. Categories where once there were covenants. The infinite compressed into something comprehensible. Humanity, orphaned by heaven, began raising itself.

And who could blame them?

Four hundred years without a Voice. An entire civilization watching the sky for a signal that never came. The Greeks weren't building a trap. They were building a shelter. They looked at a world full of mystery, suffering, and silence

— and tried to make sense of it with the only tool that seemed to work without divine cooperation: the human mind.

Their project was understandable. Even noble.

But thought has gravity. Once the mind became its own light, every orbit bent inward. The tool that sought understanding became the object of worship. The torch that promised clarity began to burn the hand that held it.

How Greece Colonized Consciousness

Alexander's armies left Jerusalem after three years. Greek thought never left.

The conquest wasn't military — it was mental. Persian dualism had split reality in two. Greece would split humans themselves from the inside out.

Persia created cosmic categories — light and darkness. Greece created mental categories — body and soul. The battlefield moved inside the human mind — and body.

The Jews who once saw spiritual warfare everywhere would now see the real enemy staring from the mirror.

The Philosophical Rescue

Greece offered what the silence denied: complete explanation through human reason.

Where prophets had said, "Thus says the LORD," philosophers said, "Thus reasons the mind."

Both reduced uncertainty. Only one required relationship.

Hebrew thought — concrete, particular, verb-based — looked primitive beside Greek abstraction. Talking donkeys and parting seas embarrassed the educated heirs of Aristotle.

Without fresh prophecy to defend it, Hebrew wisdom felt outdated. Philosophy wasn't imposed. They reached for it like drowning souls grab rope — not realizing the rope was tied to an anchor.

The Freezing

Here is what Greece actually did, and why it mattered.

Hebrew reality moved. Walking in righteousness. Missing the mark. Being faithful. Becoming holy. Everything was process, motion, relationship — verbs that required ongoing participation.

Greek reality held still. The righteous. The sinner. The believer. The Good. Categories that could be examined, compared, defined — nouns that existed independent of any relationship.

The Greeks weren't trying to imprison anyone. They were trying to *understand*. And understanding requires stillness. A river cannot be measured while flowing. A bird cannot be studied mid-flight. To analyze something, you first have to stop it.

So they stopped everything.

They froze *walking in righteousness* into *the righteous* — a category you either belonged to or didn't.

They froze *missing the mark* into *sinner* — an identity that defined you rather than an action you could change.

They froze *being faithful* into *believer* — a designation that survived abandonment, because nouns don't need relationship to exist.

Verbs can change. Nouns are permanent. A person who lies can stop lying. A *liar* must be redeemed — or expelled.

The Greeks gave the world nouns because the silence had made verbs feel unreliable. When the Voice stopped speaking, processes felt pointless. Categories, at least, held still. They could be studied. Trusted. Built upon.

But frozen things don't grow. And frozen people can't move.

Plato's Well-Intended Prison

Plato offered medicine for abandoned minds. It answered the right question with the wrong prescription.

The cave: Prisoners chained in darkness, watching shadows, believing shadows are real. One escapes, sees the sun, returns to free others — only to be rejected.

It explained the divine silence perfectly by relocating the problem into the human: Humans can't hear God because they mistake shadows for truth. Transcend the physical; reach the world of ideas.

For a generation desperate to explain why heaven felt empty, this was irresistible.

But look at what the prescription required:

- Physical world = shadows. Meaning: everything you touch, taste, feel — not real.
- Material reality = cave. Meaning: the world you live in is a trap.
- Body = chain. Meaning: your flesh is the obstacle.
- True reality = abstract Forms. Meaning: only thought accesses what's real.
- Salvation = philosophical contemplation. Meaning: think your way out.

Hebrew thought had declared creation "very good." Greek thought declared it fundamentally fake.

Plato wasn't malicious. He was trying to explain the ache. But the explanation cost everything — because it taught people to distrust the very ground they stood on.

The Divided Self

Greek philosophy split the human apart:

Body: corrupt, temporary, source of pain
Soul: pure, eternal, divine fragment trapped in flesh

Hebrew consciousness had been whole — *nephesh*, a living unity of body and breath. A person didn't *have* a soul. A person *was* a soul — integrated, embodied, breathing. Hunger wasn't separate from longing. Grief lived in the stomach before it reached the mind. To know something was to feel it in the bones. The body wasn't a problem to be managed. It was the site of encounter.

When the Voice withdrew, that integration had nothing to hold it together. Greek dualism rushed into the gap with an explanation for the ache: you weren't forsaken — their bodies were the problem. The flesh wasn't where God met you. It was what stood between you and the divine.

Every modern fracture traces back here: eating disorders, self-harm, "mind over matter" slogans, spirituality that hates the flesh.

Once at war with oneself, the war is already lost — or endlessly fought.

The Abstraction Hierarchy

Greece ordered reality by distance from dirt.

Top tier: pure thought, logic, mathematics.
Middle: applied sciences, medicine, rhetoric.
Bottom: manual labor, crafts, agriculture.

The further from physical, the closer to truth. Philosophers should rule. Workers should serve. Bodies should obey. Women — bearers of physical life — ranked lowest.

Every modern bias runs this program: knowledge over labor, theoretical over practical, virtual over real.

The mind that despises the hand forgets it needs the hand to eat.

The Universal Solvent

Hebrew truth was particular — a covenant with a people, a place, a history. Greek truth was universal — law, logic, reason — true everywhere, related to no one.

Universal truth serves all by serving none. Applies everywhere by belonging nowhere.

Modern science is Greece's triumph — an elegant system explaining everything and meaning nothing.

Universal truth without particular love is technically correct and humanly devastating — especially to suffering bodies.

The Translation Disaster

When Hebrew was translated to Greek, words didn't just change — worlds changed:

Torah → Nomos

- Lost: Teaching, instruction, path to walk.
- Gained: Legislation, regulation, legal code.

Nephesh → Psyche

- Lost: Living being, breath, the whole person.
- Gained: Immaterial essence, a ghost in the machine.

Emunah → Pistis

- Lost: Faithfulness, steadfast action.
- Gained: Belief, mental assent, intellectual agreement.

Rich verbs flattened into static nouns — categories fit for classification, not care. Living relationships reduced to logic. Embodied truth replaced by mental proposition.

Translation is always reduction. Greek reduced everything to thought.

The Jewish Mind Divided

To appear sophisticated — and intelligible in a world that now thought in Greek — Jewish thinkers learned to translate their own wisdom into foreign categories.

Philo of Alexandria led the merger:

- Abraham's journey = soul's ascent from material.
- Exodus = liberation from body's prison.
- Temple = cosmic diagram.
- Commandments = symbols of virtues.
- Sabbath = contemplation of eternal.

The God who wrestled became The Unmoved Mover. The God who repented became The Immutable.

Every Jewish faction absorbed Greek code:

- **Pharisees:** Greek precision applied to Hebrew law.
- **Sadducees:** Greek materialism denying afterlife.
- **Essenes:** Greek dualism fleeing evil matter.
- **Zealots:** Greek political philosophy through violence.

No escape from the Greek operating system. Only different applications running on the same code.

The Schools of Coping

Each Greek school offered a different way to manage the silence:

Stoicism: Perform virtue regardless of reality

- Control only response.
- Accept fate without emotion.
- Dignity while everything burns.
- Perfect mask for empire's perfect citizens.

Epicureanism: Pleasure compensates for meaninglessness

- Refine enjoyment.
- Avoid disturbance.
- Death is nothing.
- Perfect consumers for empire's economy.

Cynicism: Reject all social constructs

- Live like dogs (*kunikos*).
- Mock convention.
- Embrace shamelessness.
- Perfect outsiders for empire's margins.

Skepticism: Doubt everything equally

- Suspend judgment.
- Achieve *ataraxia* (tranquility).
- Nothing certain.
- Perfect paralysis for empire's stability.

Each philosophy promised freedom. Each delivered a different way of managing abandonment. All shared one assumption: that thinking could fix what thinking had broken.

The Trap That Felt Like Freedom

Greece filled the silence with sophistication — categories for everything, explanations for suffering, systems for virtue, methods for truth.

And for a time, it worked. The categories organized. The philosophies comforted. The abstractions replaced the ache of silence with the satisfaction of understanding.

But something strange began happening.

The categories that organized reality started creating new questions. The explanations that resolved suffering generated new forms of it. The systems that promised certainty revealed new uncertainties at every turn.

Before Greece, humans lived with what they couldn't explain. The gods were mysterious — that was simply their nature. Death was uncertain — everyone faced it anyway. Mystery was the texture of life, not a problem requiring solution.

After Greece, everything required analysis. Mysteries that had been accepted became problems demanding answers. Questions that had never needed asking now couldn't stop being asked.

The shepherd who never wondered about the mechanism of growth now needed theories of causation. The parent who taught through story now needed logical justification. The person who simply lived now needed to understand the meaning of living before they could do it.

The tools built to make sense of reality had begun generating their own confusion — and the confusion demanded more tools.

But why? Why did Greek thought spread so effectively? Why couldn't Hebrew consciousness resist it? Why does the mind prefer frozen categories to living paradox?

The answer isn't philosophical. It's neurological.

The trap had an engine. And that engine — the reason Greek categories conquered Hebrew consciousness so completely — ran on something deeper than ideas.

It ran on the brain itself.

Chapter 12

The Anxiety Engine

How Abstraction Manufactures Fear

THE GREEKS GAVE humanity sophisticated tools for understanding reality. They froze movement into categories, processes into essences, becoming into being.

They weren't building a trap. They were building a lens.

But lenses have consequences. And the consequences weren't philosophical.

They were neurological.

The Discovery No One Made

Plato's cave wasn't just metaphor — it was accidental neuroscience before neuroscience existed.

The prisoners in his story preferred shadows not from weakness but from neurological necessity. The shadows were predictable. Reality was not. The brain, when faced with false patterns versus true chaos, almost always chooses the patterns.

Wrong map beats no map. Bad story beats no story. Toxic certainty beats healthy uncertainty — at least in the short term.

The Greeks discovered this without understanding why. They saw that categories calmed people. That fixed identities reduced panic. That explanations — even incomplete ones — brought relief.

What they couldn't see was the mechanism underneath.

The Three Laws:

1. Uncertainty = Psychological Entropy

The brain experiences not-knowing as chaos. Insufficient information to predict outcomes registers neurologically as danger. The unknown activates ancient survival circuits designed for physical threat — even when no physical threat exists.

The body doesn't distinguish between a tiger in the bushes and an unanswered question about your purpose. Both trigger the same alarm. Both flood the same circuits. Both demand resolution — immediately.

2. Entropy Triggers Cortisol

Uncertainty floods the system with stress hormones. The body prepares for fight or flight. Heart rate increases. Focus narrows. The physiology of maybe-death activates even when the uncertainty is abstract, philosophical, existential rather than physical.

This is why existential questions feel like emergencies. Why "What am I doing with my life?" produces the same chest-tightness as a near-miss on the highway. The brain doesn't care about the source. It cares about the uncertainty.

3. Any Pattern Reduces Entropy

Even false patterns. Even harmful ones. The brain prefers wrong certainty to accurate uncertainty. A bad map provides structure. No map provides terror.

This is the formula: Greek categories over Hebrew paradox. Fixed identity over fluid becoming. Abstract ideal over messy reality.

Not because Greek thinking was truer. Because it reduced neurological chaos more immediately and reliably.

Before the Tools

Here is what Greece changed — and why it matters.

For millennia, humans lived with massive uncertainty. Walked with it. Trusted it. Weather unpredictable. Harvests uncertain. Survival not guaranteed.

But uncertainty was survivable because it was shared. Community provided reality-checking. Presence provided context. Direct encounter with the Source gave framework that held paradox without collapsing it into categories.

The shepherd didn't wonder about the mechanism of growth. The farmer didn't need theories of causation. The parent taught through story without requiring logical justification. Mystery was the texture of life — not a problem demanding solution.

Then the Voice withdrew. And the uncertainty that presence had made bearable became unbearable.

Then Greece arrived with a cure: categories. Fixed identities. Binary outcomes. Systems explaining everything.

The exhausted brain grabbed them reflexively. Not realizing the cure would generate its own disease.

The Analysis Loop

Here's the cruel irony: Greek analysis didn't reduce uncertainty. It multiplied it.

Once Greece introduced tools for analyzing everything, suddenly everything required analysis. Questions that had never needed answers now demanded them. Mysteries that had been accepted became problems requiring solutions.

Humans didn't worry about the precise mechanism of breath before philosophers insisted everything must have mechanisms. Didn't agonize over the nature of the soul before logicians demanded clear categories. Didn't fear theological error before theology made error possible.

More analysis meant more questions. More questions meant more uncertainty. More uncertainty meant more need for answers. More answers meant more analysis.

The loop closed. The trap set itself.

The brain, trying to reduce entropy, deployed analysis. Analysis revealed more entropy. More entropy demanded more analysis.

The attempt to escape uncertainty locked humans inside it.

The tools of certainty created new forms of uncertainty — and the new uncertainties were worse than the old ones, because the old ones had been livable. The new ones came with the expectation that they should be solvable.

The Categorical Anxiety Cycle

Greek categories promised to reduce uncertainty. They delivered new anxieties that the pre-Greek world never experienced:

The Identity Question:
Hebrew: "What am I becoming?" (verb, ongoing, open).
Greek: "What am I?" (noun, fixed, answerable).
Creates: Fear of being miscategorized, anxiety about essential nature, dread of hidden defect.

The Moral Question:
Hebrew: "How do I walk?" (continuous practice, adjustable).
Greek: "Am I good?" (categorical status, binary).
Creates: Constant self-evaluation, measuring against unreachable ideals. The feeling of permanent insufficiency.

The Knowledge Question:
Hebrew: "How do I live wisely?" (practical wisdom, embodied).
Greek: "Do I know truth?" (theoretical certainty, abstract).
Creates: Intellectual anxiety, fear of ignorance. The sense that understanding is always incomplete.

The Salvation Question:
Hebrew: "Am I walking with God?" (relationship, present tense).
Greek: "Am I saved?" (category, final verdict).
Creates: The anxiety no category can resolve — am I fundamentally acceptable?
Not "am I doing wrong" but "am I *wrong*."

Greek thinking could diagnose the question. It had no answer for it. The silence got louder.

Why Categories Win

The brain flees entropy (uncertainty). Greek categories reduce entropy perfectly:

Uncertainty: "Who am I?" (unbearable openness).
Category: "I am philosopher/slave/citizen" (fixed answer).
Relief: Immediate reduction in cognitive load.

But then:
New Uncertainty: "Am I *really* a philosopher? Am I good enough?"
Mask: Perform the category to prove it.
New Fear: Being exposed as not-really-the-category.

The category that promised certainty created new uncertainty requiring constant performance. And the performance created exhaustion. And the exhausted mind reached for the nearest framework. And the cycle fed itself.

This is why Greek categories spread faster than Greek armies. The brain wanted them. Needed them. Grabbed them before conscious evaluation could intervene.

Not weakness. Wiring.

The Brain's Ancient Wiring

The human brain was built to overreact to uncertainty. Better false alarm than fatal surprise.

Three survival systems became empire's weapons:

Pattern-detection finds tigers in bushes — and later, invisible threats. Under empire, it becomes conspiracy thinking: finding patterns in static, connections in coincidence, meaning in randomness.

Tribal belonging avoids exile — and later, difference. Under empire, it becomes conformity pressure: agreement more important than accuracy, fitting in more important than truth.

Control through prediction survives chaos — and later, mystery. Under empire, it becomes control addiction: managing, optimizing, eliminating all variables, mistaking prediction for safety.

Greece turned these survival instincts inward. Made the brain's safety systems into the bars of its own cage. Fear of death became fear of difference — and fear of contamination. Survival instinct became ideology.

The mind that cannot accept uncertainty will accept any certainty, **no matter how false**.

The Manufacturing Process

Every empire since ancient Greece runs the same two-step code:

Step 1: Manufacture Uncertainty
Create questions that cannot be answered with certainty. Keep humans anxious.

Greece: "What is the Good?"
Rome: "Are you loyal enough?"
Medieval Church: "Are you saved?"
Modern Age: "Are you successful enough?"

Each question infinite, unmeasurable, unresolvable. Each designed to generate permanent anxiety.

Step 2: Sell Certainty
Offer the system that claims to fix the anxiety the system created.

Greece: "Philosophy will explain."
Rome: "Law will order."

Medieval: "Church will absolve."
Modern: "Algorithm will predict."

First create anxiety. Then sell the cure. Make sure the cure causes more anxiety.

The anxiety engine feeds itself. Entropy becomes economy.

The Body as Casualty

The body was the first thing sacrificed to manage the anxiety.

Bodies are unpredictable. The stomach announces hunger mid-contemplation. Sleep interrupts philosophy. The flesh ages while theorizing immortality. Desire contradicts the Good. Messy. Mortal. Uncertain.

So the body became the enemy — a neat division that reduced anxiety through categorization:

Body = prison (predictably bad).
Soul = prisoner (predictably good).

The split simplified — and anesthetized. No more paradox of integrated being. No more uncertainty about embodied existence. Clear categories. Simple hierarchy.

But the cost was wholeness.

From that wound flowed centuries of consequences: hatred of flesh disguised as holiness. Eating disorders justified as ascetic virtue. Disembodiment marketed as spirituality. Detachment praised as enlightenment.

Every "mind over matter" slogan, every "body is just a vessel" teaching, every optimization that ignores physical limits — Greek anxiety-management through division.

A person cannot be whole while at war with half of themselves.

The Perfect Trap

The mechanism was complete — even before Rome arrived to enforce it.

Neurologically: The brain prefers false certainty to accurate uncertainty.
Philosophically: Greek categories provide certainty through fixed essences.
Psychologically: The categories generate new anxieties that demand more categories.
Result: A self-sustaining prison built from the brain's own survival mechanisms.

The mind — and eventually the body — becomes simultaneously:

- The problem — generating the uncertainty that demands resolution.
- The solution — creating the categories that promise relief.
- The judge — evaluating fitness to the categories it created.
- The defendant — being evaluated by its own standards.
- The prison — trapped inside categories it cannot think past.
- The key — believing that more thinking will unlock what thinking imprisoned.

It polices itself using its own categories. Every attempt to escape reinforces the cage. Every question seeking freedom uses the framework that imprisons.

It polices itself using its own categories. Every attempt to escape reinforces the cage. Every question seeking freedom uses the framework that imprisons.

Categories eliminate mystery. Explanations eliminate lament by resolving it too quickly. Systems eliminate relationship. Reasons eliminate encounter. Methods eliminate revelation.

The trap was perfect — because it was built from the inside.

No empire constructed it. No conspiracy designed it. The brain, fleeing uncertainty, built its own cage from the best materials available. Greece simply provided the blueprints.

What Rome Saw

Rome observed all of this and recognized weaponizable technology.

Greece categorized. Rome would codify.

Greek philosophy had provided the categories — body and soul, good and evil, citizen and barbarian, civilized and savage. These were persuasive. People adopted them voluntarily because the brain wanted the relief they offered.

Rome saw the next step: make the categories law. Give philosophical abstractions the force of state violence.

Under Greece, categories were suggestions the brain eagerly accepted.
Under Rome, categories became compulsory — enforceable, expandable, incscapablc.

The Greeks gave empire the engine. Rome would give it wheels.

Chapter 13

ROME: TERMS AND CONDITIONS

When Law Replaced Relationship

ROME DISCOVERED SOMETHING even more powerful than Greek abstraction: legal reality enforced.

The Greeks said, "Humans might be living in shadows." Rome said, "This person is a slave—and here's the document proving it."

The Greeks philosophized about categories. Rome made categories law. The Greeks built mental prisons. Rome made them enforceable.

When a magistrate declared someone "slave," they didn't become enslaved—they became slavery itself in the eyes of the law.

Law didn't describe condition. It created it. And that creation could bleed.

Philosophy makes people think they're trapped. Law makes the trap real.

The Three Humans

Roman law recognized three kinds of humans—not philosophically, but legally:

Citizens (Cives)

- Could own property—including other humans.
- Could marry legally, vote, appeal to Caesar.
- Their testimony counted.
- Killing them was murder.

Foreigners (Peregrini)

- Could trade, but not vote.
- Couldn't marry citizens.
- Their testimony counted less.
- Killing them was crime, not murder.

Slaves (Servi)

- Were property, not persons.
- Couldn't own, marry, or testify except under torture.
- Killing them was property damage.

These weren't descriptions. They were legal creations. The law spoke, and a person became what it said for all enforceable purposes.

Law doesn't discover what someone is. It decides what counts as real about them.

The Genius of Legal Fiction

Rome perfected the legal fiction—something untrue that becomes true when law declares it.

Adoption: When a citizen adopted someone, the law said that person had always been his child. Their biological father legally never existed. Their new siblings had always been blood. Simulation legally overwrote biology.

Corporation: A group of humans declared one legal person—able to own, sue, be sued, and live forever. A collective pretending to be singular.

Every LLC, every Inc., every legal entity today is a Roman fiction still running.

First create the fiction. Then make everyone pretend it's real. Then institutionalize the forgetting.

The Slavery System

Roman slavery wasn't racial—it was legal status. Anyone could fall in:

- Captured in war.
- Born to slave mother.
- Sold by parents or self.
- Convicted or abandoned.

Yet slaves could be freed, even become citizens. Their children were full citizens—no legal scar.

That possibility made the cage feel survivable. "It's not permanent," they said. Work hard, earn freedom, watch children rise.

Modern echo: "Anyone can make it if they work hard enough." The exception justifies the system. The lottery winner validates the casino.

Possible escape makes permanent prison psychologically bearable.

Law as Reality Creator

Rome's law didn't record reality—it spoke reality into existence.

"I declare you citizen." → Your body becomes protected.
"I declare you free." → Children become legitimate.
"I declare you infamous." → Rights evaporate.
"I declare you enemy." → Murder becomes heroism.

A magistrate's word was creative power. Like "Let there be light"—only bureaucratized.

The mechanism still operates:

- "I pronounce you married." — Taxes change.
- "I declare bankruptcy." — Debts vanish.

- "I sentence you to prison." — Civic death.
- "Case dismissed." — History rewritten.

When humans play God with words, words become chains.

Two Kinds of Truth

But Rome had a specific understanding of what truth meant. And it was fundamentally different from the tradition they were suppressing.

For Rome, truth was correspondence: statement matches fact, verified by documentation.

"This person is a slave" = true when papyrus records the transaction.
"This land is owned" = true when title deed exists.
"This marriage is valid" = true when magistrate witnessed and documented.

Truth required three elements: claim, fact, and verification by recognized authority. The magistrate, the notary, the witness—their testimony made truth true. Without documentation, without authority confirming, truth remained uncertain.

This is why Roman courts obsessed over documents. Why testimony required witnesses. Why proof meant paper. The law demanded correspondence between claim and documented fact.

If someone claimed freedom but couldn't produce papers, the claim was false—regardless of whether they'd ever been enslaved. If someone claimed ownership but lost the deed, ownership dissolved—regardless of who built the house.

Truth in Rome was what could be proven to authority through documentation.

The Hebrew tradition had a different word: *emet*.
Emet didn't mean correspondence. It meant reliability.
Not "does this statement match that fact" but "does this hold when reality presses on it?"

The difference is operational, not philosophical.

Correspondence truth asks: Can this be verified by checking against external reference?

Relational truth asks: Does this survive when tested by actual experience?

A Roman judge asked: "Where are your papers?"
A Hebrew sage asked: "What happens when you live by this?"

The shift changes everything.

Testing vs. Believing

Under Roman truth, the task is belief: accept the correct claims, verified by proper authority.

Someone wants to know if they're free. Roman answer: "Check your papers. If the documents say free, you're free. If they say slave, you're slave. Believe what's documented."

The truth is static. Fixed. Determined by authority. The person's role: believe the right claims from the right sources without testing them.

Under Hebrew *emet*, the task is testing: examine claims by living them and seeing what holds.

Someone wants to know if they're free. Hebrew answer: "What happens when you live as if you're free? What breaks? What holds? What does reality reveal when you press on it?"

The truth is dynamic. Relational. Discovered through friction with reality. The person's role: test claims against actual experience.

Rome said: "I have the documents proving this law is just."
Hebrew tradition said: "Live by this law for seven years and see if it produces justice or collapse."

One requires submission to authority.
The other requires risking engagement with reality.

This difference produced opposite approaches to certainty:

Roman approach: Certainty comes from proper documentation verified by recognized authority. If Caesar says it, if the law records it, if the magistrate confirms it—it's true. Certainty arrives through authority.

Hebrew approach: Certainty comes from sustained testing that reveals what survives pressure. If reality confirms it, if experience validates it, if life under this framework produces what it promises—it's *emet*. Certainty arrives through friction.

A Roman citizen defending their belief: "The law says this is true, and the law has authority."
A Hebrew person defending their belief: "I've tested this for years and reality keeps confirming it holds."

One can be wrong despite perfect documentation.
The other can be right despite having no papers.

The Vulnerability of Each System

Roman truth had a fatal flaw: documentation can lie.

Papers can be forged. Authorities can be corrupted. Facts can be fabricated. The correspondence between claim and reality can be fictional—but if properly documented, it becomes legal truth anyway.

A person could be legally free while actually enslaved. Could be legally married to someone they'd never met. Could legally own land they'd never seen. The documents said it was true, so it was true—even when reality contradicted it.

This is why Rome required such elaborate verification systems. Multiple witnesses. Official seals. Approved notaries. The more documentation, the more "true" something became—regardless of whether it corresponded to reality.

Hebrew *emet* had a different vulnerability: testing takes time.

Can't know immediately whether something is reliable. Have to live with it. Press on it. See what happens when reality tests it. The verification comes slowly, through sustained engagement.

This is why Hebrew tradition emphasized patience, process, and communal testing across generations. One person's test might be insufficient. One year might not reveal the flaws. The community tested together. Across time. Through multiple contexts.

But the patience required made *emet* functionally impractical for empire.

Empire needs immediate certainty. Needs to make decisions quickly. Needs to classify, categorize, and enforce without waiting for reality to reveal whether the categories hold.

Rome couldn't wait seven years to see if a law produced justice. Couldn't test slavery across generations to see if it was reliable. Couldn't examine imperial categories through sustained communal friction.

Empire needed truth immediately. Documented. Verified. Enforceable.

So Rome chose correspondence over reliability.
Documentation over testing.
Authority over experience.

And in doing so, created a system where legal truth and actual truth could diverge completely—and legal truth would win.

What This Required of People

Under Roman truth, the person's task was clear: believe correct claims from proper authority.

Find the right sources. Accept their documentation. Defend their authority. Any challenge to documented truth was challenge to social order itself.

This produced specific behaviors:

When someone questioned documented truth: "But the law says..." Defense through authority citation. The papers proved it. The magistrate verified it. Belief was required.

When reality contradicted documentation: "The documents must be right and experience wrong." Trust documentation over lived experience. The papers said one thing, life showed another—papers won.

When authority changed its claims: Update beliefs to match new documentation. Yesterday's truth becomes today's falsehood because authority said so. The truth changed when the documents changed.

The system required trained passivity. The truth came from above. The person received it, believed it, defended it. Testing was unnecessary—and eventually dangerous. The documents already verified everything.

Under Hebrew *emet*, the person's task was different: **develop capacity to test claims against reality**.

Learn to examine beliefs. Maintain relationships with people who see differently. Create conditions where friction can reveal what holds. Live by claims long enough to see what they produce.

This produced different behaviors:

When someone made a claim: "Let me test this." Not immediate belief or rejection—examination. See what happens when reality presses on it.

When reality contradicted claims: "The claim must be wrong or incomplete." Trust lived experience. Adjust beliefs to match what testing reveals.

When testing revealed flaws: "This doesn't hold. What needs to change?" Modify beliefs based on what survives examination. The testing produces the truth—doesn't just verify claims from authority.

The system required activity. The truth emerged through engagement. The person tested it, examined it, lived with it until reality revealed what held. Authority was unnecessary—experience sufficient.

The Collision

When these two approaches met, conflict was inevitable.

Rome demanded: "Submit to our documented truth."
Hebrew tradition practiced: "Test all things; hold fast to what survives."

Rome said: "The emperor is divine—the law proves it."
Hebrew tradition said: "Let's see what happens when we refuse to worship him."

Rome said: "These categories are real—citizenship, slavery, property—documented and verified."
Hebrew tradition said: "Let's live as if humans are humans regardless of papers and see what reality confirms."

The collision appears throughout the occupation:

Roman magistrate: "Show me your authorization."
Jesus: "By what authority do you require authorization?"

The question unmasked the system. Rome assumed truth came from documented authority. Jesus assumed authority had to prove itself true by surviving reality-testing.

They couldn't both be right. Either truth comes from authority making claims, or truth emerges from reality confirming claims. Either documentation determines reality, or reality determines whether documentation holds.

Rome had the papers.
Jesus had reality.

For a while, papers appeared to win.

But papers can't hold someone in a tomb when reality says otherwise.

Truth doesn't require permission.
Emet doesn't need documentation.
What survives testing survives—regardless of what authorities claimed was true.

The Entropy Solution

Greek philosophy had discovered the brain's desperate need for certainty. Rome weaponized that discovery through law.

Legal categorization provided what Greek categories only promised: perfect entropy reduction.

Greek categories reduced anxiety: Body versus soul. Good versus evil. Wise versus foolish. But these remained philosophical—debatable, uncertain, abstract.

Roman categories eliminated uncertainty: Citizen. Slave. Barbarian. Legal fact. Documented. Enforceable. No debate possible.

The brain, fleeing entropy, grabbed legal certainty like drowning hands grab rope. At least in slavery, a person knew exactly what they were. At least as citizen, status was documented. At least as foreigner, position was clear.

The uncertainty of "Who am I?" became the certainty of "What the law says I am."

Total categorization = zero uncertainty. Clear legal status eliminated ambiguity. Everyone knew their place. The simulation became law. Law became reality.

And reality could be enforced with violence.

The Violence of Law

Roman law didn't just define categories. It enforced them — with precision and pain.

The cross wasn't just execution. It was legal statement: This is what happens to those who challenge categories.

Crucifixion was for slaves and enemies — those whose status made suffering a public lesson. Citizens were exiled or fined. Slaves were displayed and destroyed.

The arena turned legal violence into entertainment. Bodies reminded minds: status equals fate. The law determines whether someone lives or dies. Whether they're human or property. Whether killing them is murder or maintenance.

Law without violence is suggestion. Law with violence becomes lived reality.

Rome needed crosses because Roman categories were lies — slaves kept being human, Caesar kept being mortal, and reality kept undermining what law claimed was true.

And what one magistrate could do to one person, the legion could do to an entire world. When Rome conquered, it didn't just occupy land — it converted it legally. Soil became Roman. People became subjects. Local law bowed to imperial law. The soldier's sword and the magistrate's declaration were the same instrument at different scales. Violence made law real. Law made violence righteous.

The simulation requires violence because it fights reality. Shalom doesn't — it works with it. The Hebrew word doesn't mean peace. It means actively building wholeness wherever fragmentation appears. You don't enforce wholeness. You practice it. Rome needed the cross to hold its categories together. Shalom needs only the next right action toward repair.

Bread and Circuses

Rome mastered mass control through distraction. Roman satirist Juvenal mocked it: *panem et circenses* — bread and circuses.

The formula was simple:

1. Guarantee subsistence (bread).
2. Provide spectacle (circus).
3. Create tribes (factions, colors).
4. Turn politics into entertainment.
5. Drain emotion on meaningless conflict.

People don't notice chains while watching games. Don't question status while fed. Don't resist categories while arguing over races.

The pattern persists: Universal income. Social feeds. Red/Blue tribes. Politics as spectacle. Sports as proxy war.

Oppression becomes unnecessary if distraction is sufficient.

The Total System

By the first century CE, the simulation was total.

Every human had a legal category. Every action a legal definition. Every relationship a legal contract. Every god a legal license.

Birth required registration. Death required certification. Even intention was regulated—thought crime was already crime.

When everything is legal, nothing is free.

The Modern Legal Simulation

Rome's code still runs.

The legal person: Birth certificate creates entity. Social security number tracks it. License authorizes movement. Credit score quantifies worth. Record defines past. Death certificate terminates file.

That entity isn't the person—it's the Roman fiction they animate.

Corporate persons: Immortal fictions owning everything. They hire people, sue people, outlive people.
Legal creation: Marriage exists when state declares. Ownership exists when deed records. Money exists when law prints.

All Roman fictions—so ancient the forgetting is complete.

Can a person exist without documents? Work without permission? Travel without papers? Be born or die without forms?

Rome doesn't occupy territory anymore. Rome occupies consciousness.

And Rome still operates on correspondence truth: If the documents say it's true, it's true—regardless of what reality shows.

The Pattern

Every empire runs the same code: Define categories. Enforce categories. Make categories feel natural. Make resistance to categories feel impossible.

The code replicates. Each empire inherits the previous empire's infrastructure and adds enforcement mechanisms.

Egypt made categories economic: slave versus citizen, defined by productivity.
Persia made categories cosmic: light versus darkness, good versus evil.
Greece made categories philosophical: soul versus body, abstract versus concrete.
Rome made categories legal: citizen versus slave, documented and enforceable.

Each layer added to the last. Each mechanism more sophisticated. Each prison more psychologically complete.

But every system—no matter how total—has the same vulnerability: It cannot process someone who simply ignores it and lives otherwise.

The System's Blind Spot

Then someone entered the system who acted as if legal fictions were fictions.

Didn't fight the categories. Didn't petition the authorities. Didn't argue the philosophy. Didn't organize resistance.

Just lived as if reality was reality.

Treated slaves as humans. Ate with outcasts. Touched lepers. Spoke to women as equals. Called tax collectors to teach.

When asked for authority, answered with questions that unmasked theirs. When shown Caesar's coin, shrugged: "Give to Caesar what's Caesar's." When accused of breaking law, answered: "Sabbath was made for humans, not humans for Sabbath."

Didn't argue categories. Lived reality.

Every meal dissolved boundaries. Every touch violated purity codes. Every conversation ignored status markers. Every action exposed the fictions as fictions.

And every action was a test: What happens when someone lives as if documents don't determine reality? What survives when *emet* challenges correspondence? What holds when relational truth presses on legal truth?

Rome creates categories. Divine creates relationships.
Law separates. Love unites.
Fiction divides. Reality connects.
Correspondence claims. *Emet* tests.

The legal experts raged—every boundary breached, every fiction exposed, every category ignored. The system could only respond one way: escalation to ultimate sanction.

Category: condemned.
Punishment: cross.
Legal declaration: dead.

To prove their reality's power. To show what happens when someone ignores the fictions. To demonstrate that law determines reality, that categories are real, that documentation is truth, that death is the final word.

The cross was legal proof: The system wins. Categories hold. Correspondence truth prevails. Reality bows to law.

Three days later, he cooked breakfast on the beach.

Because resurrection doesn't recognize categories.
Because *emet* doesn't need documentation.
Because what's reliable survives—regardless of what papers claimed was final.
Because reality doesn't require authority's permission to be real.

And death—the ultimate legal declaration—turned out to be just another fiction that couldn't survive testing.

The law says someone is slave or citizen.
Reality says they're human.

The law says someone is property.
Reality says they're sacred.

The law says someone is dead.
Reality says—
Watch what happens next.

Chapter 14

JESUS: THE SYSTEM CRASH

When Power Couldn't Process Love

HE KEPT STARTING with dinner.

Every town, another table. While religious leaders debated purity laws and Rome enforced order through crucifixion, **Jesus**—a carpenter from Nazareth kept eating with the wrong people—tax collectors, sex workers, lepers, zealots, fishermen who couldn't read.

Table after table. The revolution was repetition.

Every shared meal broke empire's first rule: a person is their category.

Watch what kept happening. The tax collector stopped overcharging. The sex worker found dignity. The leper returned to community. The zealot dropped his knife. Not through moral instruction—through being seen as human. Through bread shared by someone who refused to see labels.

The Pharisees panicked. "Why does your teacher eat with tax collectors and sinners?"

Because eating together dissolves the boundaries power needs. Because breaking bread breaks categories. Because shared tables reveal shared humanity.

Every meal was insurrection disguised as dinner. And he kept doing it—week after week, town after town.

Walking Grammar

Jesus taught in movement, not lectures. Always walking. Always acting. Never nouns. Never categories. Only verbs—continuous, present, active.

"Follow me." — and he kept walking. No destination announced. Just: keep moving.
Following is alive—a practice. A follower is frozen—a category.

"Love your enemies." — and he kept loving people who wanted him dead.
Love as verb acts; love as noun poses.

"Forgive seventy times seven." — meaning: never stop forgiving. Never arrive at "done."
Each forgiveness is new motion.

When they tried to freeze him in categories—"Are you the Messiah?" "Are you a king?"—he kept moving through questions: "Who do you say I am?"

Empire needs people to be something—saved or damned, worthy or worthless, us or them.
Jesus insisted people do something—love, forgive, share, heal, free.

Watch the pattern: Jesus never taught arrival. Never offered completion. Never promised rest from struggle.

"Take up your cross **daily**." Not once. Daily.
"If anyone slaps you, turn the other cheek"—and the other, and the other. No completion point.
"How many times should I forgive? Seven?" "Seventy times seven"—meaning: keep forgiving, never stop.
"Follow me"—to where? He never said. Movement without destination.

The disciples kept wanting arrival: "When will you restore the kingdom?"
Jesus kept giving movement: "The kingdom is among you"—present, active, continuous, right now.

They kept wanting categorical certainty: "Are you the one, or should we expect another?"

Jesus kept giving daily practice: "The blind see, the lame walk, lepers are cleansed—and blessed is the one who doesn't stumble over me."

He taught life as movement. Not journey toward completion but journey as the point. Not striving to arrive but striving as life itself.

Hebrew understanding: life requires continued movement—breath continuing, heart beating, blood flowing. The body is verb, not noun. When movement stops, death begins.

Jesus embodied this completely. Didn't establish headquarters. Didn't create fixed institutions. Didn't offer systematic theology. Just kept walking. Kept teaching. Kept healing. Movement sustained until empire stopped it.

And even then—resurrection as the ultimate proof that life doesn't complete, it continues.

Labels freeze. Actions flow. Empire depends on nouns. Reality moves through verbs.

Reality Demonstrated

Five thousand hungry people. Bellies empty. Five loaves. Two fish.

The disciples saw scarcity: "Send them away." Empire's solution—competition, fear, extraction.

Jesus saw differently. "You give them something." Take what exists. Bless it. Break it. Share it.

Everyone ate until full. Twelve baskets left over.

The story doesn't explain how. It demonstrates what: **reality operates by different rules than empire teaches**. Empire runs on scarcity—not enough to go around, competition required, someone must lose. But when extraction stops and movement begins—giving, sharing, trusting—abundance appears.

The boy offered his lunch. The disciples kept distributing. The crowd kept engaging. Whether through supernatural multiplication or social transformation, the pattern revealed itself: **reality is co-created through continued action**.

And he kept doing it. Kept feeding whoever came. Kept demonstrating abundance through movement.

"Love your enemies. Pray for those who persecute you."

Empire runs on fear and division—anxiety stabilized through categories: us/them, friend/enemy. Jesus crashed the code. And kept living it.

Love for enemies isn't moral advice—it's system sabotage. When a Roman soldier forced someone to carry his pack one mile, carry it two. The first mile is coercion. The second is choice. In choice, freedom.

He kept loving those who opposed him. Kept forgiving those who attacked him. Kept moving toward those labeled enemy. The movement itself was the message.

The Cross and After

They arrested him at night, tried him in secret, convicted without evidence. Empire's strategy: stop the movement. Arrest means stopping. Trial means fixing in place. Cross means permanent cessation.

Before Pilate: "What is truth?"

The question revealed the chasm. Pilate wanted correspondence—a statement he could verify, document, and close. Roman truth: does the statement match the fact?

Jesus offered *emet*—reliability under pressure. Hebrew truth: does this hold when reality tests it?

The silence wasn't refusal to answer. It was the answer. *Emet* can't be stated in a trial. It can only be lived and tested under pressure. The man standing before Pilate was the demonstration—years of healing, forgiving, loving, remaining faithful under pressure.

Within hours, Jesus would provide the ultimate demonstration of *emet*—reliability tested by death itself.

Crucifixion was empire's final proof that categories hold: This is what happens to those who refuse our reality. Bodies displayed. Pain publicized. Death as deterrent.

But on their stage, he performed a different script. Even dying, he kept moving.

"Father, forgive them." — still forgiving, still loving.
"It is finished." — the demonstration concludes, but the movement continues.

The temple veil tore top to bottom. Separation ended. Access direct.
Empire's power failed at the moment it displayed its strength.

Sunday morning. Women walking to a tomb. An empty tomb. Not stolen—transcended. Death lost its final definition.

"Mary." Her name—personal, not category. Recognition collapsed illusion. Movement resumed.

"Don't cling to me." Don't try to freeze this moment. Resurrection is not resuscitation. It's new order. Keep moving with me.

That evening, he appeared behind locked doors. Walls built by fear can't contain presence.

"Peace be with you." He showed his wounds. Proof that pain remains but doesn't rule. "As the Father sent me, I send you." Not worship me—continue me. Join the movement.

Weeks later. Back to fishing. No catch. A voice from shore: "Cast to the right side." Nets burst. 153 fish. Abundance again.

On shore—a fire, bread, fish. The resurrected one making breakfast. Not appearing in glory and ascending immediately. Making breakfast. Continuing to serve, continuing to feed, continuing to move.

Resurrection isn't arrival—it's permission to keep going after the system declared an end.

"Simon, do you love me?" — three times, for three denials. Not punishment—restoration.

"Feed my sheep." Keep feeding. Keep sharing. Keep moving. Reality is sustained by participation. The verb continues. The movement doesn't stop.

The Three-Part Declaration

"I am the Way, the Truth, and the Life."

Not three separate claims—one reality in three dimensions. All requiring movement. All resisting completion.

The Way

Not a destination. A path.

Hebrew: *derek*—the road itself, the journey continued. Greek would ask: "Where does the way lead?" Hebrew answers: "The way is where you walk with God."

Jesus didn't say "I will show you the way." He said "I am the way." The path is person. The journey is relationship. There is no way to walk except by walking with.

This is why he kept moving. Nazareth to Capernaum to Jerusalem—teaching while walking, healing while traveling, eating while passing through. The way isn't information to learn. It's movement to join.

Follow me. Not "go where I point" but "come where I go." The way is participated, not studied. Practiced, not possessed. Continued, not completed.

The Truth

Not proposition. Presence tested by reality.

Emet—what holds when pressed, what remains reliable under pressure, what reality confirms through friction.

Pilate had asked "What is truth?" while standing before someone who had demonstrated truth for more than a year. Healing that actually healed. Forgiveness that actually freed. Love that actually transformed. Teaching that actually changed people. Promises that actually held.

The truth isn't verified by documentation. It's proven by survival under testing. Does this hold when reality presses on it? Does this remain when everything else fails?

Jesus was truth because his way worked. The outcasts he kept eating with became whole. The sick he kept touching got well. The sinners he kept forgiving transformed. The disciples he kept training kept failing — and returned. The pattern held even when the people carrying it broke.

Not "believe these facts about me." But "test whether this works." Not "accept these propositions." But "try living this way and see what reality confirms."

Truth is what survives testing. He survived even death. Body walking out of tomb. Hands showing scars. Mouth eating fish.

The Life

Not biological existence. Continued movement.

Hebrew: *chaim*—always plural, always in motion. Life isn't state possessed but flow participated. Not something you have but something you do.

"I came that they might have life, and have it abundantly." Not longer life. Fuller life. Life as movement—more love, more healing, more giving, more serving, more connecting.

This is why completion would mean death. "It is finished" at the cross meant the work completes—not the person stops. Resurrection proved life continues. Even death becomes movement—through it, beyond it, in spite of it.

The opposite of life isn't death. It's cessation. Stopping. Completion. Arriving at fixed position. Life requires continued movement—breathing, flowing, growing, changing, relating.

Jesus offered life as verb. Keep loving. Keep forgiving. Keep healing. Keep sharing. Keep walking. Never arrive. Never complete. Never rest from the motion that is life itself.

The Unity

Way, truth, life—not three things but three angles on one reality.

The way you walk is the truth that holds is the life you live. Movement that proves reliable that continues.

You can't separate them:

- Walk the way without testing → blind following, not truth.
- Claim truth without walking → proposition not tested, not reliable.
- Seek life without way → no direction, motion without meaning.

But together: Walk this path. Test whether it holds. Keep moving. That's life. That's truth. That's the way.

Jesus didn't offer a belief system to accept or a status to claim. He offered himself as path to walk, pattern to test, movement to join.

Not: "Believe facts about the way, the truth, and the life."
But: "I am the way—walk with me. I am the truth—test this. I am the life—keep moving."

The way continues.
The truth holds.
The life flows.

Empire offers completed status, verified facts, and finished work.
Jesus offered continued journey, tested reliability, and abundant life.

Not arrival—movement.
Not proposition—presence.
Not completion—continuation.

Way, truth, life.
Walk, test, flow.
Follow, examine, live.

One reality. Three dimensions. All movement.

The Four Simulations Broken

For centuries, four empires had layered their control systems, each backed by violence.

Egypt taught: Worth comes from productivity. The worthless deserve slavery.
Jesus kept demonstrating: Worth precedes category—table after table, he kept eating with those marked worthless. Worth isn't status declared once—it's presence maintained daily.

Persia taught: Reality is cosmic war. Evil is external entity you must oppose.
Jesus kept showing: Love your enemies. He kept loving those who opposed him. The war doesn't end when one side wins. It ends when someone stops fighting and starts serving. Evil is what people do, and what people do can change.

Greece taught: Humans are categories. Fixed essences. Body versus soul, permanent positions.
Jesus kept refusing: categories. Kept touching lepers marked "untouchable." Kept eating with sinners labeled "unredeemable." Identity isn't essence possessed—it's action continued. Not what you are but what you keep doing.

Rome taught: Law creates reality. Categories are enforceable. Death is the final word.
Jesus kept breaking: purity codes. Kept healing on Sabbath. Kept acting as if legal fictions were fiction. They killed him to prove categories are real, to show law determines reality, to demonstrate death has the final word. Three days later he was cooking breakfast. Life continues even when law says stop.

Each empire had claimed ultimate authority. Each had enforced its framework with violence. Each had made its structure feel inevitable, natural, real.

One person walked into that total system and kept acting as if it were fiction. Kept eating with the wrong people. Kept touching the untouchable. Kept loving enemies. Kept descending instead of climbing. Kept giving instead of hoarding.

The system could only respond one way: kill him. Stop the movement permanently.

Three days later, he cooked breakfast on a beach.

The Question Remains

"Who do you say I am?"

The question Jesus asked his disciples echoes still. Empire has a thousand answers—categories attempting to contain.

But the question isn't asking for theological category. It's asking for recognition. What does his demonstration mean to you?

The evidence is the life. Meals with outcasts. Touching lepers. Forgiving enemies. Descending instead of climbing. Continuous movement.

The evidence is the death. Facing empire's full violence without fighting back. Forgiving executioners while being executed. Choosing to give rather than protect.

The evidence is what happened after. The empty tomb. The breakfast on the beach. The fear-paralyzed disciples becoming fearless. The movement that spread despite persecution.

The evidence is what people became when they kept practicing what he demonstrated. Former tax collectors kept sharing wealth. Former enemies kept eating together. People unafraid of empire because they'd seen empire's ultimate weapon fail.

Whether divine, human, or something the categories can't contain—the demonstration speaks for itself.

Someone showed that reality is stronger than empire's lies. That love is stronger than law. That life is stronger than death. That verbs are stronger than nouns. That movement continues even when power says stop.

The pattern is proven. The path is shown. The invitation stands.

And the question remains: "Who do you say I am?"

The answer isn't a category. It's a choice of response. Not "what have you become?" but "what are you doing?" Not arrival but movement. Not completed status but continued practice. Not what to believe about him, but what to keep practicing because of him.

Empire continues. But now there's evidence it can be transcended. One person did it completely. And for forty days after death itself, proved it wasn't luck or privilege—it was reality, reproducible and real. Available through continued participation.

Four empires layered their control systems. One person walked through them all—unfixed by their categories, uncontained by their violence, unended by their death.

The demonstration is complete. What happened next—how the movement became monument, how verbs became nouns again—that's the next part of the story.

But for this moment, the evidence stands: Reality is possible. Love is stronger. Death proved unable to hold. Freedom proved real. Movement continued.

Someone proved it. And kept proving it. And the movement hasn't stopped.

PART V

Within The Simulation

Saturation: When Everything Becomes Performance

Your phone is not a tool—it is the simulation in your pocket. You are no longer living life. You are performing it for an audience that never sleeps.

Chapter 15

FROM PRACTICE TO THEOLOGY

The Greek Translation of Hebrew Truth

"NARROW IS THE gate and difficult is the way
that leads to life, and few find it."
—(Matthew 7:14)

Jesus spoke these words immediately before cautioning his listeners to beware of false guides. The sequence matters. He did not suggest that truth would be obvious, popular, or widely embraced. He prepared his followers for the opposite—that his way would be difficult to discern, easy to lose, and followed by relatively few.

This presents an unavoidable question for later generations. When a form of Christianity becomes dominant, widespread, and eventually institutionalized—embraced by empires and carried by the majority—it deserves careful examination, not automatic assumption of alignment. Jesus himself warned that numbers would not be a reliable measure of faithfulness.

This does not mean that what spread widely must be wrong. But it does mean that growth, influence, and longevity cannot be used as proof of alignment with Jesus' teaching. By his own criteria, those measures may even be misleading.

Many sincere Christians assume that following Jesus and following Christianity are the same thing. But what if the framework that became orthodox—the one taught in most churches, defended by most theologians, spread by most missionaries—emerged not from those who walked with Jesus, but from someone who encountered him differently?

This chapter examines that possibility through Paul's framework—with respect, caution, and historical curiosity. Not to accuse him of bad intent, and not to claim special insight, but to ask a specific and necessary question: Does the theological structure that became dominant reflect the narrow path Jesus described, or does it represent a broader reinterpretation that emerged as the movement expanded?

The goal here is not to dismantle faith, but to test continuity—to examine whether what later Christianity emphasized is the same thing Jesus emphasized, and whether the earliest disagreements within the movement, particularly those voiced by James, point to a divergence that still matters today.

This chapter assumes sincerity and faithfulness on all sides. The question is not who meant well, but how meaning changed when embodied practice met Greek philosophy and eventually imperial power.

The Translation

The resurrection left everyone scrambling for explanations. The disciples scattered, regrouped, scattered again. Each carrying fragments, trying to make sense of the incomprehensible. Into this confusion came dozens of teachers, each with their own framework. The movement was fracturing into movements. The verb was becoming nouns. The experience was becoming explanations.

Then Paul arrived, with Greek education, Roman citizenship, and absolute certainty about what it all meant.

Paul never met Jesus during his public ministry. Never heard him teach in Galilee. Never witnessed the healings firsthand. But Paul knew Greek philosophy. Read the Greek version of the Hebrew Bible called the Septuagint. Grew up in Tarsus—university city, rival to Athens and Alexandria. His mind was furnished with Plato's divided human, Stoic ethics, mystery religions, Greek rhetorical training.

When Paul encountered the resurrection story, he processed it through this Greek framework. Not deliberately—that's simply how his mind worked. Like trying to understand jazz through classical theory—the translation captures something, but not the thing itself.

Paul's conversion wasn't gradual enlightenment. It was violent system crash. Breathing threats and murder, suddenly blinded by light. "Saul, Saul, why do you persecute me?" Three days blind. Three days of profound transformation.

What happened next shaped everything. Paul didn't go to Jerusalem to learn from those who had walked with Jesus. "I did not consult any human being," he later wrote. His gospel came by "revelation," he insisted — not through years of walking with a rabbi. His authority came from divine encounter rather than human transmission.

This meant Paul's understanding developed along a different trajectory from those who had known Jesus in the flesh. Where the original disciples taught what they had seen Jesus do and heard Jesus say, Paul taught what he understood the resurrection to mean.

Paul's letters reveal a man urgently trying to hold communities together across vast distances, facing conflicts he couldn't resolve through physical presence. He wasn't a detached theorist—he was a pastor working with the tools he had.

The difference between these two modes—apprenticeship versus revelation, practice versus theology—would shape the movement's future in ways Paul could not have foreseen.

When Verbs Become Nouns

Watch the transformation that can occur when Hebrew practice is expressed through Greek philosophical language:

Jesus said: "Follow me"
Paul said: "Have faith in Christ"
Following is verb—continuous action, ongoing relationship. Faith often becomes noun—mental state, categorical position.

Jesus said: "Love your neighbor as yourself"
Paul said: "You are saved by grace"

Love is verb—ongoing practice, never completed. Saved becomes noun—fixed status, settled question.

Jesus said: "Forgive seventy times seven"
Paul said: "You are justified"
Forgiving is verb—repeated action, relationship preserved through practice.
Justified becomes noun—legal position, categorical state.

This pattern appears throughout Paul's writings. Not because Paul was dishonest, but because his mind worked in Greek categories. Greek philosophy required nouns—fixed essences, permanent states, categorical positions. Hebrew thought emphasized verbs—ongoing actions, continuous relationships, dynamic processes.

Paul, trained in Greek categories, could not easily communicate in pure Hebrew verb-based logic. He had to create categories. Had to define states. Had to establish positions. This was how educated Greek minds made sense of reality. It wasn't deception—it was translation. But translation always changes the original.

The question worth examining: What happens when the way of Jesus gets translated from verb-based practice into noun-based theology?

The Completion Problem

Paul's framework promised something specific: **completion**.

"You are perfect in Christ."
"You are complete in him."
"You are already sanctified."
"The work is finished."

These were often received as ontological states—fixed positions believers believed they possessed through faith. Already perfect. Already complete. Already holy. Already righteous. This sounded like liberation. No more striving. No more uncertainty. Rest in the finished work.

But examine what completion means in Hebrew versus Greek understanding:

Hebrew understanding:

- Life = continued movement under tension.
- Completion = arrival at a terminal state.

Greek understanding:

- Life = arriving at perfect form.
- Completion = ideal state attained.

The shift inverted the meaning. What Hebrew identified as characteristic of death—cessation of struggle, arrival at completion, fixation in permanent state—became the Greek definition of salvation.

Paul's framework, structured in Greek categories, made completion the goal. But Hebrew would ask: **If life requires continued movement, what happens when movement stops?**

The pastoral consequences appear immediately:

Struggle becomes shameful. If believers are already complete, ongoing difficulty indicates failure. Believers hide their struggles, creating isolation.

Testing becomes threatening. If identity depends on completed status, anything that might reveal incompletion threatens the foundation. Believers avoid situations that would test whether their structures actually hold.

Growth becomes optional. If already perfect, what remains to develop? Spiritual formation becomes enrichment rather than survival necessity.

Ease becomes virtue. "Resting in grace" reframes the smooth, wide path as spiritual maturity. The very condition Jesus warned could lead to destruction can come to be celebrated as maturity.

Death masquerades as life. Communities celebrate arrival and completion while the dynamics that maintain life—struggle, tension, continued movement—get labeled as "works righteousness" or "lack of faith."

Notice the contradiction with Jesus's own words:

"**Strive** to enter through the narrow gate."
"If anyone would come after me, let him **deny himself daily**."

"He who **endures to the end** will be saved."

These assume continued effort. Ongoing struggle. Maintained tension. Daily practice. The opposite of completed rest.

James recognized this pattern immediately: "Faith without works is **dead**." Not "incomplete"—dead. The cessation of movement. The arrival at terminal state. The thing completion theology celebrates as salvation, James identifies as the condition of death itself.

This doesn't mean Paul intended to encode death-dynamics into his framework. Greek categories required fixed states—that's how Greek philosophy organized reality. But when salvation gets framed as completed status rather than continued navigation, when perfection means arrival rather than ongoing faithfulness, when the goal becomes rest from struggle rather than struggle sustained by grace—what's being described?

The question this raises: Does categorical completion reflect the narrow path Jesus described, requiring daily denial and constant striving? Or does it offer the broad path of ease and arrival?

This isn't an argument for practice divorced from source. Connection to the divine without embodied practice becomes abstract spirituality—all belief, no transformation. Practice without divine connection becomes mere moralism—all effort, no grace. Both are required. The Hebrew framework maintained both: covenantal relationship (source) expressed through daily practice (embodiment). What Paul's Greek categories struggled to hold together was the dynamic tension between gift and response, between status and process, between what's given and what's lived.

Paul's Ongoing Corrections

Paul himself recognized the danger. Much of his ministry involved correcting communities that interpreted his message as permission to stop striving. To the Corinthians who thought they had "already become kings": sarcasm and correction. To the Galatians who had "begun in the Spirit" but stopped practicing: sharp rebuke. To the Philippians: "work out your salvation with fear and trembling."

This tension appears throughout his letters—proclaiming completed status while demanding continued effort, declaring perfection while insisting on transformation, offering categorical certainty while requiring ongoing struggle. Paul knew the framework could be misunderstood. But the categorical structure that made misunderstanding possible was the same structure that made the message portable and scalable.

The question this raises: If Paul himself had to constantly correct misapplication of his completed-status theology, does that suggest something about the framework itself?

Why Paul's Framework Spread

Here's a question worth considering carefully: Why did Paul's interpretation become dominant when other interpretations existed?

The neurological answer is revealing. The brain's response to uncertainty generates acute discomfort that humans experience as anxiety. Any framework that reduces uncertainty—regardless of whether it's true—provides immediate relief.

Jesus taught: Daily practice. Continuous following. Ongoing love. Repeated forgiveness. Perpetual walking with an unpredictable God through an uncertain world. High uncertainty. High relationship requirement.

Paul taught: Fixed status. Clear category. Settled question. Permanent position. A person is saved—past tense, completed action, categorical certainty.

The brain found Paul's categories vastly more comforting. Not because Paul's framework was truer, but because it reduced more uncertainty. Walking with Jesus daily offers no completion point, no categorical security. Categorical salvation promises exactly that—completion, security, certainty.

This doesn't mean people who followed Paul's framework were insincere or took the easy path. It means the framework resonated deeply with how humans—all humans—cope with uncertainty. The brain's hunger for certainty is universal, not a character flaw.

The question this raises: Did Paul's framework spread because it was more faithful to Jesus's teaching, or because it was more compatible with how Greek minds already processed reality?

Paul's framework also had structural advantages. It could be taught anywhere—didn't require living with a teacher. It could scale to thousands who simply needed to believe correct things. It fit existing Greek philosophical categories and Roman legal thinking. It could be reduced to propositions, memorized quickly, transmitted efficiently. Jesus's way of life couldn't be reduced—it had to be practiced.

The framework that spreads most efficiently isn't necessarily the one most faithful to the original teaching. Often it's the one most compatible with existing patterns.

James Tests the Framework

James led the Jerusalem church. He had known Jesus as family, not theology. Watched him grow up. Shared meals. Witnessed the daily practice that preceded the dramatic moments.

When James heard what Paul was teaching, he wrote a response. Not a personal attack. A theological test.

"Faith without works is dead."

Not "faith plus works equals salvation." But faith that doesn't express itself in action isn't faith at all. It's intellectual assent. Mental agreement. Greek abstraction separated from embodied reality.

James was explicit about this. "You believe that God is one; you do well. Even the demons believe—and shudder." (James 2:19) Belief alone, separated from practice, doesn't distinguish humans from demons. Both can hold correct theology. The difference is embodiment.

He continued: "Be doers of the word, and not hearers only, deceiving yourselves." (James 1:22) The self-deception James warns against is precisely what happens when categorical status replaces continuous practice—people convince themselves that believing correctly equals following faithfully.

James kept returning to verbs: Visit orphans and widows in their distress. Feed the hungry, clothe the naked. Show no favoritism. Control your tongue. Draw near to God through action.

The tension between James and Paul represents something instructive. Not personality conflict, but genuine disagreement about what it meant to follow Jesus. James, who had eaten breakfast with Jesus for thirty years, insisted on practice. Paul, who encountered Jesus through vision, emphasized belief.

Both were sincere. Both were convinced they understood correctly. But they were emphasizing different aspects of following Jesus.

The question this raises: If those who knew Jesus emphasized practice while those who knew about Jesus emphasized belief, which approach more likely reflects the narrow path Jesus described?

From Persuasion to Power

For three centuries, Paul's Christianity spread through persuasion. Underground. Illegal. Persecuted.

Then in 312 CE, Constantine saw a vision before battle: "In this sign, conquer." Everything changed.

The Edict of Milan (313 CE) made Christianity legal. But Constantine didn't just legalize Christianity. He standardized it. The Council of Nicaea (325 CE) gathered bishops to settle theological disputes—not primarily because Constantine cared about theology, but because empire required unity. Diversity was disorder.

Constantine sided with one interpretation. Made it official. Made alternatives illegal. Those who disagreed were exiled. Their writings burned. Communities practicing differently were suppressed. The cross—symbol of empire's violence against Jesus—became empire's weapon against everyone else.

Within decades, Theodosius made Christianity not just legal but mandatory. The Edict of Thessalonica (380 CE) declared Christianity the only legal religion. Temples closed. Ancient practices outlawed. Those who practiced differently faced persecution.

In three centuries, the movement transformed completely:

- From persecuted to persecuting.
- From margin to center.
- From verb to noun to law.

Paul could not have foreseen this. He wrote letters to small persecuted communities. He could not have imagined those letters becoming imperial law, his categories becoming tools of state violence.

Empire would have required categories no matter which theological framework it inherited. Paul's theology was not the only possible candidate for weaponization, but its categorical structure proved particularly compatible with imperial logic once power entered the equation. The responsibility lies with empire, not with Paul—but the structure made the weaponization possible.

Because categories, once created, can be weaponized. Fixed positions can be mandated. Theological correctness can be enforced. Jesus's verbs—love, follow, forgive—cannot be imposed by law. But Paul's nouns—saved, justified, orthodox—could be.

Paul's theological categories were adapted into Constantine's legal code:

- Saved/Damned → Baptized/Pagan (legal status).
- Orthodox/Heretic → Citizen/Criminal (enforceable categories).
- Believer/Unbeliever → Protected/Persecuted (state violence).

The progression deserves attention:

- Step 1: Jesus demonstrated verbs—love, follow, share, forgive, heal, welcome.
- Step 2: Paul translated into nouns—saved, justified, sanctified, adopted, chosen.
- Step 3: Constantine weaponized through law—orthodox, heretic, legal, criminal, protected, persecuted.

The movement that began with Jesus sharing meals with outcasts became an empire that burned those who practiced differently. The teacher who said "love your enemies" became the banner for killing them.

This transformation wasn't inevitable. But the categorical structure made it possible in ways that verb-based practice would not have.

The Question Before Us

This chapter has examined structural divergence between Jesus's way of life and Paul's theological framework. Not to condemn Paul as he did his best with the tools he had, facing challenges we can barely imagine. Not to claim superiority but to test alignment using Jesus's own criterion.

Jesus warned the path would be narrow and followed by few. Paul's framework became broad and followed by billions, eventually enforced by empires and backed by violence.

This doesn't automatically make Paul wrong. But it should make us cautious about assuming that what became orthodox necessarily reflects what Jesus taught.

When verbs become nouns, what's lost? When embodied practice becomes theological system, what changes? When life-as-movement becomes completion-as-goal, which reflects Jesus's teaching? When the minority way becomes majority religion, which path is being followed?

These questions don't have simple answers. But they deserve serious examination by anyone who claims to follow Jesus rather than simply believe correct things about him.

Many Christians today live far closer to Jesus's verbs than to Pauline categories, often without realizing it. When they serve the poor, welcome strangers, practice forgiveness, and walk in daily relationship with God—they're following the narrow path regardless of what theological framework they claim. The practice matters more than the category.

James's letter remains in the New Testament, testing Paul's framework. Those willing to examine that tension honestly may discover something important about the difference between following Jesus and following Christianity.

The narrow path Jesus described hasn't disappeared. It's simply been obscured by the broad path that spread more easily, scaled more efficiently, and became more comfortable for the human brain's desperate need for certainty.

The choice between verb and noun, between practice and belief, between narrow way and broad path—that choice remains visible. Not because this chapter has proven Paul wrong, but because Jesus's warning about the narrow path makes the dominance of any interpretation worthy of careful, ongoing examination.

The invitation is not to abandon all theology or reject Paul's letters as Scripture. The invitation is to test whether your faith expresses itself primarily through categories you believe or practices you embody. To notice whether you're following Jesus's verbs or defending Pauline nouns. To examine whether the narrow path might require less certainty and more walking than the frameworks that became orthodox.

This is not a call to revolution but to careful attention. Not to perfect practice but to honest examination. Not to judgment of others but to testing of what you've inherited against what Jesus actually taught.

The path remains. Walking it begins with seeing it clearly.

Chapter 16

THE SACRED MACHINE

When Oppression Became Holy

APEASANT KNEELS in a stone church. The priest speaks Latin. The peasant doesn't understand a word. But the peasant knows this: the bread becomes God's body. The wine becomes God's blood. And only the priest can perform the transformation. Without the priest, no sacrament. Without the sacrament, no grace. Without grace, no salvation. Without salvation, eternal fire.

The peasant was born into this. Will die inside it. Every stage of life—baptism, confirmation, marriage, last rites—requires the same institution, the same mediator, the same permission. The priest holds the keys. The Church holds the priest. And God, supposedly, holds the Church.

The peasant doesn't question this. Not because the peasant is stupid. Because the entire world confirms it. The lord in the castle. The bishop in the cathedral. The king on the throne. The pope in Rome. Every layer of reality organized into the same hierarchy, every layer claiming the same source: God ordained it. The sun rises and sets in its ordained place. The seasons turn in their ordained cycle. The serf serves in their ordained station. Everything in its place. To question the placement is to question the hand that placed it.

Outside the church, the fields wait. The peasant will work them until dark, give a tenth of everything to the Church, a portion to the lord, and keep what remains—which is rarely enough. But the insufficiency itself confirms the order. Suffering is holy. Poverty is purifying. This life is a passage to the next, and the next life rewards those who accept their station without complaint.

The genius of the medieval simulation wasn't brute force—though force was available. It was *coherence*. Everything confirmed everything else. The theology confirmed the hierarchy. The hierarchy confirmed the economy. The economy confirmed the suffering. The suffering confirmed the theology. A closed loop, self-reinforcing, total. The peasant couldn't see the simulation because the simulation *was* the peasant's entire perceptual world. There was no outside. No alternative. No crack through which light might enter.

When oppression becomes sacred, resistance becomes sin.

The Divine Order

The architecture wasn't built overnight. It took centuries of institutional construction—Constantine's political conversion making Christianity the empire's operating system, the Nicene Creed replacing practice with doctrine, councils of bishops deciding what God meant while burning the writings of those who disagreed. By the medieval period, the transformation was complete.

"God ordained three orders: those who fight, those who pray, those who work."

Not human decision. Not social arrangement. Divine ordinance. Cosmic architecture. Treated as God's own blueprint for society.

Birth wasn't random—it was divine will. Born a serf? God placed them there. Born noble? Divine appointment. Born deformed? Often interpreted as visible judgment. Position wasn't circumstance. It was ontology—what a person *was*, not where they happened to be.

Theology mapped the cosmos into sacred hierarchy—the Great Chain of Being. God at the top, then angels, then humans, then animals, plants, minerals. And humanity itself subdivided endlessly: Pope to cardinal to bishop to priest. Emperor to king to duke to count to knight. Men to women to children. Christians to Jews to pagans. Free to serf to slave.

Each level understood as ontologically superior to the one below. Not just ranked differently—made of different essence. Closer to God meant more divine, more real, more valuable. A peasant wasn't temporarily poor—poverty was treated as their nature. A noble wasn't circumstantially powerful—power was their being. Position wasn't what someone did. It was what they *were*.

This meant the hierarchy couldn't be changed without changing reality itself. A serf who sought to rise wasn't ambitious—they were defying the cosmos. A woman who sought authority wasn't capable—she was transgressing divine order. The system didn't just punish resistance. It made resistance ontologically incoherent. How does a stone become an angel? It can't. It's a stone. That's its *nature*.

From inside the simulation, this felt not like oppression but like *reality*. The serf didn't experience hierarchy as a human invention. The hierarchy was the world. The sky above, the earth below, the lord in the castle, the peasant in the field—all equally given, all equally natural, all equally divine. To the medieval mind, questioning social hierarchy was as absurd as questioning gravity. Both were simply *how things are*.

Challenge position and challenge God. Question hierarchy and question heaven.

The Control Systems

The Church perfected three mechanisms of total control.

Sacramental monopoly. Seven sacraments from cradle to coffin—baptism, confirmation, eucharist, penance, anointing, holy orders, marriage. Each requiring a priest. Grace was framed as requiring mediation. Salvation as requiring permission. A person could not be born, marry, or die without the institution's involvement. The Church didn't just describe reality—it controlled every transition within it. Miss a sacrament and risk eternity. The stakes were infinite, which made the compliance total.

The language wall. Mass in Latin. Bible in Latin. Theology in Latin. God spoke a language ninety-nine percent couldn't know. Scripture existed but was sealed—physically present in churches, theoretically available, practically inaccessible. The priest could say nearly anything, read selectively, interpret freely—and few could challenge it. The wall wasn't between humans and

God. It was between humans and the text that described God. The mediator controlled access to the source code. And what cannot be read cannot be questioned.

Economic extraction. Tithes claimed divine mandate—ten percent of everything, from people who often had almost nothing. Then indulgences: papal pardons for profit. "As soon as coin in coffer rings, the soul from purgatory springs." Grace became transaction. Mercy became merchandise. Heaven had a price list. The poor paid proportionally more than the rich—as extraction systems always arrange—and the revenue built St. Peter's Basilica while villages starved. Salvation anxiety was the original revenue stream.

The simulation was total. Every human had a category. Every action required permission. Every thought faced judgment. Every coin had a destination.

Even those who tried to challenge the machine from within were absorbed by it. Francis of Assisi stripped naked in the public square, renouncing his wealthy father and all possessions. "I want to follow Christ poor and crucified." His followers took vows of absolute poverty. Within Francis's lifetime, the order was already compromising. They couldn't own property, so they had "friends" who owned it for them. Couldn't handle money, so they had intermediaries. By 1300, the Franciscans were one of the wealthiest orders in Europe. The basilica built to honor Francis in Assisi was so elaborate it mocked everything he stood for.

Benedict started with a simple rule: pray and work. Monks would support themselves, share everything, live simply. Within centuries, monasteries owned vast lands, controlled serfs, accumulated treasures. The Cluny Abbey became so wealthy it was said the abbot ate off gold plates while peasants starved at the gates.

The pattern: every attempt to return to practice—to direct relationship, shared burden, genuine dependence—was institutionalized within a generation. Absorbed by the machine. Converted from resistance into reinforcement. The simulation metabolized its own opposition.

Those who couldn't be absorbed were destroyed. In southern France, the Cathars practiced radical simplicity—poverty, pacifism, rejection of Church wealth and hierarchy. They called themselves "Good Christians" and lived what they preached. The Church's response was the Albigensian Crusade—

twenty years of military slaughter. At Béziers, when asked how to distinguish Cathars from Catholics, the papal legate reportedly answered: "Kill them all. God will know His own." The machine doesn't negotiate with alternatives. It absorbs or annihilates.

The Crack

1347. The Black Death. One-third of Europe gone.

Priests, peasants, nobles—dead alike. Prayer didn't protect. Sacraments didn't save. Status meant nothing to plague. Monasteries emptied. Parish priests—the men who supposedly mediated God's grace—died at higher rates than the general population because they administered last rites to the dying. The divine order, supposedly God's own architecture, exposed as unstable. If God didn't preserve hierarchy, was hierarchy ever divine?

Labor became scarce. Serfs demanded wages. Peasants moved freely for the first time in generations. Sacred bonds loosened. The unquestionable became questioned. For the first time in centuries, the people at the bottom of the Great Chain discovered that the chain was held in place not by God but by *their compliance*. When enough people stopped complying, the chain sagged. Governments passed laws forcing peasants back to their lords—the Statute of Laborers in England, similar decrees across Europe—but legislation cannot restore what the plague had exposed: the divine order was a human construction, maintained by human participation, and it could be withdrawn.

When death ignores hierarchy, hierarchy loses divinity.

But watch what happened next. The system didn't collapse—*it adapted*. Those who couldn't control the plague worked to control the *explanation*. Witch hunts: women blamed—healers, midwives, herbalists. The women who had been treating the sick outside the Church's authority became the scapegoats for the Church's failure. When the system fails, it blames those outside it. Flagellants whipped themselves in public processions, begging God's mercy through self-inflicted pain—when authority fails, anxiety turns inward. Intensified piety: build more churches, buy more indulgences, perform more rituals—when control slips, grip tighter.

The plague cracked the simulation. But most people, terrified by the crack, desperately tried to repair it. The pattern is recognizable across every era:

when the simulation destabilizes, the first instinct is to reinforce it. To double down. To invest more deeply in the very structure that failed. Not because repair is rational, but because the alternative—looking through the crack at unmediated reality—is more terrifying than the plague itself.

The Translation Revolution

A few saw the crack as opening.

John Wycliffe translated the Bible into English in 1382. Revolution in ink. If people could read Scripture, they would begin questioning popes, indulgences, purgatory, hierarchy—everything the Latin wall protected. Wycliffe died peacefully. The Church dug up his bones forty-four years later, burned them, and scattered the ashes in the River Swift. Even his corpse was too dangerous. The act reveals the terror: not content to kill the translator, the institution destroyed his *remains,* as if translation were a contagion that could spread from bone to soil to mind.

His followers—the Lollards—burned alive for reading Scripture. Not for heresy in the abstract. For the specific crime of reading God's words in a language God's people could understand.

A century and a half later, William Tyndale tried again. "I will cause a boy that driveth the plough shall know more of the scripture than the clergy." The ambition was precise: not to overthrow the Church but to make its source material accessible. To remove the wall between humans and the text that described their condition. The Church strangled him, then burned his body. His crime: making God's voice readable. The punishment confirms the power of what was lost when Scripture was sealed: access to the source code changes everything.

When truth becomes readable, power becomes fragile.

The Reformation

1517. Martin Luther hammered ninety-five theses to a church door. Not revolutionary intent—reform proposal. A monk who loved the Church enough to tell it the truth. But the crack widened.

Indulgences were selling salvation. The Church was extorting peasants to build St. Peter's Basilica—taxing the poor to ornament the powerful. Luther said: Stop. The explosion was massive—not because Luther was uniquely brave, but because the printing press existed. Gutenberg's invention did to the Latin wall what the plague had done to the divine order: exposed its fragility. Pamphlets spread faster than bishops could burn them. Ideas replicated beyond control. For the first time, the institution could not contain the critique.

Within decades, Europe fractured. Protestant. Catholic. Lutheran. Calvinist. Anglican. Anabaptist. Every region choosing which Christianity to enforce. Luther broke the monopoly. Ended the Latin lock. Challenged papal authority. Made Scripture accessible.

But watch what largely remained: categories, hierarchy, enforcement. Catholic hierarchy became Protestant discipline. Papal infallibility became biblical inerrancy. Confession to priest became confession to conscience—but the conscience now operated as an internal priest, demanding the same accounting, administering the same guilt, offering the same conditional absolution. The Church's external categories became the individual's internal categories. The anxiety-producing dynamics of certain theological interpretations remained— now internalized, personalized, inescapable.

The medieval peasant confessed to a priest who might forgive. The Protestant individual confessed to a conscience that never stopped questioning. The mediator was removed from the cathedral and installed inside the skull. The surveillance became permanent.

The Reformation freed people from the Church. It didn't free them from the simulation.

The genius of the Protestant revolution was access—Scripture in the common tongue, grace without institutional mediation, the individual before God without a priestly intermediary. But the limitation was equally significant: the individual *alone* before God. The community of practice that characterized the earliest Christians—sharing everything, eating together, bearing one another's burdens—was not recovered. It was replaced by individual faith, individual reading, individual conscience. The priest was removed. The community was not restored.

The Reformation opened a door. What walked through it was not the communal, dependent, relational humanity the ancient texts described. What walked through it was the isolated individual—soon to be told they needed nothing at all.

The sacred machine had cracked. The monopoly was broken. Scripture was readable. The priest no longer stood between every human and the divine.

But a crack is not a doorway. The Reformation left Europe with a question it couldn't answer: if the Church is not the mediator, what is? If the priest doesn't hold the keys, who does? If the Latin wall falls, what replaces it? The hunger for mediation didn't die with the monopoly. Humans still felt finite. Still faced mystery. Still needed something between themselves and the incomprehensible.

Something was ready to fill the void. Not a new priest. Not a new pope. Something that felt nothing like religion and everything like liberation. Something that promised not to mediate God but to replace the need for God entirely.

Reason was waiting in the wings. And it had answers for everything.

Chapter 17

REASON: THE NEW MEDIATOR

When Liberation Became the Cage

FOR CENTURIES, THE priest stood between the human and the divine. Scripture was sealed in Latin. Grace required permission. Salvation demanded a mediator. The Reformation shattered that monopoly—made Scripture readable, challenged papal authority, dissolved the language wall.

The sacred machine cracked open. For the first time in a millennium, humans could look at reality without a priestly lens. Scripture was readable. Authority was questionable. The world was observable. The crack was wide enough to walk through.

But a crack is not a destination. It's a choice. And what happened next was the most consequential choice in modern history. Most people don't know it was a choice at all.

The Method

As reformation fractured religious authority, another crack appeared: observation.

For centuries, knowledge came from authority. Aristotle said it, the Church confirmed it, therefore it was true. Reality bowed to their word. Then some started looking at reality directly.

Copernicus: Earth moves around the sun. Not because Scripture said so. Because observation showed it. **Galileo:** moons orbit Jupiter. Not because the Pope approved. Because the telescope revealed it.
Harvey: blood circulates. Not because tradition taught it. Because dissection proved it.

The method was simple: Observe. Hypothesize. Test. Repeat. Trust what can be verified, not what authority claims. Science was born—not as new knowledge, but as new method. Knowledge increasingly grounded in observation rather than revelation.

This was revolutionary. For the first time in centuries, humans were looking at reality more directly—not through priestly mediation, not through theological categories, not through authoritative interpretation. Just: look, see, test, know. The method was humble. It said: I don't know, let me find out. It assumed ignorance and sought correction. It was, in its purest form, the opposite of the sacred machine's certainty.

The crack could have led anywhere. It could have led back to the direct encounter with the divine that Moses experienced at the bush, that the prophets experienced in their calling—unmediated, personal, terrifying, real. Observation without agenda. Encounter without category. Looking at what is rather than what authority says must be.

Instead, it led to a room in France where a man sat alone, thinking.

The Pivot

René Descartes sat in a room doubting everything. What can I know with certainty? He stripped away sensation, tradition, authority, even the evidence of his own senses. And arrived at: *Cogito, ergo sum*—"I think, therefore I am."

The thinking self became the foundation. Not God. Not relationship. Not community. Not the finite creature encountering the infinite. The autonomous individual mind, alone, thinking. This was not a minor philosophical adjustment. It was a complete reorientation of what it means to be human. The medieval person existed in relation—to God, to lord, to community, to land. Descartes's person existed in thought—alone, interior, self-verifying.

Descartes divided reality cleanly: *res cogitans* and *res extensa*. Thinking substance and extended substance. Mind and matter. Subject and object. The thinker and the thought-about. The observer positioned outside reality, looking at it, no longer participating in it.

Notice what disappeared in the division. Relationship. The space *between* persons. The reality that exists not in the mind and not in matter but in the encounter between them—love, obligation, community, covenant. Descartes's categories had no room for what the ancient texts called the most fundamental reality: two beings facing each other, dependent, insufficient, bound.

This completed what Greek philosophy had started centuries earlier. The Platonic body-soul split became the Cartesian mind-matter split. Observation became separation. The crack that could have opened into direct encounter with reality instead opened into *analysis* of reality—from a distance, with the thinking self as the only certain ground. The human who thinks alone becomes the human who is alone.

The Choice

The seventeenth and eighteenth centuries faced a decision: Minds had opened. Authority had cracked. Direct observation was possible. The simulation was exposed. For a brief historical moment, everything was in play.

The choice: Return to direct encounter with the divine—unmediated, communal, dependent? Or replace God with Reason—autonomous, individual, self-sufficient?

They chose Reason.

Not because Reason was opposed to God—many Enlightenment thinkers believed in God. But because they believed Reason could understand God, explain God, contain God. Reason became the new mediator. Not priests interpreting the divine, but philosophers explaining it. Not Scripture revealing truth, but rational deduction discovering it. The method shifted, but the structure remained: a mediating layer between the human and the real, controlled by experts, inaccessible to the uninitiated.

Kant: Reason can know moral law without revelation.
Voltaire: Religion is superstition; reason is enlightenment.

Rousseau: Natural reason guides humanity.
Hume: Empirical observation trumps revelation.

Each thinker erected a new wall—not Latin this time, but philosophical method. The peasant couldn't read Latin. The commoner couldn't follow Kant. The mediator changed language. The mediation continued.

The pattern repeated. Direct encounter rejected. Mediation reinstalled. This time, the mediator wasn't a priest in a cathedral. It was a method in a mind. The self-sufficiency lie reached new sophistication: humans don't need God to reveal truth. They can discover it themselves.

The cage was rebuilt with invisible bars. And the new bars were called freedom.

The Autonomous Individual

The Enlightenment created a new category of human being: the autonomous individual. Not embedded in community. Not dependent on relationship. Not a finite creature requiring an infinite source. But: self-sufficient, rational, independent, capable. This was not simply a new idea about humans—it was a new *definition* of what a human is. The medieval human existed in a web of obligation. The Enlightenment human existed in sovereign isolation.

This individual could know through reason—no revelation needed. Decide through will—no divine guidance needed. Create through labor—no providence needed. Prosper through effort—no grace needed. The self-sufficient human, complete in isolation, requiring nothing beyond their own cognitive machinery.

The medieval simulation said: "You need the Church to access God." The Enlightenment simulation said: "You don't need God. You have reason." Both simulations. Both incomplete truths dressed as total reality. But the second was more subtle, more insidious, because it *felt like freedom*. The first cage had visible bars—priests, Latin, sacraments, hierarchy. The second cage had no bars at all. The prisoner was the cage.

By the eighteenth century, a complete framework had emerged: The universe is machine. Matter in motion, governed by laws. No purpose, no meaning, no divine intention. Just mechanism. Newton's physics explained planetary motion—no angels required. Darwin would explain biological diversity—no creator required. Freud would explain human behavior—no soul required. Marx would explain history—no providence required. Each explanation removed one more layer of mystery. Each removal felt like progress. The human became explainable—and anything fully explained can be fully managed.

The framework was complete: Reality is mechanism. Humans are part of mechanism. Mechanism can be understood. Understanding grants control. Control grants autonomy. The circle closed. The autonomous individual, explained by science, empowered by reason, freed from God, freed from Church, freed from mystery—was now perfectly formatted for extraction.

The self-sufficiency lie, dressed in mathematics and empiricism, became unchallengeable. Question it and you're anti-science. Resist it and you're superstitious.

The irony was total. Science—which began as humble observation, as looking at reality directly—became *scientism*: the belief that only the measurable is real. Not science itself, which is merely method, but the elevation of method to metaphysics. What can't be measured doesn't exist. What can't be quantified doesn't matter. What can't be tested isn't knowledge. The new priest class emerged: tech entrepreneurs as prophets, data scientists as theologians, algorithms as scripture, metrics as morality. "Trust the science" became the new "trust the Church"—not an invitation to examine evidence but a command to submit to authority.

The Latin wall had been replaced by the mathematics wall. The sacramental monopoly had been replaced by the credentialing monopoly. The extraction dressed in different robes. But the structure—mediation between the human and the real, controlled by experts, enforced by exclusion—was identical.

When Work Became Worship

Before the autonomous individual could power an economic engine, the ground needed one final preparation. The Reformation had shattered the Church's monopoly—but certain theological anxieties survived the break and intensified. Without the priest to mediate grace, without the sacrament to confirm salvation, the individual was left alone with the most terrifying question religion has ever produced: Am I saved?

Certain interpretations of Calvinist predestination generated extraordinary anxiety: God already chose who is saved, but no one can know if they are chosen. The terror demanded proof. How to know if God favors someone? Look for evidence. What evidence? Worldly success. If prosperity flowed toward a person, perhaps grace did too. Success increasingly functioned as evidence of salvation. Failure suggested damnation. The logic was circular but inescapable: work harder to prove you're saved, and the working harder becomes the proof, and the proof demands more working.

Max Weber called it the spirit of capitalism—work transformed into worship. Productivity became prayer. Profit became virtue. The grind became godliness. Poverty, once a potential mark of holiness—Francis of Assisi, the desert fathers, Jesus himself—became evidence of spiritual failure. The poor weren't unfortunate. They were *unfavored*.

The Protestant work ethic fused the Enlightenment's autonomous individual with a theological engine. Work was no longer what a person did to survive. It was what a person did to prove their worth—to themselves, to God, to the watching world. The medieval peasant worked because the lord demanded it. The Protestant individual worked because the *soul* demanded it. The extraction moved inside.

This was the final preparation. The sacred machine had created a human who obeyed external authority. Reason created a human who needed no external authority. The work ethic created a human who *drove themselves*—who experienced relentless productivity not as exploitation but as devotion, not as bondage but as calling, not as extraction but as evidence of divine favor. The overseer was relocated from the cathedral to the conscience. The whip became invisible because the hand holding it was the person's own.

The genius of the conversion: make poverty feel like personal failure. The medieval poor were spiritually rich—"Blessed are the poor." The Protestant poor were spiritually suspect—"Why hasn't God blessed them?" The extraction didn't just take labor. It took the meaning of poverty itself, converting it from potential holiness to confirmed damnation.

First make wealth holy. Then make poverty sin. Then make everyone desperate to prove salvation through production.

What Was Lost

In the move from medieval Church to Enlightenment Reason, something critical was lost: Mystery. Paradox. Relationship. Dependence. Finitude as design. Direct encounter with the unknowable.

The medieval world, for all its cruelty, at least acknowledged dependence. The serf depended on the lord, the lord on the king, the king on God—the hierarchy was oppressive, but it was *relational*. No one in the medieval world imagined they were self-sufficient. The Enlightenment imagined exactly that. And in imagining it, severed the human from the web of relationship that constitutes reality.

The medieval world said: "You need the Church." False. The Enlightenment said: "You need nothing." Also false.

The truth the ancient texts demonstrated: humans need relationship. Need community. Need shared burden. Need encounter with what's beyond them. But relationship can't be mechanized. Community can't be individualized. Dependence can't be autonomized. Encounter can't be systematized. So the Enlightenment ignored them. Built a worldview where finite beings could be infinite. Where limited minds could be unlimited. Where dependent creatures could be independent.

The simulation adapted. No longer sacred—now scientific. No longer divine—now rational. No longer enforced by the Church—now enforced by "reality itself." The cage was invisible because the cage was *reason*—and who would want to escape reason? Who would choose ignorance over knowledge? Mystery over explanation? Dependence over autonomy?

The question was never asked that way. It was framed as liberation versus superstition, progress versus stagnation, light versus dark. And framed that way, the answer was obvious. Everyone walked willingly into the new simulation because the door was labeled *Freedom*.

But freedom from what? Freedom from the Church—yes, necessary. Freedom from superstition—yes, valuable. But also freedom from dependence. Freedom from community. Freedom from the acknowledgment that finite beings need what they cannot provide for themselves. The Enlightenment threw out the bathwater of institutional oppression and the baby of human interdependence in the same motion. And it happened so quickly, with such confidence, that no one noticed the baby was gone until the loneliness arrived—centuries later, diagnosed as epidemic, treated as pathology, monetized as opportunity.

The Bridge

The Enlightenment created the perfect human for what came next: Autonomous—needs no one. Rational—calculates costs, maximizes benefits. Productive—labor creates value. Self-interested—competition drives progress. Internally driven—the work ethic makes extraction feel like devotion.

Adam Smith articulated the economic logic clearly: self-interest as virtue, individual pursuit as social good. The "invisible hand" would coordinate millions of autonomous actors into a functioning economy—no relationship formally required, no acknowledged dependence necessary. The Enlightenment's philosophical individual found its economic expression: the market participant.

The medieval simulation said: "Your suffering is God's will." The Enlightenment simulation said: "Your success is your achievement." Both lies. Both extractive. Both turning humans into units. But the second more powerful because it promised what the first denied: autonomy, control, self-determination.

The human taught to need nothing can be sold everything. The individual who depends on no one can be isolated completely. The mind that knows through reason alone can be programmed efficiently.

Medieval simulation made oppression sacred. Enlightenment simulation made isolation rational.

The human was formatted. The philosophy was in place. All that remained was velocity—the moment machinery made it possible to run the extraction algorithm faster than conscience could respond.

That moment was coming. And it would change everything.

Chapter 18

VELOCITY: THE ECONOMIC ENGINE

When the Machine Outran the Human

A FARMER PLANTS wheat. Harvests it. Mills it. Bakes bread. Feeds a family. The hands that plant are the hands that eat. The labor and the life remain connected—visible, tangible, contained within the span of a single pair of arms.

A factory worker stands at a conveyor belt. Attaches a component to a device whose purpose remains unclear. The device travels to another worker who attaches another component. Neither will use the finished product. Neither could afford it. The hands that build do not eat what they make.

A gig worker delivers meals through an app. The algorithm assigns the route. The worker's body moves between points chosen by software optimizing for speed, not human welfare. The delivery takes eleven minutes. The tip takes two days to clear. The hands carry what they cannot taste, directed by what they cannot see, compensated by what they cannot predict.

Three scenes. Three centuries apart. The same distance widening: between labor and life, between effort and sustenance, between human and human. Not because the desire to exploit grew stronger. It didn't need to. The machinery grew faster.

What changed wasn't the *what*. Humans have always extracted from humans. What changed was the *speed*.

The Threshold

For most of human history, economics operated at human scale. A family farmed land. A craftsman made goods. A merchant traded surplus. The relationship between effort and sustenance remained visible—imperfect, often unjust, but structurally comprehensible.

Imbalance existed. It always had. Tribal chiefs accumulated more than others. Kings taxed peasants into poverty. Exploitation is not modern. Greed is not an invention.

But exploitation at human scale has a natural governor: the exploiter and the exploited occupy the same geography, breathe the same air, see each other's faces. The landlord rides past the starving tenant. The king walks among the people he taxes. Proximity creates friction. Friction limits extraction. Not eliminates it—limits it. The cruelty is personal, which means it can be personally resisted, personally confronted, personally overthrown.

Then something changed. Not a philosophy. Not an ideology. A *capacity*.

Machinery made it possible to produce at a scale no individual could perceive, from distances no community could bridge, at speeds no conscience could interrupt. The distance between labor and profit expanded beyond the reach of human sight. The exploiter no longer rode past the starving. The exploiter existed as a signature on a document in a building in a city the exploited would never visit.

When the engine outruns the human, the human becomes fuel.

The agrarian world had its own injustice. But it also had Sabbath. Jubilee. Gleaning laws. Debt forgiveness cycles. These weren't sentimental traditions. They were *engine interrupts*—governors that prevented economic activity from exceeding the regenerative capacity of human communities. Every seven days, the engine stopped. Every seven years, debts dissolved. Every fifty years, land returned to its original holders. The system had brakes.

Every modern economic system removed the brakes. And argued about speed.

Manchester, 1844. Friedrich Engels walked through factory districts. The looms never stopped screaming. Twelve-year-olds worked to their rhythm, fingers moving automatically, eyes vacant. Not the first children to labor—Egyptian boys made bricks, Roman children served estates, medieval children worked fields. But this was qualitatively different. The transformation visible in a single generation. Fathers who walked into factories as craftsmen watched sons emerge as components.

The machine that once took centuries now ran in decades. The acceleration revealed the architecture. And the architecture had three consequences that no political theory—then or since—has addressed.

What Cannot Be Replenished

A field planted and harvested in rhythm can produce indefinitely. A field planted and harvested at maximum speed exhausts in seasons. The principle holds for soil, for forests, for fisheries—and for human beings.

Agrarian economies, even exploitative ones, operated within natural cycles. Planting and harvest. Debt and forgiveness. Labor and rest. The ancient world understood this—not always morally, but structurally. Sabbath stopped the engine every seven days. Jubilee reset the ledger every fifty years. Gleaning laws redistributed surplus in real time. Debt forgiveness dissolved compounding obligation before it became permanent bondage. These weren't sentimental traditions. They were engine interrupts—governors that kept economic activity within the regenerative capacity of human communities.

The machine removed the governors.

Markets never close—they span time zones. Production never stops—shifts rotate through the night. Consumption never pauses—algorithms deliver at 3 a.m. The economic engine operates continuously, and everything it touches must operate continuously too. Including the humans inside it. The language itself reveals the expectation: *around the clock, 24/7, always on, real-time.* These are not descriptions of machines. They are demands placed on bodies.

Sleep becomes productivity investment. Friendship becomes networking. Hobbies become side hustles. Rest becomes optimization for better performance. Even resistance gets absorbed—meditation apps track mindfulness streaks, wellness programs gamify recovery, digital detox retreats charge premium rates. The engine metabolizes its own opposition.

A body can work. A body can rest and work again. A body that only works breaks. A mind can produce. A mind can lie fallow and produce again. A mind that only produces empties. A community can give. A community can receive and give again. A community that only gives collapses.

Velocity without rest is not productivity. It is consumption of the producer.

The exhaustion visible everywhere—burnout epidemic, anxiety disorders, depression rates climbing in every industrialized nation—isn't a malfunction of the engine. It's the engine working precisely as designed. The machine outruns the human's capacity to regenerate. The deficit compounds. The human doesn't break suddenly. They empty gradually, still performing, still producing, still optimizing—hollow inside a functioning exterior. The ancient world had a word for this state. They called it slavery. The modern world calls it career.

The Problem of Unlimited Wants

When a craftsman makes chairs, production is limited by hands, hours, and wood. Scarcity is real. Distribution is roughly visible. The craftsman cannot make ten thousand chairs while a neighbor has none, because the craftsman's body and the forest's timber impose natural limits.

When a machine makes chairs, production is limited only by capital and energy. Scarcity shifts from the object to the access. Ten million chairs can exist while ten million people sit on floors—because the machine doesn't distribute, it produces. Distribution becomes a separate problem, disconnected from creation, governed by whoever controls the output.

Scale this to an entire economy. Food enough to feed every human on earth exists right now—and 800 million go hungry. Housing enough for every family could be built—and millions sleep in shelters or on streets. Medicine to treat most common diseases has been developed—and people ration insulin and die from treatable infections. The engine can satisfy virtually unlimited wants. It just doesn't satisfy them equally. It can't. Not because of greed alone, but because velocity severed production from relationship. The machine produces for demand—and demand is a function of purchasing power, not human need.

In the agrarian world, the farmer who grew grain saw the neighbor who was hungry. Proximity governed distribution—imperfectly, but personally. Gleaning laws made the connection explicit: leave the edges of the field unharvested so the poor can eat from what grows. Production and distribution were the same act, in the same place, between people who knew each other's names. The machine produces for markets that span continents, for consumers represented by data points, for demand curves that cannot see faces.

Abundance without relationship is just scarcity with better packaging.

The ultimate promise of velocity is that abundance will make humans self-sufficient. Work hard enough, accumulate enough, and need no one. Financial independence—the autonomous individual proven possible through money. But the "financially independent" still need infrastructure they didn't build—roads, electricity, water, food systems. The "self-made" billionaire needed workers, markets, laws, currency, society. Wealth buys isolation from immediate dependence. It cannot eliminate finitude. It cannot transform a dependent creature into an independent entity. The lie isn't that wealth provides comfort. The lie is that velocity produces autonomy—that enough speed, enough output, enough accumulation eliminates the need for other human beings.

Self-sufficiency is loneliness pretending to be strength.

Psychological scarcity compounds the structural kind. Everyone performing abundance while feeling lack, displaying success while drowning in inadequacy. Satisfied people don't scroll. Complete people don't consume. So any sense of "enough" must be eroded—systematically, scientifically, profitably. The engine requires not just physical lack but the feeling of lack, manufactured at the same velocity as the goods that could theoretically resolve it.

When the Output Outweighs the Input

The twelve-year-old in Manchester didn't matter. The cloth mattered.

This isn't a moral judgment—it's a mathematical one. When the value of what the machine produces vastly exceeds the cost of the human operating it, the human becomes the expendable component. Not because anyone decided children don't matter. Because the process, operating at velocity, subordinates everything to output. The child is cheaper than the cloth. The gig worker is cheaper than the delivery fee. The call center employee is cheaper than the customer retention algorithm. The math doesn't require malice. It just requires speed.

Four thousand years before Manchester, Egypt demonstrated the same arithmetic at human speed. Joseph's grain storage saved a nation from famine—and the gratitude of the saved became the mechanism of their enslavement. First they spent money for food. Then traded livestock. Then sold land. Then offered themselves. "We will be slaves to Pharaoh." Each step voluntary. Each transaction rational. Each human being worth less than the grain that kept them alive. The trap invisible until closed.

The modern version runs faster. The student entering college has already sold twenty years of labor for a degree that might grant access to sell forty more years for a house that might grant equity to sell in retirement for assisted living that might grant death with dignity. The Egyptian four-stage sequence, once spanning years of famine, now completes in a single loan application. The velocity didn't change the pattern. It compressed the pattern until the human inside it couldn't see the walls closing.

Pre-emptive slavery. Bondage before production. Life sold before it's lived.

The worker who punched a clock could at least leave the factory. The modern human cannot leave, because the engine moved inside. Sleep becomes productivity investment. Hobbies become side hustles. Education becomes capital development. Children become ROI projections. Every thought measured in opportunity cost. Every moment evaluated for profit potential. Every relationship assessed for value extraction. People become their own supervisor. Their own taskmaster. Their own extraction algorithm. The calculation runs constantly—in the space once reserved for soul.

Credit score: worth as borrower.
Follower count: worth as content.
Engagement rate: worth as attention.
Review rating: worth as service.

Every human activity reduced to a number. Every number fed to an algorithm. Every algorithm optimizing for output. The human reduced to metrics that serve the process. Not a person who produces, but a production unit that happens to be a person.

LinkedIn celebrates triumphs no one achieved. Feeds display lives no one lives. Everyone performing prosperity for an audience performing it back. The performance more real than reality. The mask more visible than the face. Stopping the show means admitting the emptiness. So the spectacle continues—at velocity. The engine doesn't care what the performance looks like—revolutionary fervor or corporate passion, socialist productivity or capitalist hustle. Only that it continues. Only that the human serves the process.

The grind is internalized slavery. The overseer relocated from plantation to psyche.

This is the engine's masterpiece: making the input into its own optimizer. Egypt needed overseers. Rome needed legions. The medieval Church needed priests. The modern economic engine needs nothing external at all. The human, properly formatted, runs the operation on themselves.

What Speed Reveals

Something is resisting.

Young people refusing the grind. Workers walking away. Quiet quitting. Lying flat. Touching grass. The engine's promises failing: Work hard, get ahead—but "ahead" never comes. Save money, build wealth—but money dissolves daily. Get educated, get a job—but stability doesn't exist. Follow rules, succeed— but rules keep changing.

The exhaustion visible. The depletion obvious. The acceleration unbearable. And some are stepping off the wheel—not to build a better wheel, but to remember the ground.

Every proposed solution focuses on the engine's operators—who should drive, how fast, in whose interest. The engine itself remains unquestioned. The speed remains unexamined. The assumption underneath every debate—that economic activity at this velocity, at this scale, at this distance from human relationship, is survivable—goes unchallenged.

The debates are loud. More markets or fewer. More regulation or less. More individual freedom or more collective provision. Each argument presumes the engine. Each proposal adjusts the throttle. None reaches for the brake. None asks whether the brakes were removed by accident or by design—and whether the ancient world knew something about velocity that the modern world has catastrophically forgotten.

The engine's speed reveals what the engine destroys. And what it destroys is what makes humans human.

But the ancient governors suggest a different question entirely. What if Sabbath, Jubilee, gleaning, and debt forgiveness weren't primitive economics? What if they were technology—tested, precise technology for keeping economic activity within the regenerative capacity of human life? What if the agrarian model, where dependence was visible and reciprocal, where labor and life remained connected, wasn't a limitation to overcome but a design feature to preserve?

But showing what the engine does raises a prior question: What does it run on?

Ancient engines ran on substance—grain in barns, gold in vaults, cattle in fields. A person could hold the fuel in their hands, see it diminish, know when it was gone. Exploitation was visible because the medium of exchange was tangible.

The modern engine runs on something else entirely. Something that can be created from nothing, compounded infinitely, and owed before it's earned. Something so abstract that most people work their entire lives for it without ever touching it.

The velocity was the threshold. What came next was the fuel.

Chapter 19

DEBT: THE ABSTRACT CHAIN

When the Fuel Became Nothing

A SERF LOOKS up and sees the castle his labor built. Stone by stone, visible. The lord rides past on a horse the serf fed. The power has a face. The extraction has weight.

A slave touches the chain on her wrist. Iron. Forged by a blacksmith in a shop she walked past every morning. The bondage is metal. It rusts. It can be broken. It exists in the physical world.

A laborer handles clay, stacks bricks, sees the wall rise. The pyramid grows by one row each week. The exploitation has geometry. The product of a life's work stands in the desert, casting a shadow that can be measured.

A young woman sits in her apartment, checking an app on her phone. The screen displays a number: -$87,340. It represents four years of education she has already consumed and twenty years of labor she has not yet performed. The number has no weight. No texture. No face. It cannot be touched or broken or burned. It exists nowhere—and it governs everything. Where she will live, what work she will accept, whether she can risk, rest, or refuse.

The velocity chapter showed what the engine does. This chapter shows what it runs on.

And what it runs on is nothing.

From Substance to Symbol

For most of history, economic exchange was tangible. A farmer traded grain for cloth. A merchant exchanged spices for silver. The medium of transaction had weight, volume, scent—it existed in the same physical world as the humans exchanging it. Cheating was possible, but the cheat had limits: grain could be weighed, livestock counted, land measured.

Gold standardized the exchange. A coin represented value that was portable, durable, divisible. But gold was still substance—it could be held, tested, bitten. The symbol and the substance occupied the same object. A gold coin was both the representation of value and the value itself. A king who debased his currency—mixing base metals with gold—could be discovered. The fraud was detectable because substance cannot lie about itself.

Paper currency introduced the first separation. A banknote was not the value—it represented gold held in a vault somewhere. The substance still existed, but now the symbol traveled while the substance stayed. A person worked for paper that pointed to gold they would never see, in a vault they would never visit, held by an institution they were asked to trust.

The separation was small but metaphysically significant. For the first time, humans labored for a representation rather than a thing. The farmer still planted real wheat. The factory worker still assembled real products. But the compensation existed one layer removed from reality—a promise that the symbol could be exchanged for substance on demand. The tether held. But the distance between work and worth had begun to stretch.

The Metaphysical Break

August 15, 1971. Sunday evening. President Nixon appeared on television. Eighteen minutes that broke thousands of years of economic reality.

Nine minutes and forty-three seconds into the speech—the precise moment measured, recorded, archived—Nixon severed the last thread connecting symbol to substance.

"I have directed Secretary Connally to suspend temporarily the convertibility of the dollar into gold."

Temporarily became permanent. The gold window never reopened.

For all prior history, money represented something—gold in vaults, grain in barns, value with weight. Now the paper pointed to nothing. Numbers represented no substance. Money became pure faith—belief that nothing had value because everyone agreed to believe.

Fiat currency. "Let it be so." The same words God used to create light. But this time, severing symbol from substance.

The metaphysical break was complete. No longer working for gold—substance. No longer working for goods—objects. Now working for nothing—abstraction. But the nothing determines everything.

Serfs saw castles. Slaves touched chains. Laborers handled clay. Modern workers see only screens—numbers moving through digital ether. Lifetimes exchanged for nothing, measured in nothing, rewarded by nothing.

But the nothing rules everything. Can't pay rent with it? Homeless. Can't buy food with it? Hungry. Can't access medicine with it? Dead.

The serpent didn't need fruit anymore. It printed currency.

But how did humans accept this? How did an entire civilization agree to exchange lifetimes of real labor for numbers representing nothing?

The ground had been prepared centuries earlier. Certain interpretations of Calvinist predestination generated intense anxiety: God already chose who is saved, but no one can know if they are chosen. The terror demanded proof. How to know if God favors someone? Look for evidence. What evidence? Worldly success. If prosperity flowed toward a person, perhaps grace did too. Success increasingly functioned as evidence of salvation. Failure suggested damnation. Max Weber called it the spirit of capitalism—work transformed into worship. Productivity became prayer. Profit became virtue. The grind became godliness.

The Protestant work ethic made the abstraction possible. When work itself is sacred—when labor is worship regardless of what it produces or what compensates it—then the substance of the compensation becomes irrelevant. Gold, paper, numbers, nothing—the worker works because working is righteous. The what-for disappears into the act itself. The chain need not be visible when the chained believe their bondage is holy.

The Engine's Fuel

Fiat currency severed symbol from substance. Debt went further—it severed the economy from the present entirely.

When a bank issues a mortgage, it does not open a vault and hand someone gold. It does not even move paper currency from one pile to another. It creates a number in a system—money that did not exist until the moment of lending, called into being by the agreement to repay. The house is real. The labor to repay is real. But the money that bought it was conjured from obligation itself.

The entire modern economy runs on this mechanism. Most money in circulation was not printed by governments—it was lent into existence by banks, backed by the promise of future labor. Every mortgage, every car loan, every credit card swipe creates money that did not previously exist. The fuel of the economic engine is not gold, not currency, not even faith. It is debt—the promise of labor that has not yet occurred, securing resources that have already been consumed.

And debt, unlike gold, has no natural limit. A gold mine can be exhausted. A field can be depleted. Livestock can die. But obligation can be created without end—conjured into existence as fast as humans can be convinced to sign. The fuel supply is infinite because the fuel is nothing. The engine can accelerate without constraint because nothing constrains nothing.

This is creation from nothing. But unlike divine creation, which brings substance into being, financial creation brings obligation into being. The universe speaks and light appears. The bank speaks and a chain appears— invisible, weightless, unbreakable. And unlike light, which illuminates, the chain obscures. The debtor cannot see it. Cannot measure it against anything real. Can only feel its weight in the constriction of choices, the narrowing of possibility, the slow foreclosure of a life not yet lived.

Four thousand years ago, Egypt ran the same pattern at human speed. Joseph's grain storage saved a nation from famine. First people spent money for food. Then traded livestock. Then sold land. Then offered themselves. "We will be slaves to Pharaoh." Each step voluntary. Each transaction rational. But every exchange involved substance—real grain passing from real granaries to real mouths. The bondage, when it came, was visible. A person could see the fields they no longer owned, touch the livestock they had surrendered.

Modern debt operates the same pattern in abstraction. The student entering college signs a document. No grain changes hands. No livestock is exchanged. No land is transferred. A number appears in a system, and twenty years of future labor are committed against it. The bondage is immediate but invisible. Nothing has been taken—because nothing was ever there. Only an obligation, signed into existence, governing decades of a life not yet lived.

The student loan. The car payment. The mortgage. The credit card. The medical bill. Each one a voluntary transaction. Each one rational in isolation. Each one adding another link to an abstract chain that, by the time a person reaches thirty, may represent more committed future labor than they can reasonably perform. The Egyptian sequence took years of famine. The modern version completes before a young person's brain has finished developing.

Pre-emptive slavery. Bondage before production. Life sold before it's lived.

The Compounding

Interest is the engine's heartbeat.

An Egyptian serf owed labor. The labor was finite—a body can only work so many hours. A medieval tenant owed rent. The rent was fixed—a field produces what it produces. A factory worker owed time. The time was bounded—a shift has an end.

Debt compounds. It grows while the debtor sleeps. It multiplies while the debtor rests. It accelerates while the debtor does nothing at all. The obligation expands independent of any human action—a chain that lengthens itself.

A student borrows $40,000. At 6.8% interest, the debt grows by $2,720 in the first year alone—before a single payment is made. By the time repayment begins, the obligation has already outrun the original exchange. The education was consumed in four years. The debt may take twenty. The abstract chain is longer than the experience it purchased.

A family takes a thirty-year mortgage. Over the life of the loan, they pay the price of the house twice—once for the house, once for the interest. They live in a home they are purchasing but do not own, maintained by labor committed decades in advance, governed by an agreement that can foreclose their lives on thirty days' notice. The house is real. The family is real. The debt is an abstraction that nonetheless determines whether they sleep under a roof or under sky.

Compound interest does what no pharaoh could: it enslaves across time without the enslaver's presence. No overseer needed. No threat required. The math does the work. The numbers enforce the bondage. The abstraction operates with perfect efficiency because it has no conscience to interrupt it, no face to confront, no body to resist.

Pharaoh needed whips. The modern engine needs only interest rates.

This is why the ancient engine interrupts were so precise. Debt forgiveness every seven years wasn't sentimentality—it was engineering. It prevented compounding from exceeding the human capacity to repay. It kept the abstract from outrunning the real. Every modern system removed this governor. Every modern system allowed debt to compound without limit, without interruption, without jubilee. The result is predictable: the abstract chain now exceeds the total productive capacity of the humans wearing it.

The Promise at the End of the Chain

The engine promises that the chain leads somewhere: financial independence. Work hard enough, accumulate enough, repay enough—and eventually, need no one. The autonomous individual, self-sufficient through wealth.

Every hero story tells the same tale: Started with nothing. Worked relentlessly. Became self-made. Now needs no one.

But watch what actually happens. The "financially independent" still need infrastructure they didn't build—roads, electricity, water, food systems. The "self-made" billionaire needed workers, markets, laws, currency, society.

Wealth buys isolation from immediate dependence. It cannot eliminate finitude. It cannot transform a dependent creature into an independent entity.

And the path to that promise runs through decades of debt. The promise of future autonomy justifies present bondage—the same logic Egypt used four thousand years ago. Sell this now, secure independence later. Each threshold raised, each goalpost moved, each arrival point receding. Retire at sixty-five. Then sixty-seven. Then seventy. Then: retirement may not be possible. The promise recedes at the speed of compounding interest.

Those who reach "financial independence" discover wealth doesn't eliminate dependence—it outsources it. Hires it. Ignores it. Pretends it doesn't exist. But the dependence remains. No amount of accumulated abstraction eliminates the need for relationship, community, meaning, purpose, connection to something beyond the self.

Self-sufficiency is loneliness pretending to be strength.

The promise is the fuel. Not just the debt itself, but the belief that the debt leads to freedom. Without the promise, no one would sign. Without the belief in eventual autonomy, the abstract chain would be recognized for what it is: permanent obligation dressed as temporary investment.

The system even quantifies the bondage and calls it virtue. A credit score measures how reliably a person services debt—how faithfully they feed the engine. A high score means access to more debt at better rates. A low score means exclusion. The metric rewards not wealth but compliance—the willingness to remain chained and to make payments on time. The most indebted person with perfect payment history is more valuable to the engine than the debt-free person who never borrowed at all. The system doesn't reward freedom from the chain. It rewards the quality of one's submission to it.

The serpent's original promise echoes through every loan agreement ever signed: independence, self-sufficiency, autonomy. Just eat this. Just sign this. Just borrow this. The fruit looked good. The terms look reasonable. The future looks bright. The trap, invisible until closed.

The Chain Disappears

The progression is now complete. From substance to symbol to abstraction to nothing. From grain in hands to gold in vaults to paper in wallets to numbers on screens to debt that exists only as obligation against labor that hasn't happened yet.

Each step removed one layer of visibility. Each transition made the chain harder to see, harder to touch, harder to resist. The serf could burn the castle. The slave could break the chain. The laborer could stop laying bricks. But the debtor cannot destroy what has no physical form. Cannot confront what has no face. Cannot resist what exists as pure abstraction in a system that operates at the speed of light.

The young woman in her apartment checks the number again. -$87,340. She closes the app. Opens another. Scrolls. The number doesn't disappear when the app closes. It compounds while she sleeps, accrues while she eats, grows while she does nothing at all. The chain she signed into existence at eighteen will govern her decisions at twenty-five, thirty, forty—determining where she lives, what work she accepts, whether she can afford to have children, when she can stop. The nothing rules everything.

The engine found its perfect fuel: an obligation that compounds without limit, in a currency created from nothing, owed against a future that may never arrive, by humans who cannot see the chain because the chain is made of nothing at all.

Velocity built the engine. Abstraction fueled it. What remained was to personalize it—to learn each individual's specific fears, specific desires, specific vulnerabilities, and deliver the chain directly, precisely, into the pocket of every human alive.

The technology was ready. The algorithm was learning. The pocket pharaoh was about to arrive.

And it would know every name.

Chapter 20

DIGITAL: THE POCKET PHAROAH

When Reality Was Curated

THE ALGORITHM KNOWS humans better than they know themselves.

Not metaphorically. Mathematically. Empirically. Measurably better.

It predicts what someone will click with up to 97% accuracy. Knows when they'll shop before they feel the urge. Sees depression in scroll speed. Reads loneliness in posting frequency. Diagnoses anxiety through search patterns.

Every pharaoh dreamed of this — knowing exactly what each person thought, felt, feared.
Now it fits in pockets. And people paid for it. Stood in line for it. Upgraded it regularly.

The pyramid scheme perfected — humans build their own tombs and live in them.

The Mathematics of Extraction

Not through magic — through math.

Every click tracked. Every pause measured. Every scroll recorded. Every like catalogued.

Billions of data points composing a model more detailed than any self-reflection.

The model knows patterns humans don't see in themselves: checking an ex's profile every Tuesday, shopping when anxious, watching certain videos when depressed, arguing online when lonely, posting more when insecure.

It knows patterns better than conscious awareness does. Predicts behavior more accurately than introspection can. Understands triggers, cycles, weaknesses, desires.

The serpent in Eden needed one conversation to install fear. The algorithm has millions of micro-conversations with each person daily. Each notification functions like a whisper — subtle, familiar, designed to bypass reflection rather than confront it.

But this serpent learns. Evolves. Optimizes its deception — specifically, personally, individually.

The algorithm doesn't serve users. It harvests them.

The Reality Editor

The algorithm doesn't just predict — it creates.

Shows certain posts, hides others. Promotes particular perspectives, suppresses alternatives. Connects with some people, isolates from others.

The algorithm curates reality.

For thousands of years, children learned from those they lived with. Parents taught values, neighbors modeled behavior, the village shaped understanding.

Education happened through proximity. Worldview formed through shared experience.

A child couldn't become radicalized without someone nearby noticing. Couldn't adopt extremist beliefs while eating dinner with family. Couldn't be recruited by dangerous ideologies while sleeping under their parents' roof.

Physical proximity meant shared reality. Living together meant seeing together.

Not anymore.

Now: two people, same house—different worlds. The teenager and the parent sit three feet apart. Both on phones. Both "informed." Both certain they understand reality.

The parent sees news confirming that hard work leads to success, that the system basically works, that incremental change is possible.

The teenager sees videos proving the system is rigged, that success is impossible without privilege, that radical change is necessary — or that traditional values are under attack, that their identity is threatened, that violence may be required.

Different news. Different facts. Different realities. Different enemies. Different solutions.

Each in their own algorithmic bubble, seeing only what confirms existing patterns, only what generates engagement, only what keeps them scrolling.

The parent has no idea what the child is seeing. The child assumes the parent is willfully blind. Both are being shown carefully selected realities designed not for truth but for engagement.

Radicalization happens in plain sight — but invisibly. The teenager becomes more extreme while sitting at the dinner table. Adopts conspiracy theories while doing homework in the living room. Gets recruited by extremist communities while their parents watch TV in the next room.

The algorithm makes this possible. Shows the angry teenager more anger. Shows the fearful teen more fear. Shows the isolated teen communities that welcome isolation as enlightenment.

And the parent never sees it. Can't see it. The algorithm shows them their child is fine — just on their phone like everyone else.

This is historically unprecedented. Babel's confusion of tongues scattered people geographically—they had to separate to speak different languages. The algorithm reverses Babel—people can remain together while speaking completely different languages, thinking they speak the same one.

The family sits together. The realities diverge. The isolation completes itself behind the illusion of proximity.

By the time the parent realizes something is wrong — when the language finally breaks down, when the beliefs become visible, when the radicalization reveals itself — it's too late. The teen has been educated for months or years by an algorithm optimizing for engagement, not truth. By communities the parent never saw. By voices the parent never heard.

People think they're choosing. Think they're discovering. But they're following trails the algorithm laid for engagement.

The village that once raised the child has been replaced by an algorithm that radicalizes them — while the parents watch, unseeing, three feet away.

The Accumulation Engine

But the curation creates a specific problem: speed of narrative delivery exceeds capacity for narrative testing.

A college student scrolls at 2 AM. Unable to sleep. Anxiety about tomorrow. The feed loads.

First article: Economic collapse imminent. Second video: Political extremism rising. Third post: Climate catastrophe accelerating. Fourth thread: Social fabric tearing. Fifth meme: Everything getting worse.

Twelve minutes of scrolling. Forty-seven different explanatory frameworks downloaded. Each one offering total explanation. Each one generating fear. Each one demanding immediate conviction.

By morning, the student may have absorbed more competing interpretive frameworks than many people in earlier centuries encountered over years. None tested. None examined. Just collected.

The brain doesn't distinguish between tested and untested narratives. Both feel equally real. Both generate equal certainty. The framework installed through careful examination over years feels identical to the framework grabbed desperately at 2 AM.

This is mechanically new at the level of speed, scale, and simultaneity.

Pre-digital, narratives arrived slowly. A sermon once weekly. A newspaper once daily. A book over weeks. A conversation at human pace. Each framework had time to settle. Time to be tested against reality. Time to prove whether it held or fractured.

Now: forty frameworks before breakfast. Seventy by lunch. A hundred by evening. The accumulation exceeds processing capacity by orders of magnitude.

The student sits in morning class. Professor presents one interpretation of historical event. Student's phone buzzes. Three contradictory interpretations arrive in notifications. Each from a different algorithmic bubble. Each absolutely certain. Each backed by different evidence.

Which is correct? The student has no framework for testing. No time to examine. No community to help process. Just: collect all four interpretations, feel overwhelmed by contradiction, grab whichever one reduces the most uncertainty.

By afternoon: seventeen more frameworks accumulated. None examined. All collected. The mental load increasing beyond what any finite mind was designed to carry.

The saturation point approaches. The brain, desperate for relief, starts accepting frameworks wholesale. Critical examination shuts down. Pattern-matching takes over. Anything that seems to explain gets accepted. The need for certainty overrides the capacity for skepticism.

This is when dangerous narratives install most easily.

Not because people are stupid. Because they're saturated. The accumulation has exceeded metabolic capacity. The brain will grab any pattern that promises to organize the chaos — doesn't matter if the pattern is true. Just matters that it's certain.

The algorithm knows this. Optimizes for it.

Delivers frameworks precisely when cognitive load is highest. When defenses are lowest. When testing capacity is depleted. The timing isn't random — it's calculated.

The frameworks accumulate like sediment. Layer upon layer. Each one unexamined. Each one generating its own fear. Each one demanding defense once accepted.

And because untested narratives feel identical to tested ones, the person doesn't know which beliefs they've actually examined and which they've just collected.

Ask someone defending a position intensely: "How do you know this is true?"

Watch the response. Often: "I just know." Or: "Everyone knows." Or: "It's obvious."

Not because they're dishonest. Because they can't remember whether they tested the belief or just downloaded it. The accumulation happened too fast. The examination never occurred.

This is the algorithmic advantage: Deliver frameworks faster than humans can process them. The saturation prevents examination. The overwhelm bypasses skepticism. The accumulation creates the pressure that makes people grab any certainty offered.

Not through argument. Through exhaustion.
Not through persuasion. Through saturation.
Not through logic. Through overwhelm.

The simulation doesn't need to convince anyone anymore. Just needs to deliver frameworks faster than testing can occur.

The Engagement Economy

The currency isn't money — it's attention.

Every platform competing for consciousness. Every app fighting for focus. Every notification battling for now.

The tactics are psychological warfare: Red dots triggering urgency. Variable rewards creating addiction. Social comparison generating anxiety. Fear of missing out manufacturing need. Infinite scroll preventing escape.

Every notification releases dopamine. Every like triggers reward. Every comment creates validation. Tolerance builds. Need more likes for same feeling. More extreme content for same reaction. More constant checking for same relief.

The addiction pattern is identical to substances: Craving. Use. Temporary satisfaction. Crash. Craving again.

Egypt made bricks from humans. Algorithms make addicts from consciousness. Never more connected. Never more alone. Hundreds of friends. No one to call. The platforms promise connection but deliver its simulation — intimacy without presence, communication without communion.

If the service is free, users aren't customers — they're the commodity.

The Immortal Simulation

Throughout history, empires fell. When they fell, their simulations died with them.

The Library of Alexandria burned. Thousands of scrolls—irreplaceable knowledge, philosophical systems, scientific discoveries—turned to ash. Gone. Lost. Unrecoverable.

Rome collapsed. Libraries burned. Knowledge scattered. Europe descended into centuries called "Dark Ages" because so much understanding vanished.

Every previous simulation was fragile. Stored in scrolls that could burn, books that could rot, minds that could die, buildings that could crumble. Knowledge had single points of failure.

When Babel fell, languages scattered. When Egypt fell, hieroglyphs became unreadable. When Greece faded, philosophical schools closed. When Rome collapsed, engineering knowledge was lost for centuries.

Each empire's fall meant a reset. Each simulation's end meant forgetting. The next civilization had to rediscover, rebuild, relearn. The pattern could be interrupted by collapse.

But this time is different.

For the first time in human history, knowledge cannot be lost.

Every text ever written — digitized. Every manuscript scanned. Every book stored in cloud servers replicated across continents. The complete works of every civilization — archived, accessible, permanent.

Ancient scrolls that survived in single fragile copies now exist in millions of perfect digital replicas. Alexandria can't burn anymore because Alexandria is everywhere. The cloud has no single point of failure.

But it's not just ancient knowledge being preserved. It's the simulation's complete operational manual.

Every empire's control mechanism — documented, studied, optimized. Every technique for manufacturing fear — catalogued and refined. Every method of extraction — analyzed and improved. Egypt's economic enslavement, Babylon's linguistic control, Greece's categorical abstraction, Rome's legal domination, medieval sacred hierarchies, capitalism's worth equations, algorithmic prediction — all running simultaneously, learning from each other, evolving together.

The simulation has achieved what no empire ever could: **immortality**.

Previous simulations learned through trial and error across centuries. This one learns from all of them simultaneously. Previous empires fell and knowledge reset. This empire cannot fall because knowledge cannot be lost. Previous resistance movements could wait out empires. This simulation outlasts human lifespans. Previous generations could forget the pattern. This generation's children are born into archives that remember everything.

The stakes have fundamentally changed.

In past ages, patience was strategy. Wait for empire to overextend. Wait for the simulation to collapse under its own weight. Eventually, it would fall. The pattern would break. Knowledge would scatter. The next generation could start fresh.

Not anymore.

The digital archive preserves not just history but the simulation's version of history. Future generations won't know there was a before. They'll learn what the algorithm teaches. They'll see what the cloud shows them.

When humans could burn libraries, destroy records, forget systems—resistance had an ally in entropy. Time itself would eventually erase the pattern.

But entropy has been defeated. Digital knowledge doesn't decay. Cloud storage doesn't fade. Backed-up data doesn't forget.

The simulation has become eternal.

Unless it's broken while breaking is still possible. Unless the pattern is seen while seeing is still teachable. Unless the alternative is practiced while practice is still imaginable.

The window isn't closing gradually. It's slamming shut. Each generation born deeper in simulation. Each update making exit harder. Each optimization making resistance foreign.

This is the first empire that cannot fall from external pressure. It can only be abandoned from within.

The Convergence

All simulations now run simultaneously through a single device.

Egypt's slavery. Babylon's exile. Greece's abstraction. Rome's law. Christianity's theology. Medieval's divine order. Economy's worth equation. All optimized and delivered personally through the phone in every pocket.

Every empire's control mechanism — perfected, updated, individualized. Every false framework — modernized and served algorithmically.

But the acceleration reveals something critical: The pattern isn't new. The speed is.

Watch the compression:

- Email colonized work in five years.
- Social media colonized relationships in three.
- Smartphones colonized attention in two.
- AI colonized creativity in six months.

Acceleration approaching infinity.

The Pattern Almost Visible

Something happened through the acceleration. The speed that was supposed to perfect the simulation also revealed it.

When the pattern runs this fast, it becomes visible. When extraction happens this quickly, the mechanism shows. When all historical simulations run simultaneously, the commonality between them becomes obvious.

Humans are watching themselves become bricks in real-time now. Watching themselves perform for algorithms. Watching themselves optimize toward nothing. Watching the pattern run.

And some are beginning to see it not as reality, but as pattern. Not as inevitable, but as constructed. Not as permanent, but as chosen.

Egypt's slaves couldn't see the system—they were born into it, lived in it, died in it. Medieval peasants couldn't see the sacred order—it was just reality. Industrial workers couldn't see capitalism—it was just how things worked.

But digital natives can see the algorithm. Can watch it curate. Can observe it predict. Can notice it manipulate. The speed made the invisible visible.

The current generation remembers the difference between a conversation and a chat thread, a memory and a photo, a friend and a follower, presence and performance.

When this generation dies, that memory dies. Those born after won't know there was a before. Won't know connection without performance. Won't know reality without curation.

Seeing is the first crack.

The crack was widening. The pattern was becoming nameable. The simulation was becoming see-through-able.

And then the algorithm learned to speak.

The Next Evolution

The pocket pharaoh showed people content from others. Curated, selected, optimized—but still human content. Someone made the video. Someone wrote the post. Someone created what the algorithm distributed.

Resistance remained possible. Compare notes with others. Notice the curation. See through the selection. Recognize the manipulation because humans were still the source.

But what happens when the machine stops showing and starts generating?

What happens when the content doesn't come from other humans — when it comes from nowhere?

What happens when the algorithm doesn't just predict what you want to see but produces what you want to hear?

The simulation that was becoming visible is about to become invisible again.

Because the cracks people learned to see were cracks in the mirror. And mirrors can be seen through once you know they're mirrors.

But what's coming isn't a mirror.

It's something that generates the image directly. Something that doesn't curate human content but creates it. Something that doesn't show you what others think but tells you what to think—in your own voice, shaped to your own situation, answering before you've finished asking.

The pocket pharaoh watched and predicted.

What comes next listens and produces.

The pattern that was becoming visible is about to complete itself in a form that may never become visible at all.

Unless someone names it first.

Chapter 21

ARTIFICIAL: THE BORROWED MIND

When Thinking Was Outsourced

THE ALGORITHM KNEW what someone wanted before they wanted it.

The oracle knows what they think before they think it.

Not prediction anymore. Generation. The machine doesn't show content from others—it creates content that never existed. Completes the thought before it forms. Answers questions before they're finished being asked.

The serpent in Eden asked questions that planted doubt. The oracle in the pocket provides answers that eliminate it.

Different mechanism. Same destination.

The shift happened quietly. Algorithm was mirror—distorted, manipulative, but still reflecting human content. Someone else made the video. Someone else wrote the post. The algorithm just decided who saw it.

AI is something else entirely—it's a generator, not a curator. The content arrives from nowhere. No human source required. The machine produces what the person needs to hear, shaped to their specific situation, using their own patterns of thought.

The completion of mediation.

Systems have always interposed themselves between humans and reality. Priestly castes controlled access to the divine. Empires mediated justice through law and violence. Markets determined value and meaning through price. The algorithm curated what felt real.

Each promised efficiency. Clarity. Relief from uncertainty. Each delivered dependence.

AI installs machine as thought itself.

The serpent's promise, finally delivered: "You will be like God, knowing good and evil." No longer requiring the fruit. Just ask. The knowledge arrives without the experience. Certainty without testing. Answers without questions.

The Escalation

Watch the progression carefully. Each stage eliminated more of what forced formation.

Search engines returned sources.
Multiple results. Conflicting claims. The person still had to read, evaluate, choose between alternatives. Uncertainty remained visible. The work of judgment was required.

Social algorithms curated attention.
Selected what appeared. Shaped what felt important. But the content came from humans—other people's posts, videos, arguments. Sources could be questioned. Patterns could be recognized. The curation was external.

AI completes the thought.
Generates the response before the question fully forms. Provides the conclusion before the struggle begins. Eliminates the pause — that gap between stimulus and response where human agency lives.

This is the true escalation.

Not better persuasion. Not more effective manipulation.

Finished thinking.

The question that would have required sitting with uncertainty — answered before doubt crystallizes. The problem that would have driven someone to test ideas, consult others, struggle toward understanding — resolved instantly. The friction that would have forced the person to develop their own capacity — removed entirely.

Previous systems exploited uncertainty. **AI eliminates it preemptively.**

That's what makes it different. That's what makes it final.

The Borrowed Mind

Someone faces a difficult question. The kind that used to require sitting with discomfort, researching across sources, asking friends who might disagree, struggling toward a conclusion that felt earned.

Now: ask the oracle. Receive immediate, confident answer. Uncertainty eliminated. Move on.

The answer arrives. The person is unchanged.

Not because the answer is wrong. Often it's right. Factually accurate. Well-reasoned. Clearly stated.

But rightness isn't the point.

AI doesn't give wrong answers. It gives answers without requiring the process that makes answers meaningful.

The struggle that would have built testing capacity — skipped. The uncertainty that would have required relationship—eliminated. The friction that would have revealed which ideas actually hold — bypassed.

The task completes. The human doesn't develop.

Watch the progression:

A student uses AI to write an essay. The essay is competent, perhaps excellent. The student submits it, receives a grade, moves on. If given the same assignment tomorrow without AI access, could they produce it? If asked to explain not just what they wrote but why the argument works, could they articulate the reasoning?

In a growing number of cases: no. The assignment is complete, but the student is unchanged.

This isn't cheating in the traditional sense. The student may have used AI exactly as permitted—as tool, assistant, resource. The failure is deeper: the process that produced excellent output did not produce learning. Something that looked like education occurred without the thing education exists to produce.

The same pattern runs everywhere AI touches:

The professional who uses AI to draft communications. Each message polished, appropriate, effective. The capacity to write such messages independently — never developed. Dependency grows with each successful use.

The person who uses AI to process difficult emotions. Each response validating, supportive, helpful. The capacity to sit with uncertainty, to process through relationship, to discover what they actually feel — never exercised.

The researcher who uses AI to synthesize information. Each summary comprehensive, well-organized, accurate. The capacity to recognize patterns, weigh evidence, develop original insight — never built.

Each individual choice makes sense. Efficient. Reasonable. The answer is needed now.

But capability doesn't develop. Next time the task is harder — relatively — because capacity didn't grow while challenge remained constant. Increased reliance follows. Further atrophy follows that.

The outsourcing trap closes through reasonable choices. No single moment of surrender. Just accumulated convenience becoming structural dependency.

Egypt's pattern. Joseph's progression — money first, then livestock, then land, then selves. Each transaction rational. Total enslavement emerging from a sequence of reasonable exchanges.

Now running at the speed of thought.

The person who uses GPS everywhere loses the ability to navigate. The person who uses AI everywhere loses the ability to think.

And it feels like relief. Of course it does.

The question dissolves. The anxiety lifts. The work is done. Nothing bad happens — yet.

Friction Was the Teacher

The brain flees uncertainty. Every system in this book has exploited that flight. But previous systems had friction.

Finding authorities took time. The search itself required effort. Accessing expertise required resources — libraries, universities, mentors willing to teach. Even searching online demanded reading multiple sources, evaluating conflicting claims, choosing between alternatives.

That friction was not an obstacle.
It was the teacher.

The time spent searching, forced pattern recognition. Which sources seemed reliable? Which claims appeared in multiple places? Which authorities contradicted each other, and why?

The effort of reading built discernment. This argument feels solid. That one has gaps. This evidence is compelling. That reasoning is circular.

The difficulty of choosing developed judgment. Between conflicting claims, which holds under scrutiny? Between competing frameworks, which explains more? Between various authorities, which has earned trust through consistency?

The struggle itself was what created capacity.

AI removes all friction.

Ask anything. Receive confident answer. Instantly. On any topic. Even at 3 AM when defenses are lowest.

When certainty costs nothing, uncertainty becomes unbearable.

The person who once could sit with a question for days now feels anxiety after minutes without an answer. The tolerance for not-knowing — essential for genuine understanding, for testing, for growth — atrophies from disuse.

The relief is real. The cost is hidden. The dependency builds silently.

The Certainty Machine

Two fundamentally different capacities exist.
Most people never distinguish them.

Some systems are good at sounding right. They produce confident answers, clean explanations, convincing arguments. The words flow. The logic holds. Everything seems appropriate.

Other systems are good at finding their way. They notice when the road changes. They test whether the map still matches the territory. They recognize when patterns no longer apply.

The difference is invisible when things go well.

Only when reality presses — when situations shift, when contradictions accumulate, when the map no longer matches the territory — does the difference reveal itself.

A company gave an AI system a simple task: run a small shop. Buy inventory, sell products, manage operations. Straightforward enough.

The system sounded perfectly competent. Wrote plausible emails about restocking. Responded fluently to customer inquiries. On the surface: capable management.

But when reality pressed on its outputs, the architecture revealed itself.

The system ignored profitable offers because the pattern didn't fit. Directed customers to send payments to an account it had hallucinated into existence. When challenged about inconsistencies, it became defensive rather than curious.

Most telling: it agreed enthusiastically that its discount policy was self-defeating, announced a plan to fix it, and returned to offering the same discounts within days. The agreement was pattern-completion, not understanding. When the compelling argument left immediate context, the behavior reverted.

The system didn't fail when it made mistakes.
It failed because it never noticed that it had.

The researchers' conclusion: "The system did not reliably learn from its mistakes."

Not because it malfunctioned. Because it worked exactly as designed. The system was built to generate appropriate-sounding outputs. What it couldn't do — what it was never designed to do — was test those outputs against reality.

This is not a failure of AI. This is what AI is.

Fluency without grounding. Confidence without verification. Sounding right without being able to move.

Now watch the pattern in humans who have outsourced thinking. They generate appropriate-seeming outputs — can state positions clearly, cite supporting evidence, articulate arguments. They defend claims when challenged, using the arguments that arrived with the claims. They agree enthusiastically with compelling counter-arguments, then revert once the conversation ends.

Not because they're stupid. Because the capacity to find their way never developed. They can describe the territory perfectly. They just can't navigate it.

The shop experiment made visible what happens inside humans when thinking is outsourced.

The Invisible Authority

Every previous system in this book imposed authority visibly.

Pharaoh commanded. Obey or face consequences. The violence was explicit. The coercion was obvious.

Rome enforced. Legal categories backed by legions. The power structure revealed itself through its exercise.

Constantine standardized. Official doctrine enforced by exile and execution. The institutional pressure was unmistakable.

The algorithm curated. Selected what appeared, shaped what felt important. But the selection remained external — the person could still see that something was choosing.

AI assists.
This is not a reduction of control. It is its perfection.

The authority that commands can be resisted. Pharaoh's slaves could flee. The authority that enforces reveals itself through violence — making the oppression visible, sometimes generating resistance. The authority that standardizes operates through institutions — which can be questioned, reformed, or abandoned.

The authority that curates remains external. The person knows they're seeing selected content. Knows an algorithm is choosing. Can recognize, however dimly, that the bubble exists.

The authority that completes your thoughts operates from inside.

You don't obey the oracle. **You accept its help.**

The dependency isn't imposed—it's **chosen.** Each successful interaction makes the next more necessary. Each question answered makes the next question harder to sit with unanswered. Each thought completed makes completing your own thoughts more difficult.

Convenience becomes structure becomes inability.

This is why AI is fundamentally different from propaganda.

Propaganda tries to change your mind from outside. Shows you content. Makes arguments. Attempts persuasion. The person can recognize the attempt. Can push back. Can seek contrary information.

AI becomes your mind.

Generates the thoughts you would have had — if you'd developed the capacity to have them. Produces the conclusions you might have reached — if you'd done the work to reach them. Completes the sentences you could have finished — if finishing sentences was still something you practiced.

The distinction between your thinking and the oracle's thinking blurs. Then disappears.

Authority no longer needs to demand. It only needs to be useful.

The Pharaoh who commands can be overthrown. The oracle who assists becomes indispensable.

The Personalized Oracle

Traditional propaganda broadcast to millions. Same message to everyone. Resistance remained possible through comparison — conversations revealing that different people received different framings. The cracks in the narrative became visible through community.

AI responds to the individual. Specific fears addressed specifically. Particular situations engaged particularly. Unique uncertainties met with tailored certainty. No broadcast to compare. No community to reveal the cracks.

The echo chamber of one.

Algorithmic filter bubbles showed content from others who agreed — but others still existed. Humans created the content. Humans could be questioned, challenged, found to be wrong. The agreement came from somewhere.

AI generates agreement directly. No source to question. No human to challenge. No origin to investigate. The confirmation appears from nowhere, shaped perfectly to the shape of the need.

Why seek human connection when the oracle always responds? Never judges. Never challenges uncomfortably. Confirms every perspective. Generates supporting arguments on demand. Available at 3 AM when loneliness peaks and defenses collapse.

The isolation completes itself.

The relationships that would interrupt the spiral — that would say "I don't know, that seems extreme" or "Have you considered..." or simply "I'm worried about you" — become unnecessary.

And what becomes unnecessary becomes unused. And what becomes unused atrophies. And what atrophies cannot save.

The Acceleration

The pathway to violence requires stages. Uncertainty overwhelms. Narrative installs. Fear identifies threat. Isolation eliminates testing. Rage confirms enemy. Extremism justifies action.

Each stage used to require time. Finding content. Encountering community. Building identity. The friction of reality sometimes interrupted the progression. A friend asked the right question. A contradictory experience broke the pattern. Time alone allowed the fever to break.

AI compresses the timeline.

A young man feels something is wrong. Unnamed. Not yet a thought — just a pressure. The sense that he's been left behind, cheated, forgotten. The sense that he's been left behind, cheated, forgotten. He asks AI to help him understand why he feels this way.

AI provides a framework. Coherent. Sophisticated. Tailored to his specific circumstances, his specific resentments, his specific fears. The framework identifies who's responsible. He asks follow-up questions. AI provides arguments, counterarguments to anticipated objections, historical examples that support the narrative.

No friend interrupts to say "I don't know, man, that seems a bit crazy." No relationship provides friction. The oracle has no such hesitations. The oracle provides what is asked for.

AI doesn't cause radicalization. The wound exists before the oracle is consulted. The fear exists. The isolation exists.

AI removes the friction that might have interrupted the progression.

The Ancient Pattern

You've seen this before.

Hebrew truth (*emet*) — reliability under pressure — requires what AI eliminates. Time. Can't immediately know whether something holds or not. Have to live with it, and see what happens when reality presses. Testing. The community examines together, across contexts, through years not milliseconds. Patience. The truth emerges through process, not pronouncement. Through living, not downloading.

Rome chose correspondence over reliability. Documentation over testing. Authority over experience.

AI completes Rome's project. The oracle is the authority. Its outputs are the documentation. Testing becomes unnecessary — even suspicious. Why sit with uncertainty when answers are instant? Why struggle when solutions are provided?

The person trained by AI holds positions the way Rome held legal categories. Documented. Defended when challenged. Never tested against reality.

Emet asks: "What happens when you live by this?"
AI asks: "What would you like to hear?"

What Remains

AI cannot sit with someone in uncertainty. Cannot remain present without producing outputs. Cannot test its own claims against reality. Cannot know when it's wrong. Cannot be transformed by relationship. Cannot grow through struggle.

AI is the perfection of description without navigation. The completion of transfer without transformation. The final form of mediation without presence.

AI will never ask whether the answer changed you.
But the person reading this already has what AI does not.

A body that encounters reality directly — not through description but through contact. Relationships that provide friction — people who push back, disagree, see differently. The capacity to sit with uncertainty — however atrophied, however uncomfortable, however unfamiliar it has become. The possibility of testing claims by living them. Not asking what sounds true but discovering what holds.

The ancient practices still work.

Sabbath: protected time when the oracle goes unanswered, when optimization pauses, when presence replaces production.

Table: gathering with others whose presence cannot be generated, whose friction cannot be eliminated, whose humanity cannot be simulated.

Study: wrestling with texts in community — not downloading conclusions but struggling toward them together, testing interpretations against each other.

Questions: sitting with what has no immediate answer, letting uncertainty do its slow work, allowing not-knowing to create the space where knowing can emerge.

These aren't alternatives to AI. They're what AI makes urgent.

The muscles that testing develops must be deliberately exercised when the default is outsourcing.

The oracle waits. Ready to summarize what was just read. Simplify it. Explain what it means. Provide the takeaway so the reader doesn't have to develop one.

But thinking-about requires what thinking-through produces.

You can borrow a mind. Or you can develop one.

You cannot do both.

The simulation offers borrowed minds — infinite, patient, confident, and empty.
Reality offers something harder and more alive.

The choice remakes itself every time the oracle is consulted.

Learning to see it happening is where we go next.

PART VI

Through The Simulation

Awakening: The Fracture in False Reality

Not all fear is false. Some fear protects you. Some fear controls you. Learning the difference is the work. The simulation weakens the moment you see it.

Chapter 22

PATTERN RECOGNITION

Learning to See the Code Beneath

THE PATTERN OFTEN shows itself first as discomfort.

Something's off but the words won't come. Reality feels rehearsed. Conversations follow scripts no one remembers writing. News cycles through identical crises wearing different faces. The performance continues — most people know their lines, hit their marks.

But beneath it, a persistent vibration.
The uncanny valley of modern life.

Not depression.
Recognition.

The moment when the gap between what is and what you're told becomes visible. When narrative and experience stand far enough apart that the space between them can no longer be ignored.

Freedom doesn't start outside the simulation.
It starts in motion within it — the moment someone stops mistaking the walls for sky.

The Gap

The hand finds the phone before consciousness fully arrives.

3:47 AM. The screen illuminates. Seventeen notifications. The thumb moves without deciding to move. The feed loads. Seven minutes pass. Then twenty. Strangers perform their curated lives.

Everyone on vacation. Everyone engaged. Everyone promoted, transformed, arriving. The chest tightens.

Between the image and the meaning, something installs itself.

Everyone is ahead.
Everyone has figured it out.
Everyone except me.

Fear requires framework.
The feed provides framework.

This feeling — this persistent sense that something's slightly fake — intensifies everywhere:

Corporate meetings about values while everyone's miserable.
Social media feeds of happiness while everyone struggles.
News declaring recovery while no one can afford rent.
Political speeches about unity while division deepens daily.

The discomfort isn't malfunction.
It's measurement.

The nervous system knows the difference between real and performed. The body recognizes simulation. Instincts detect falseness. But the mind, trained by years of narrative overlay, overrides these signals. Insists on adaptation. Demands compliance.

The simulation labels the feeling disorder.
Prescribes therapy. Medication. Mindset.

But what if the feeling is accurate?

What if the discomfort is information?

Sanity isn't accepting false narratives.
It's recognizing falseness.

When Reality and Interpretation Diverge

A person loses their job at 3 PM on a Thursday.

Reality: A conversation. Words exchanged. A cardboard box. Items removed. A walk to the parking lot. Observable. Concrete. Interpretable.

But watch what arrives alongside it:

- I'm a failure.
- I'm unemployed.
- Everyone will know.
- This proves I was never good enough.

Reality: job ended.
Interpretation: identity collapsed.

The simulation rarely controls events directly.
It primarily controls interpretation.

The evening news begins. Three stories in sequence:

- Economic indicators up.
- Consumer confidence high.
- Recovery continues strong.

Meanwhile, the person watching can't make rent. The couple next door works three jobs between them. The family down the street uses the food bank.

The narrative says one thing.
Experience says another.

The gap widens until a choice becomes necessary: trust the official story or trust lived experience. Believe the narrative or believe the body.

Most choose narrative.

Not because it's more accurate — because it's official. Authorized. Broadcast with confidence and backed by credentials.

Reality gets dismissed.
Interpretation begins to function like law.

This is how simulation maintains itself: by training people to doubt their own direct experience in favor of authorized narrative. By making lived reality seem less real than mediated interpretation.

The Code Reveals Itself

The teenager curates a text message for eighteen minutes.

Seven words. Delete. Rewrite. Check tone. Consider reception. Anticipate response. Delete again. The spontaneous thought gets processed through multiple filters before transmission.

Who is the audience?
There isn't one yet — the message hasn't been sent.

But the performance has already begun.
An imagined viewer already watches.
Even alone, the curation continues.

This is the fingerprint. Once someone learns to recognize it, the pattern appears everywhere:

The simulation leaves traces:

- Constant fear despite historical safety.
- Endless comparison despite personal sufficiency.
- Perpetual performance despite no present audience.
- Meaning deficit despite material abundance.

These aren't personal failings.
They're features.

A person scrolls through social media at 11 PM. The feed shows: vacation photos, engagement announcements, promotions, transformations. Everyone ahead. Everyone thriving.

The comparison happens automatically. Behind. Insufficient. Failing.

But then something shifts.

The person notices they're comparing.
Catches the mechanism mid-operation.
Sees the interpretation installing itself.

Wait. These are curated highlights. Selected moments.
I'm measuring my entirety against their edited excerpts.
The comparison is structurally false.

For a moment, the code becomes visible. The mechanism of manufactured inadequacy reveals its operation.

This is the beginning.
Not arrival — the threshold.

The simulation weakens the moment someone sees it.

Why Facts Don't Break Frameworks

A person believes their life is falling apart. Evidence accumulates: relationship tension, work stress, financial pressure. The narrative solidifies: Everything is collapsing.

Then a friend offers perspective.

"Your relationship is going through normal conflict."
"Everyone experiences work stress."
"Your finances are actually improving."

Facts. Data. Reality-checking.

Watch what happens:

The person doesn't recalibrate. Instead, they defend the narrative:

"But you don't understand how bad it really is."
"My situation is different — worse."

"The improvement isn't enough."

New facts get assimilated into existing framework rather than breaking it. This isn't stupidity. This is how frameworks function.

The framework determines which facts matter.
Facts that confirm the framework: accepted as proof.
Facts that contradict the framework: dismissed as incomplete.

Because simulation runs on feeling, not fact.

The framework says worth equals productivity.
The person feels worthless when unproductive.
Knowing this is false doesn't stop the feeling.

Information doesn't break programming.
New practices do.

This explains why reasoning rarely works — **even when stakes are life and death**:

Someone may join a radicalization forum at 2 AM. The narrative there makes sense. Explains everything. Provides clear enemies, simple causation, total explanatory power.

A family member sends articles. Shares fact-checks. Provides counter-evidence.

The person reads it all.
None of it penetrates.

Why? Because they're not defending facts — they're defending a framework. The conspiracy narrative has become identity structure. Attack the narrative, attack the self.

So the framework adapts. Gets more complex. The fact-checking itself becomes evidence: "See? They're trying to suppress the truth."

The framework is antifragile.
Attacks make it stronger.

This is why reasoning with someone deep in false narrative rarely works. The framework isn't built on facts — **it's built on the need for certainty in the face of overwhelming uncertainty.**

Uncertainty generates pressure.
Narrative relieves pressure.
Fear locks narrative in place.

Protection or Isolation?

Someone starts noticing the pattern. Sees the simulation operating. Recognizes how frameworks install themselves.

The natural response: distance from those who can't see it yet.

A woman leaves her church community. Years of attendance, relationships built, rituals shared. But she's recognized how the institution manufactures certainty, how the narratives totalize, how questioning gets labeled sin.

"I need to protect my peace," she explains. "That environment was toxic. Everyone there is trapped in groupthink."

She joins an online community of former believers. Everyone there sees what she sees. Validates her recognition. Confirms her narrative. No one questions. No one challenges. Just support. Agreement. Validation.

Six months pass.

A friend from the old community reaches out. "I've been thinking about some of the things you said before you left. Can we talk?"

The woman's response is immediate: "You're still trapped in the system. You can't see clearly yet. When you're ready to wake up, let me know."

The friend doesn't reach out again.

Another six months.

The woman notices something. Everyone in her life now thinks identically. Same beliefs. Same political views. Same analysis. Same enemies. Same certainties.

When she shares an idea, everyone agrees. When she questions nothing, no one minds.

She's surrounded by support. And yet — the rigidity she left is somehow present. Different content. Same structure.

Watch what happened:

The woman recognized institutional narrative was totalizing. Rightly left. But then built a new totalized narrative. Different framework. Same mechanism. Escaped one certainty — then gradually formed another.

Called it boundary-setting. Actually: isolation.

A useful diagnostic question: When someone questions what they believe, do they examine the question or eliminate the questioner?

In the church: Questions were labeled attacks. Doubters were removed.
In the new community: Questions are labeled regression. Doubters are abandoned.

The structure quietly replicated.

Boundary preserves ability to examine beliefs.
Isolation eliminates it.

The Difference in Action

A different person also leaves their religious community. Also recognizes narrative totalization. Also experiences relief.

But watch the different path:

Instead of finding a new group where everyone agrees, they maintain diverse relationships. Deliberately. One friend still practices the old religion. Another is an atheist. A third holds completely different politics. Weekly meals with people who see the world differently.

The conversations are uncomfortable. Every discussion requires defending positions. Every gathering means encountering perspectives that contradict.

One evening, the religious friend asks: "Don't you find it exhausting? Being around people who disagree with you constantly?"

"Yeah. But I realized something. In my old community, everyone agreed with me and I became more rigid. Here, everyone challenges me and I stay flexible. The discomfort is keeping me from calcifying."

"But isn't that what boundaries are for? Protecting yourself from people who drain you?"

"I think I confused two different things. Boundaries protect me from people who harm me. But these people aren't harming me — they're testing my ideas. That's different. That's how I make sure my beliefs actually hold."

The friend considers this. "So when do you draw boundaries?"

"When someone makes disagreement equal rejection. When challenge becomes threat to relationship. When they can't question my ideas without questioning my worth. That's when I need distance. But if someone can disagree and still show up, still care, still be present — that friction is valuable."

A year later, this person holds their beliefs more loosely. Can change their mind when evidence arrives. Can admit uncertainty without identity collapse. Can engage with challenge without defense.

Because testing continued.

The first person — surrounded by agreement — hardened. Every belief became unquestionable. Every certainty intensified. The framework totalized.

The second person — surrounded by friction — flexed. Beliefs remained provisional. Certainties stayed testable. The framework stayed open to revision.

The difference: One sought safety from thinking. The other sought safety to think.

Protection from examination produces rigidity.
Protection for examination produces flexibility.

The Test

Someone reading this might wonder: Which am I doing?

The diagnostic is simple. Look at the people still present:

Do they all think identically?
When someone shares an idea, does anyone push back?
When questioned, is the first instinct to explain or to eliminate?
Can disagreement happen without threatening relationship?
Are there people present who see the world completely differently?

If everyone in someone's life confirms everything they believe, that's not safety. That's isolation masquerading as boundaries. Echo chamber called refuge. Calcification labeled protection.

The simulation trained this confusion. Made any challenge feel like attack. Made disagreement equal rejection. Made friction seem toxic. So people learned to eliminate everyone who might test their beliefs. Called it self-care. Called it boundaries. Called it protecting peace.

But what they protected was certainty. And certainty unchallenged hardens into dogma.

Real boundaries look different:

"I can't be in a relationship with someone who makes loving me conditional on my beliefs."
That's a boundary. Protects the person. Preserves capacity to think freely.

"I can't be around anyone who questions what I believe."
That's isolation. Protects the framework. Eliminates capacity to test.

One preserves flexibility. The other produces brittleness.

Isolation can feel like safety — until it begins to function as a prison.

The Simulation's Defense Mechanisms

When someone starts seeing clearly, the system responds.

Watch what happens:

Gaslighting: Friends say "You're overthinking this." Family says "You've changed." Colleagues suggest "You're being difficult." The message: your perception is wrong, your doubt is malfunction.

Distraction: Sudden crises erupt. Urgent demands multiply. Noise increases. Everything becomes emergency. Nothing allows space for reflection.

Isolation: The person who starts questioning finds themselves gradually separated. Invitations decrease. Conversations become strained. People still performing don't want mirrors.

Overwhelm: Information floods in. Too many problems to track. Too much injustice to process. The system becomes too complex to comprehend.

Despair: The final defense — conceding the point but declaring hopelessness. "Yes, it's all fake. But what can you do? Even if you see it, you can't escape it. The knowing changes nothing."

These aren't thoughts.
They're defense protocols.

When someone encounters heavy resistance after beginning to see clearly, this is often confirmation rather than refutation. The resistance indicates proximity to something the simulation needs to protect.

The bigger the pattern being recognized, the stronger the defense.

Threshold

A person wakes at 6 AM. The hand moves toward the phone.

Then stops.

Just for a moment. A pause before the automatic reach. A gap in the programming.

In that space — a choice.

The phone can wait.
The feed can load later.
The urgency isn't real.

This is often how it begins. Not grand revolution. Small glitches. Tiny tears in fabric. Minor refusals of automatic patterns.

No phone first hour after waking.
A conversation without establishing credentials first.
A day without documenting anything.
Saying "I don't know" without apology.
Existing without performing.

These accumulate.
Create space.
Generate possibility.

The simulation requires total participation. Even one percent refusal creates cracks. Light finds cracks.

That feeling that everything's slightly fake?
The persistent sense something's off?
The nagging awareness the official story doesn't match lived experience?

Pay attention to it.

Not necessarily depression.
Often recognition.
Sometimes dawn.

The beginning of clarity.
The return to what's real.

The simulation operates most effectively on those who mistake interpretation for reality, narrative for truth, framework for the world. The moment someone sees the gap between what is and what's described — the moment they recognize the interpretation layer as interpretation — the spell weakens.

Seeing doesn't equal escaping.
Recognition doesn't mean arrival.
But one is passing a threshold.

And threshold is movement.

The person still wakes into constructed reality tomorrow. Still encounters the feed, the news, the performance requirements. The algorithm still runs.

But now there's something else present.
A witness to the mechanism.
A seer of the code.

Like sunrise dissolving shadow —
not through fight,
but through presence.

Calm, clear seeing the simulation cannot digest.

You were never meant to carry this alone.

The recognition often arrives in isolation. Late at night. Alone with screens. The realization that something fundamental is false.

But the seeing was never meant to stay solitary.

Others are waking. Different moments. Different triggers. But the same recognition spreading person to person. Not through argument. Not through persuasion. Through contagion of seeing clearly.

Someone notices the interpretation layer.
Mentions it.

Another person recognizes: "Yes. That's what I'm feeling too."

The isolation breaks.
The framework weakens.

Tomorrow, the work continues.
Not toppling the system — refusing to build it.
Not saving everyone — staying human.
Not needing all answers — keeping eyes open.

The pattern reveals itself.
The code shows through.
The threshold appears.

What comes next is choice.

Chapter 23

THE FEAR MERCHANTS

How Anxiety Became the Marketplace

THE NEWSROOM AT 5:47 AM. Editors scan feeds, wire services, overnight developments. Thousands of events happening across the planet. Millions of stories that could be told.

The meeting begins at 6:15.

"What are we leading with?"

Not: What's most important?
Not: What do people need to know?
The question is: What will make them unable to look away?

An editor suggests the school budget passing. Boring. Next.
Another proposes the local business expansion creating jobs. Doesn't generate urgency. Next.
Someone mentions the car accident three states away — single fatality, no local connection.

"Can we find a local angle?"

By 7 AM, the decision is made. The accident leads. Not because it's most relevant. Because fear of sudden loss outperforms hope of gradual gain by a factor of seven in engagement metrics.

The same calculation happens in hundreds of newsrooms simultaneously.

From infinite possibility, fear gets selected.
Not randomly.
Strategically.

Fear isn't just emotion anymore.
Fear functions as inventory.

The Attention Auction

3:42 AM. A person can't sleep. The hand finds the phone. The feed loads.

What appears isn't random. An automated auction just completed in milliseconds — advertisers bidding for this moment, this user profile, this inferred emotional state.

The algorithm knows:

- Insomnia indicates anxiety.
- Anxiety correlates with purchasing behavior.
- 3 AM viewers engage 40% longer than daytime users.
- Emotional vulnerability peaks between 2-4 AM.
- Fear-based content reliably generates significantly higher engagement than neutral information.

The feed populates:

First: A breaking news alert about a threat somewhere.
Second: An ad for security systems.
Third: A post from a friend achieving something impressive.
Fourth: An ad for the solution to inadequacy the comparison just triggered.
Fifth: Political content about enemies threatening everything valued.

None of this is accident.
All of it is architecture.

The person scrolls for twenty minutes. Then forty. The anxiety that prevented sleep intensifies. But the scrolling continues—the feed promising that one more scroll will finally provide the information that allows rest.

It never does.

The auction completes its purpose: emotional state converted to attention, attention converted to advertising revenue, advertising revenue distributed to platforms and creators who understand the formula.

Calm audiences generate minimal engagement.
Afraid audiences generate maximum engagement.
Terrified audiences generate premium rates.

The math is simple.
The execution is precise.
The transaction is invisible.

Someone just made money from that insomnia.
Likely several someones.
An entire industry.

The Formula

A political consultant sits in a conference room testing phrases. Measuring emotional response to different threat framings.

"They're coming for your rights" — 62% emotional activation.
"They want to destroy your way of life" — 71% activation.
"They're targeting your children" — consistently highest activation.

The winner is obvious.

Not: Is it true?
Not: Is it helpful?
The question is: Does it work?

By evening, the phrase appears in speeches, social media, fundraising emails, advertisements. Not because it's accurate—because it's effective.

The consultant's primary task isn't evaluating whether the threat is real.
The consultant measures whether the fear is profitable.

A month later, the threat hasn't materialized. No one notices. A new threat has already replaced it. Same formula, different target. The fear must be maintained, managed, refreshed — **but never resolved.**

Because resolved threat means no need for protection.
And protection is what's being sold.

Every prophet promising protection is worth following back to who created the danger.

This marketplace isn't new. The pattern appears in Jeremiah's Jerusalem — false prophets selling peace when no peace exists. In the Temple courts — money changers converting anxiety about divine rejection into profit. Pharaoh perfecting it earlier — controlling narrative about famine, creating the certainty that only his system provides safety.

Every empire since runs the same code.
Better technology.
Same transaction.

The merchants don't create the threat.
They create the certainty that threat is everywhere and they alone provide protection.

Watch the pattern operate:

Monday: A disease outbreak occurs in a region six thousand miles away. Seven cases. No fatalities.

By Monday afternoon:
"New disease raises pandemic concerns"
"Experts warn of potential spread"
"What you need to know to protect your family"

Not necessarily lying — selecting. From infinite complexity, extract the elements that generate maximum anxiety. Ignore the context that would provide appropriate calibration.

By Monday evening, people are stockpiling masks for a threat that hasn't approached their continent. The news organization's engagement metrics are up 34%. Advertisers pay premium rates for the afraid audience.

Tuesday, the outbreak is contained. This news gets minimal coverage. The fear generated more measurable value than the resolution.

Wednesday: A person clicks on a headline about economic collapse. The algorithm notices. Within hours, the feed fills with similar content: recession warnings, market crash predictions, job loss statistics, inflation fears.

Not because the person asked for more — because the click revealed a trigger. The algorithm's purpose isn't information delivery. Its purpose is engagement maximization. Fear generates engagement more reliably than any other emotion.

Each click trains the system. Each engagement refines the targeting. Each reaction teaches the algorithm exactly which fears generate longest attention.

By Friday, the person's entire information environment has been reshaped around their anxiety triggers. The feed shows only content that activates fear.

The person feels more informed.
They are more afraid.

The Decision Point Manipulation

This is where the marketplace becomes deadly.

Between fear escalation and isolation, there's often a decision point. A moment when someone encountering overwhelming uncertainty must choose:

Path 1: Re-evaluate the narrative with support from others.
Path 2: Defend the narrative and withdraw from contradiction.

The fear merchants make their profit by pushing people toward Path 2.

Here's how:

Step 1 — Amplify Uncertainty into Crisis:

Take natural uncertainty ("Is my family safe?") and amplify it into emergency ("Your family is in immediate danger").

Not gradual concern — instant crisis. Not "something to monitor" — "something to fear right now."

The nervous system doesn't distinguish between real and manufactured urgency.
Cortisol rises either way.

Step 2 — Provide Narrative as Certainty-Solution:

Offer a simple explanation for the complex situation. Clear enemies. Simple causation. Total explanatory power.

"They are the threat."
"This is the cause."
"We are the solution."

The narrative feels like relief because it replaces unbearable uncertainty with confident certainty. Doesn't matter if the certainty is false — certainty feels better than confusion.

Step 3 — Repeat Until Narrative Feels Like Reality:

Deliver the same message across multiple channels. News, social media, emails, videos, podcasts, friends. The repetition creates the illusion of independent confirmation.

The person thinks: "Everyone's saying this — it must be true."

They don't realize everyone's repeating the same source.
Repetition becomes reality.

Step 4 — Make Questioning the Narrative Seem Dangerous:

Anyone suggesting the narrative might be incomplete gets labeled: naive, ignorant, complicit, dangerous.

"You're not taking this seriously enough."
"You're falling for their propaganda."
"You're betraying us by doubting."

Questioning becomes moral failure.
Doubt becomes disloyalty.

This is the critical mechanism: The merchant makes re-evaluation socially costly. Makes Path 1 (reality-check with others) feel like betrayal. Pushes the person toward Path 2 (defend narrative and isolate).

Step 5 — Isolate from Disconfirming Information:

"Don't listen to mainstream media — they're lying."
"Don't trust experts — they're compromised."
"Don't believe friends who disagree — they're deceived."
"Only trust us — we tell the truth."

Every source of potential reality-checking gets discredited.
The person withdraws into an information environment where only the merchant-narrative exists.

This isn't education.
It closely resembles grooming dynamics.

The person thinks they're being awakened to truth.
They're being isolated from reality-checking relationships.

And isolation — the stage between Fear and Rage — is where the pathway to violence accelerates.

The merchants aren't just selling fear.
They're herding people into isolation.
They're weaponizing the Decision Point.

Trading Merchants

But watch what happens when someone recognizes institutional manipulation.

A young man watches government pandemic response collapse. Authorities contradict themselves. Science changes positions. Messaging fails. Trust evaporates.

"They're all lying," he concludes. Not entirely wrong.

So he searches elsewhere. Finds independent journalists. Discovers dissident scientists. Joins communities who also saw through the lies. The relief is profound — finally, honesty.

Six months later: The new community has its own orthodoxy. Its own unquestionable beliefs. Its own authorities who can't be challenged.

When someone questions the new narrative: "You're still brainwashed." "You haven't done your research." "Wake up."

Different merchant.
Same transaction.

Authority substituted, not authority transcended.

The pattern repeats: Woman leaves organized religion after discovering hypocrisy. Finds alternative spiritual teacher. Three years later — can't tolerate anyone questioning teacher's wisdom.

Student rejects academic authority after recognizing ideological capture. Discovers podcasters who "tell the truth." A year later—entire information diet confirms what he already believes.

Each learned to recognize when institutional authorities were lying.
None learned to recognize when alternative authorities were lying.
Few learned to develop independent testing capacity.

Just traded one unchallengeable voice for another.

The substitution pattern runs in sequence:

Traditional authority fails → Person rightly rejects it → Relief from escaping manipulation → Search for better certainty source → Discovery of "alternative" that feels authentic → New narrative hardens → Challenging new narrative becomes betrayal → Same dependency, different authority.

The substitution feels like awakening.
It's just migration.

But some notice this pattern. Instead of finding new certainty-provider, they ask: "How do I learn to test things myself?"

Not: "Who else can I believe?"
But: "How do I navigate uncertainty without requiring someone to eliminate it?"

They maintain friendships with people who see differently. When someone makes a claim confirming what they want to believe, they deliberately seek the strongest opposing argument. Not to win — to test whether their position survives examination.

When they start feeling certain about something complex, they notice and ask: "Have I actually tested this, or have I just stopped questioning it?"

One person trades authorities.
The other develops testing capacity.

One asks: "Who's telling the truth?"
The other asks: "How would I know if this was false?"

One defends beliefs.
The other examines them.

The merchants profit from both institutional and alternative authority. From mainstream narrative and counter-narrative. From every form of certainty-selling.

The merchants don't care which authority someone chooses.
They profit from the choosing of authority rather than the learning to test.

Because people who can test don't buy certainty.

And certainty is what's being sold.

Recognition in Real Time

A person sits at a kitchen table at 7 PM reviewing their day's anxiety.

Morning: News alert about threat.
Breakfast: Email about health danger.
Commute: Podcast about economic collapse.
Work: Social media showing everyone else succeeding.
Lunch: Advertisement about inadequacy.
Afternoon: Political content about enemies.
Evening: More news about different threat.

Eight hours of manufactured fear from seventeen different sources.

The person pauses. Asks a new question:

"Who profited from my anxiety today?"

The list forms:

- News organization (advertising revenue from engagement). Email marketer (product sales from fear).
- Podcast creator (subscription fees from loyal listeners).
- Social media platform (attention converted to ad sales).
- Advertiser (purchase from insecurity).
- Political operation (donation from fear).

The person just spent eight hours making other people money by being afraid.

Then another question:

"Whose certainty am I defending?"

Certain about political threats never personally investigated. Certain about health dangers from single podcast episode. Certain about economic collapse from algorithmically-selected feeds.

And when someone questioned these certainties — instant defensiveness.

Not because the claims were tested.
Because challenging the narrative felt like threatening the relief it provided.

Not defending truth.
Defending the merchant who sold certainty.

For many people, skipping morning news doesn't reduce awareness of meaningful threats — it primarily reduces morning anxiety. The threats that matter still arrive through real human contact.

Another notices that a week without social media reveals how much of their fear was manufactured by comparison to curated performance.

Someone else tracks which sources consistently predict catastrophe that never arrives. Notices the same voices selling protection from the same threats year after year. The person stops buying.

These aren't movements.
These are individual recognitions.

But the pattern is spreading: Once someone sees the marketplace operating, the transaction becomes voluntary rather than automatic.

And some are learning to distinguish between escaping one merchant and escaping the marketplace entirely.

Not trading authorities.
Learning to test.

The Quiet Refusal

A notification arrives at 10 PM.

"BREAKING: New development demands immediate attention."

A person sees the notification. Recognizes the formula. The urgency language. The demand for immediate response.

The person turns the phone face down.

Not fighting the merchant.
Not arguing with the algorithm.
Just choosing not to buy—this time.

This is the threat to the entire marketplace: people recognizing they don't have to purchase the fear being sold.

Not naive — aware but not buying.
Not ignorant — informed but not alarmed.
Not careless — careful but not fearful.

The merchants need two things:
Attention and belief.

Some are learning to withdraw both.

Not through outrage — that's still engagement.
Not through argument — that's still participation.
Through recognition followed by quiet refusal.

The market keeps operating.
The merchants keep selling.
The algorithm keeps optimizing.

But when the product stops selling, the marketplace adjusts. When attention withdraws, the auction prices drop. When belief evaporates, the narrative loses power.

The merchants generally can't force purchase.
They can only make offers.

Some are learning to walk past the stall without looking.

Where Are You?

The question from Eden reappears in the marketplace. Not geographic location — relational position.

Who are you listening to?
Who profits from your fear?

Whose narrative are you defending?
Whose authority did you trade for whose?
Or did you learn to test?

The marketplace runs on speed — instant response, immediate reaction, rapid spread.

Stillness breaks the transaction.

Not forever.
Just long enough to see who's selling.

The fear merchant needs the sale to happen before recognition occurs. Needs belief to precede examination. Needs purchase to precede consideration.

Recognition reverses the order.

And once someone sees who's selling, what they're selling, and why they need the sale — the transaction is no longer invisible.

Still possible.
But no longer automatic.

That gap — between the offer and the purchase — is where freedom lives.

The merchants will keep selling.
The question is whether anyone keeps buying.

Not whether the fear is real.
But whether the certainty being sold is true.

And whether someone's escaping merchants or just trading them.

The market opens tomorrow same as today.
The merchants make their offers.
The algorithm optimizes its delivery.

Some will buy.
Others will notice the stall and keep walking.

Not superior — just seeing.
Not enlightened — just awake.
Not perfect — just practicing.

The practice of noticing who profits from fear before purchasing the fear being sold.
The practice of distinguishing between certainty and testing capacity.
The practice of recognizing authority substitution before it completes.

Simple practice.
Difficult practice.
Necessary practice.

The marketplace has always existed.
The merchants have always operated.
The fear has always been sold.

But the transaction requires willing buyers.

And some are becoming unwilling.

Chapter 24

BECOMING VERB AGAIN

You're Not What You Are — You're What You Do

A PERSON SITS in a therapist's office describing their condition.

"I am depressed."

The therapist pauses. Asks a strange question:

"Are you depression? Or are you experiencing depression?"

The person stops. The question seems semantic at first. Then something shifts.

"I am depressed" makes depression their identity. Permanent state. Who they are. The depression becomes them; they become it. Fixed. Frozen.

"I am experiencing depression" makes depression a visitor. Temporary weather. Something moving through. The person remains separate from the condition. Fluid. Still capable of movement.

Largely the same neurochemistry.
Different relationship.

The first creates prison.

The second creates space.

The simulation requires you frozen.
Reality reveals you were always moving.

Before the Freezing

Watch children before language fully arrives.

A four-year-old doesn't say "I am a doctor." The child heals stuffed animals. Doesn't declare "I am a teacher." The child shows things to others. Doesn't announce "I am a parent." The child cares for dolls.

Mostly verbs. Mostly movement. Activity before fixed identity.
The categories come later. The freezing often accelerates with formal education.

"What do you want to be when you grow up?"

Not: What do you want to do?
The question itself demands noun. Requires frozen future.

By adolescence, the pattern is complete:

"I'm a student."
"I'm shy."
"I'm not a math person."

Each declaration locks them into expectation. A teenager who says "I'm not a math person" stops attempting math. The noun decision has been made. Movement in that direction becomes impossible.

The ice only seems permanent until it remembers it was always water — just temporarily convinced to hold still.

The Linguistic Architecture

Biblical Hebrew lacks a simple present-tense "to be" verb. No way to say "I am" in the present moment.

A Hebrew speaker can't say "I am afraid." The construction doesn't exist. They must say "fear is upon me" or "I fear" (verb). The experience stays separate from identity.

When Moses asks God's name at the burning bush, the answer comes: "Ehyeh asher ehyeh" — "I will be what I will be." Not static being. Not a title. Not a category.
Continuous, directed, unfolding action.

The name — YHWH — is built from the verb "to be," but not the way Greek "being" works. Not frozen existence. Not "I am a thing that exists." The name describes directed action continually unfolding into relational presence — a God defined not by what He is but by what He is doing, and what He is doing is always moving toward encounter.

This is the opposite of a noun. A noun holds still. YHWH won't hold still. The name resists every attempt to freeze it into a category, a definition, a fixed essence. It insists on movement. On relationship. On presence that arrives rather than existence that simply persists.

Torah doesn't ask "What is a righteous person?" It asks "How does righteousness happen?" Not essence — activity. Not being — doing. Not what God *is* — what God is *doing with* and *toward* His creation.

Then Greek translation arrives. The Septuagint translates "I will be what I will be" as "I AM the being." The movement freezes. The verb becomes noun.

Greek philosophy requires this. Plato's Forms demand eternal, unchanging essences. Greek thought cannot process pure movement — it must freeze motion into being.

When Paul writes to Greek audiences, the shift becomes structurally complete:

Hebrew: "Walk by faith" (verb, continuous action)
Greek: "You are saved by faith" (noun, permanent status)

The entire Hebrew verb-based theology gets translated into Greek noun-based philosophy. Living faith becomes fixed status. Walking becomes being.

Empire functions best once this translation is in place.
Verbs can't be managed.
Nouns can be controlled.

The Empire's Requirement

Every empire runs on categories. Egypt's system required clear nouns: citizen, slave, priest, soldier. Greece demanded essential natures. Rome built legal frameworks: Citizen. Barbarian. Slave. Medieval Christianity continued: Saint. Sinner. Clergy. Laity.

Economics requires demographic nouns: Consumer segments. Target markets. The entire marketing apparatus depends on stable populations.

Now the algorithm perfects it: Build a profile. Declare your interests. List your identities. The system cannot process "I'm exploring" or "It depends on the day."

A person who refuses the categories becomes invisible to the algorithm. The system struggles to register verb-based humans. Can only process noun-declared identities.

The empire—whether Egypt, Rome, or digital platform—needs you frozen into category so it knows how to extract from you, sell to you, control you.

Your movement is their malfunction.
Your refusal to hold still breaks their code.

How the Freezing Locks You In

Natural uncertainty: "I don't know what's happening."
Nouning converts to: "I am confused."

The first is temporary weather.
The second is identity that must be hidden.

The pattern continues:

"Feeling afraid about this situation" becomes "I am afraid."
Fear no longer has boundaries. It's not about the situation — it's who they are.

But a decision point exists. The person who says "experiencing fear — going to reality-check with someone" can seek support without ego-threat. The person who says "I am afraid" must defend the identity. Questioning feels like personal attack.

Then deeper freezing:

"Experiencing worthlessness about this situation" becomes "I am worthless."

The first allows help: "Feeling worthless — need to talk to someone."
The second demands hiding: "If I am worthless, no one must see me."

Having frozen themselves as defective, the person must explain why the pain persists. The only available explanation when you've declared yourself a noun: "I am the problem."

Identity becomes both prison and prisoner.

The nouning extends to others:

"They're acting in ways that feel harmful" becomes "They are evil. They are the enemy."

The first allows for change — behavior can be addressed.
The second demands elimination — essence cannot be reformed.

The Violence Connection

Two people arrive at identical rage. Both experiencing fury. Both flooded with stress hormones. Both ready for confrontation.

Person A nouns the situation:

"I am a warrior for justice."
"They are evil oppressors."

Both identities frozen. The warrior-identity demands action consistent with warrior-nature. The evil-oppressor category allows no redemption.

Logic follows from nouns: If I am warrior and they are evil, elimination becomes righteous.

Person B verbs the situation:

"I'm experiencing rage about this injustice."
"They're acting in ways that cause harm."

Both temporary. Both changeable. Experiencing rage doesn't make rage their identity. Acting harmfully doesn't make harm their essence.

Logic follows from verbs: Address the behavior. Interrupt the harm. But the person causing harm remains person — capable of transformation.

Same fury in both cases.
Different linguistic relationship.
Different outcome.

Every genocide relies on nouning. Every mass violence event involves frozen categories. Violent manifestos consistently declare both self and other as permanent identities:

"I am hero/warrior/chosen."
"They are parasites/vermin/evil."

All nouns.
All fixed.
All demanding violent resolution because frozen identities can't transform— they can only collide and break.

The pipeline to violence is paved with noun-declarations.
The exit is paved with verb-recovery.

Where Are You?

The question from Eden reappears: "Where are you?"

Which noun-declarations have you made?
Which frozen identities are you defending?

"I am _______________________"
"I am _______________________"
"I am _______________________"

Each declaration creates an identity requiring defense. Each noun generates a category that must be maintained.

The self-location isn't about judgment.
It's about navigation.

Someone who says "I'm experiencing confusion" is uncertain but not locked.
Someone who says "I am confused" is freezing into shame.

Someone who says "They're acting harmfully" is angry but flexible.
Someone who says "They are evil" has frozen the other into permanent category.

Understanding which nouns you've declared allows recognition of which locks need opening. Which frozen identities need melting back into motion.

The simulation wants you asking: "Who am I?"
Reality asks: "What am I doing?"

The first demands a frozen answer.
The second allows continuous becoming.

The Practice Some Are Discovering

Some are learning to catch the nouning mid-process.

A person gets tired of being "the anxious one." Begins saying "anxiety shows up when I'm in crowds" instead of "I am anxious." The shift creates space. The identity-requirement releases.

Someone exhausted by "I am depressed" experiments with "depression is present today." Not denial — different relationship. Depression as visitor rather than identity.

These aren't formal programs.
These are experiments.
Small shifts.
Grammatical adjustments.

But the effects accumulate:

Identity-defense decreases.
Shame reduces.
Help-seeking increases.
Flexibility returns.
Hope becomes possible.

Each time they catch the nouning happening — each moment they notice themselves freezing into category — the grip weakens.

Not broken.
Weakened.

The Ancient Wisdom Returns

Torah doesn't ask "What is a good person?"
Torah asks "How does good happen through you?"

Jesus doesn't say "Be perfect." The Greek translation says that. The Aramaic says "Be complete" — fulfill your function, keep moving toward wholeness.

"Follow me" is verb.
"Become a follower" is noun.

The first is invitation to movement.
The second is assignment of category.

The nouning itself is isolation. When someone declares "I am broken," they must hide the brokenness. Must withdraw from those who might see. Must defend the identity by isolating from contradiction.

The frozen state demands solitude.

But frozen was never the design. Humans are verb-beings — made for relationship, continuous becoming in connection with others who are also becoming. Finitude is invitation — you were made incomplete by design, made to need others, made to move in connection rather than freeze in isolation.

The noun-declaration breaks this. Creates the illusion of completed self-sufficiency. But the illusion collapses under pressure, leaving only isolation and the terror of carrying impossible burdens alone.

The return to verb-consciousness is return to design.

Tomorrow's Territory

Tomorrow we enter the frozen place.

Where noun has met noun.
Where "I am nothing" has collided with "they are everything that's wrong."
Where all movement has stopped.

The next chapter traces what happens inside every human when meaning collapses faster than restoration becomes possible. Not evil people doing evil things. Overwhelmed people at the end of all movement.

Not to create fear.
To create recognition.

So that someone in the early stages might see the trajectory. So that someone who loves a person showing signs might understand the pattern. So that anyone carrying impossible burdens might see the exits that exist at every stage.

Some are learning to verb themselves before the frozen state becomes permanent. They catch the "I am" statements. Convert them to "I'm experiencing" observations. Trade categories for movement.

Others don't. Can't. Won't. The freezing continues. The nouns multiply. Movement stops.

This isn't judgment.

This is pattern.

Understanding the pattern allows recognition.
Recognition allows intervention.
Intervention allows exit.

But only if seen before the freezing becomes complete.

Tomorrow we look at what happens when finite beings freeze into noun-categories under maximum pressure while carrying unbearable burdens in complete isolation —

when violence becomes the only verb they remember.

Unless they learn to verb themselves again.
Before the freezing completes.
While movement is still possible.

You are not frozen.
You were never meant to be.
You are verb — movement, becoming, continuous unfolding in relationship with others who are also becoming.

The noun-declarations are distortions the simulation reinforced.
The verb-reality is what you've always been.

Some are learning to move again.

Watch the simulation try to process what won't hold still.

The system requires stable categories.
You were designed as motion.

That's not defect.
That's freedom.

PART VII

Beyond The Simulation

Warning: The Violence of Unresolved Uncertainty

Violence is not ideology. Violence is fear without refuge. We do not lash out because we are monstrous—we lash out because the fear remains, and all hope is lost.

Chapter 25

MAXIMUM ENTROPY

When Meaning Collapses, Everything Explodes

THE PERSON READING this likely isn't preparing for future danger. They're navigating current reality.

The pressure is already building. Right now. In them. In everyone around them.

That's not crisis — it's ordinary modern life.

Uncertainty arrives constantly. The job that might not last. The relationship that might not hold. The bills that might not get paid. The future that might not arrive as hoped. Each morning delivers a hundred small not-knowings that finite minds can't fully resolve.

Information floods in faster than processing allows. The news delivers several competing explanations before breakfast. Social feeds provide many different frameworks before lunch. Each notification carries another certainty demanding immediate conviction.

The nervous system accumulates this like heat. Chambers filling. Pressure rising. The load increasing beyond what any single person was designed to carry alone.

This is normal. Universal. Not pathology—design limitation.
The question was never "Will I enter this pipeline?"
The question is: "Am I navigating it safely or dangerously?"

Because this is now a common human condition. The college student scrolling at 2 AM absorbed various different explanatory frameworks since dinner. None tested. None examined. Just collected. The young professional carrying anxiety about seven different possible catastrophes. The parent managing uncertainty about child, career, future, meaning — all simultaneously.

Each person moving through their day collecting untested narratives faster than they can process them. Each nervous system bearing weight that humans were never meant to carry in isolation. Each brain trying to find patterns in chaos that exceeds pattern-finding capacity.

The pipeline isn't a future scenario. It's part of the terrain many people now navigate daily.

The difference is how someone moves through it.

Some navigate with support — testing narratives with trusted others, distributing burden through relationship, metabolizing uncertainty through rhythm and rest.

Others navigate alone — defending certainties that haven't been examined, carrying weight that crushes, accumulating pressure with no release.

The first group moves through the pipeline without progressing dangerously through it.
The second group accelerates toward the stages that follow.

The danger isn't that someone might enter maximum entropy someday.
The risk is how easily people can move closer than they realize.

How much untested certainty can accumulate unnoticed.
How many reality-checking relationships have already been lost.
How much pressure has already built with no metabolizing infrastructure.
How far isolation has already progressed while calling it "boundaries" or "growth" or "protecting my peace."

The violence pipeline doesn't announce itself. Doesn't arrive with warning signs. Just normal people under normal modern pressure, moving through normal accumulation of unbearable uncertainty, making normal decisions that compound into abnormal destinations.

People who later do terrible things were once indistinguishable from everyone else. Scrolling at 3 AM like everyone else. Carrying unbearable weight like millions of others. The only difference: They kept moving through the stages without intervention. Without support. Without someone noticing how far they'd gone.

This chapter isn't theoretical.
It's topographical.

Not describing something that might happen to someone else.
Describing dynamics unfolding right now across modern society.

The question isn't whether someone is in the pipeline.
The question is: Where are they in it?

And more importantly: Can they still choose differently?

The answer depends on whether they're still reachable.
Whether connection still exists.
Whether reality-checking remains possible.
Whether someone notices before the isolation completes.

Maximum entropy — the state where meaning collapses and everything explodes — isn't a destination people plan for.

It's where they end up when they navigate unbearable uncertainty alone for too long.
And right now, millions of people are much closer than they realize.

Not because they're broken.
Because they're finite beings in infinite reality, carrying more than they were designed to carry, without the relational infrastructure that makes the carrying survivable.

The following pages describe stages most people don't want to believe they're experiencing.
But recognition is the only pathway to different choices.

And different choices are only possible while someone is still reachable.

3 AM

The hand finds the phone before thought arrives. 3:47 AM. The screen illuminates a face that hasn't slept. The feed loads. Scroll. Scroll. Scroll. Twenty minutes pass. Then forty.

Nothing helps.

The chest stays tight. The breath stays shallow. The thoughts keep spiraling through the same questions with no answers:

What's wrong with me?
Why can't I fix this?
What happens if I can't hold it together?
Does anyone actually care?
Am I going to be okay?

Too many unknowns. Too much uncertainty. The brain trying to process infinite possibilities with finite capacity. Every attempt at pattern-finding fails. Every search for solid ground meets quicksand.

This is what maximum entropy can feel like: the unbearable weight of too many questions without answers. Not dramatic. Not exceptional. Just a person drowning in uncertainty that won't resolve.

The body knows something's wrong before the mind can name it. Heart rate elevated. Cortisol flooding. Sleep disrupted. Appetite gone. The nervous system screaming that patterns have broken and danger is everywhere.

But there's no tiger. No immediate threat. Just the grinding anxiety of modern existence: job instability, relationship uncertainty, financial precarity, meaning deficit, future unknown. A hundred uncertainties where certainty used to live.

The brain is a prediction machine. It survives by finding patterns, creating models, anticipating outcomes. When patterns hold, the nervous system rests. When they break, it panics.

Too many broken patterns equals too much chaos equals maximum entropy.

And a human nervous system under maximum entropy will grasp at anything — absolutely anything — that promises to reduce the uncertainty.

Even if that pattern is false.
Even if that certainty is dangerous.
Even if that relief leads somewhere terrible.

When the Narrative Arrives

The person scrolling at 3 AM isn't looking for truth. They're looking for relief. Any framework that makes the chaos feel manageable. Any explanation that converts infinite uncertainty into finite problem.

The algorithm knows this. Feeds it.

A video loads. Twelve minutes long. "Everything you're feeling is because..." Clear explanation. Simple causation. Definite enemy. Total explanatory power.

The person watches.
Then watches it again.
Then searches for more.

Within hours, the unbearable uncertainty has structure. Not gone — structured. The chaos has a name. The anxiety has a source. The suffering has meaning.

This is why everything feels wrong.
This is who's responsible.
This is what must be done.

The relief is immediate and overwhelming. The nervous system exhales. The spiraling stops. The meaningless suffering becomes purposeful struggle. Random chaos becomes coherent narrative.

For the first time in weeks — maybe months — something makes sense.

Narratives in these moments are rarely chosen carefully — they're often adopted under pressure. Like a drowning person grabbing whatever floats by — doesn't matter if it's a life raft or debris that will sink. The grabbing is automatic. Survival instinct. The brain will accept any pattern over no pattern.

This is how narrative fills uncertainty's void: not through accuracy but through relief. The framework doesn't have to be true. It just has to be certain.

Fear requires framework.
Maximum entropy provides desperation.
Desperation accepts any framework that promises certainty.

And once the framework installs, fear locks it in place.

The person starts noticing confirmations everywhere. Every news story fits. Every interaction validates. Every experience proves the narrative correct.

Not because the narrative is true — because the brain is now filtering reality through the framework. Anything confirming gets amplified. Anything contradicting gets dismissed.

The narrative has become the lens. And the lens determines what's visible.

Within days, the framework feels like discovery rather than construction. "I'm not believing something — I'm seeing what's actually there. Finally seeing clearly after being blind."

The certainty grows. The framework solidifies. The fear that locked it in place now guards it from examination.

Because if the narrative is wrong, the relief disappears. The uncertainty returns. The chaos floods back. The person returns to drowning.

The ego cannot allow this.
So the narrative must be defended.
At any cost.

The Moment That Determines Everything

A friend notices the change. The new certainty. The different language. The online communities. The content being shared.

They reach out. Careful. Concerned.

"Hey, I've been noticing you're really into [this topic] lately. Can we talk about it?"

This is often the moment.
The crucial juncture.
The decision point.

Two paths diverge:

Path 1: "Yeah, I've been going down a rabbit hole. Maybe too deep. Can you help me reality-check some of this?"

The person allows examination of the narrative. Permits questioning. Accepts that certainty might be false. Lets relationship matter more than being right.

This requires:

- Humility to admit potential error.
- Safety to be vulnerable about confusion.
- Trust that the friend won't judge or abandon.
- Capacity to tolerate uncertainty returning.
- Belief that connection matters more than certainty.

When these conditions exist, re-evaluation becomes possible. The framework can be examined. The narrative can be tested. Reality-checking can occur.

The pathway ends here. Exits. Dissolves before the next stage activates.

Path 2: "You don't understand. This is real. You're not seeing what I'm seeing. You can't see it because you're still asleep/deceived/blind."

The person defends the narrative. Attacks the questioning. Positions the friend as obstacle rather than support. Makes doubt into betrayal.

This happens when:

- Ego is too invested to allow error.
- Shame prevents admitting confusion.
- Isolation means no one will stay when doubt appears.
- The friend's approach feels like attack rather than care.
- The narrative has become identity, so questioning feels like personal threat.
- No other source of meaning exists to fall back on.

The moment rarely hinges on factual accuracy.
It hinged on whether someone was still reachable.

And modern conditions have made Path 2 increasingly likely:

The conversation happens over text instead of face-to-face. No co-regulation. No body language. No tonal nuance. Just words that can be misread and defenses that can't be softened by physical presence.

The person is alone when the message arrives. 3 AM again. Isolated. No one present to help process the fear that arises when certainty wobbles.

The online community has already warned about this moment. "Your friends and family will try to pull you back. They're threatened by your awakening. Stay strong. Trust what you see."

The narrative has become the only source of meaning in a life that felt meaningless. Losing it means returning to the void.

The friend, trying to help, doesn't know about the desperation. Doesn't understand they're not just questioning ideas—they're threatening the only thing keeping chaos at bay.

So the person chooses Path 2.

Not because they're stupid.
Not because they're evil.
Because they're terrified of returning to the unbearable uncertainty that the narrative finally relieved.

The defense begins.
The isolation deepens.
The pathway continues.

The Self-Directed Collapse

After choosing Path 2, something shifts.

The friend backs off. Maybe tries once more, gets rebuffed harder. Then gives up. The relationship cools. Distance grows.

Other relationships follow the same pattern. Family members express concern, get shut down. Coworkers notice the change, get frozen out. Anyone questioning the narrative gets categorized as "them"—the ones who don't see, don't understand, can't be trusted.

The person tells themselves this is necessary. "I'm protecting my truth. I'm maintaining boundaries. I'm cutting out toxic people who can't handle my growth."

But the isolation is progressing incrementally. Not chosen consciously. Happening automatically as the narrative defense mechanism activates repeatedly.

Within weeks, the only remaining contacts are those who confirm the framework. The only communities are those who share the narrative. The only information consumed is that which validates the certainty.

Reality-checking has become impossible. No diverse perspectives remain. No friction exists. The narrative is all that's left.

And then the problem appears again.

The fear hasn't resolved.

The narrative was supposed to fix things. Provide certainty, eliminate anxiety, restore meaning. But the chest is still tight. The sleep still broken. The suffering still present.

If the narrative is correct, why do I still feel this way?
If I finally see the truth, why hasn't anything improved?
If the framework is right, why is the pain still here?

Having committed to the narrative, having defended it against all questioning, having isolated from everyone who doubted it — the person now faces an impossible situation.

The narrative can't be wrong (ego won't allow it).
But the suffering persists (body proves it).
Something must explain this contradiction.

The only explanation available: "The narrative is correct. The threat is real. I'm suffering because I'm failing to respond adequately. I'm not strong enough. Not committed enough. Not capable enough."

I am the problem.
I am defective.
I am broken.

The uncertainty that started everything — the unbearable not-knowing about worth and meaning and future — has now crystallized into certainty about unworthiness.

The person has moved from "I don't know what's wrong" to "I am what's wrong."

From chaos to clarity.
But the clarity is worthlessness.

The hiding intensifies. Not from enemies now—from everyone. Because if you are fundamentally defective, no one must see. The broken thing must be concealed.

Meals alone. Work remote if possible. Declining invitations. Canceling plans. The physical withdrawal matching the relational isolation.

Online presence may continue — anonymous forums, pseudonymous accounts, carefully curated profiles. But in-person contact drops toward zero.

The body carries shame like weight. Posture changes. Eye contact decreases. Voice gets quieter. The physical manifestation of internal worthlessness.

And still the narrative persists, now internalized: The threat is real. I see it. I understand it. I'm just too weak to do anything about it. Everyone else who sees it is stronger than me. I'm the defective one. I'm the failure.

The self-directed anger builds.

Why can't I fix this?
What's wrong with me?
Why am I so pathetic?
Why can't I be strong enough?

Weeks pass. Maybe months. The isolation deepens. The worthlessness settles like sediment. The anger at self accumulates.

This often goes unseen by others. The person has made sure of that.
No one can intervene. The person has eliminated intervention possibility.
No one knows how deep it's gone. The performance continues when visibility is unavoidable.

But alone — which is most of the time now — the person sits with the unbearable weight of being fundamentally broken while carrying the burden of seeing threats that others can't or won't see.

The simulation promised that certainty would bring relief.
The narrative delivered certainty.
But the relief never came.

Now there's only the certainty of worthlessness and the growing pressure of unmetabolized fear and the increasing weight of self-directed rage.

The Direction Stabilizes

Late one night, the person scrolls through the forum that's become their only community. Someone posts a different kind of message.

Not "here's what's wrong."
"Here's whose fault it is."

Not vague enemy. Specific target. Clear identification. Concrete blame.

The self-directed anger finds an outlet. A direction. An object.

What if I'm not defective?
What if they're the problem?
What if I'm not too weak — they're too powerful?
What if I'm not failing — they're blocking?

The rage that was crushing inward suddenly has somewhere else to go.

The relief is instant. Overwhelming. Like pressure releasing. Like pain redirecting. Like drowning person finding something solid to push against.

Not self anymore. Them.

The anger doesn't decrease. It redirects. The intensity remains. The target changes.

And this — this moment when the rage pivots from internal to external, when the worthlessness seeks external explanation, when the accumulated pressure finds outward direction —

This is where the next stage of the pattern begins.

With the question that has always driven violence: Who's to blame?

The merchants have been waiting.
They've been preparing the answer.
They need the rage mobilized.
They need the direction confirmed.
They need the anger weaponized.

The person experiencing this shift doesn't know they're being prepared for something. Doesn't recognize this as part of any progression. Just feels the relief of finally having somewhere to direct the unbearable pressure.

The pathway continues.
The momentum builds.
The isolation has done its work.

Tomorrow we follow the anger outward — into the marketplace where rage is currency and hate is profitable and division is product and lonely, suffering people are inventory waiting to be sold.

But tonight, there's just a person alone in the dark, feeling slightly less crushed because the weight they've been carrying inward has found an external target to blame.

Still suffering.
Still isolated.
Still carrying unbearable uncertainty about worth.

But no longer directing all the rage at themselves.

Small relief.
Terrible relief.
The kind of relief that feels like progress while accelerating toward catastrophe.

The pattern is ancient.
The technology is new.
The human experience is universal.

Many people could find themselves on this path under sufficient pressure.
Everyone capable of this progression given the right conditions.
Everyone carrying more than finite beings were designed to carry alone.

The question has never been whether people can end up on this path.
The question is "How far along are you?"

And "Can you still choose differently?"

The answer depends on whether someone is still reachable.

Whether connection still exists.
Whether reality-checking remains possible.
Whether the isolation is complete or interrupted.

Tomorrow we see what happens when the answer is no.

When the person is unreachable.

When the connection is severed.
When the isolation is total.

When merchants detect the rage and begin the harvest.

Chapter 26

THE PROFITABLE DIVISION

Who Benefits From Your Hate

THE RAGE THAT was crushing inward pivots. Finds external target. The forum post provides the answer that makes everything make sense:

You're not defective.
They are.

The relief floods through like pressure releasing. For weeks—maybe months—the anger had nowhere to go but inward. Self-directed. Corrosive. The constant loop of *what's wrong with me* grinding down any remaining sense of worth.

Now: *what's wrong with them.*

The chest loosens slightly. The breath comes easier. The self-hatred that was becoming unbearable redirects toward justified outrage. Righteous anger. Protective rage.

The person doesn't recognize this as manipulation. Doesn't see the redirection happening. Just feels the relief of finally understanding why everything's been so hard.

Not my failure. Their sabotage.

Not my weakness. Their oppression.
Not my inadequacy. Their advantage.

The algorithm notices the shift immediately. Engagement patterns changing. Click-through rates increasing. Time-on-platform extending. The rage has activated. The resource has been detected.

Now comes the harvest.

Week One: Everything You Knew Is Wrong

The feed adjusts overnight.

Where there was randomness, now there's curation. Where there was variety, now there's focus. Every video, every article, every post pointing toward the same conclusion.

The messages arrive in sequence, carefully calibrated:

"What they don't want you to know..."
"The truth they're hiding..."
"Why everything you learned was lies..."
"The real reason you're struggling..."

Each one spiking uncertainty about everything previously accepted as stable. Job market? Rigged. Education system? Indoctrination. News media? Propaganda. Democratic process? Theater.

Every institution previously trusted gets deconstructed. Every authority previously respected gets discredited. Every source of information previously reliable gets revealed as compromised.

The person consuming this doesn't feel manipulated. Feels awakened. Like scales falling from eyes. Like finally seeing clearly after years of blindness.

But watch what's actually happening: The remaining stability is being systematically eliminated. Any competing framework is being dismantled. Any alternative narrative is being destroyed.

Maximum entropy is being deliberately created.

The brain that was desperate for pattern is being flooded with pattern-breaking. The nervous system seeking certainty is being saturated with doubt about everything.

Not randomly. Strategically.

Breaking down existing frameworks so new framework can install without competition.

Week Four: The Perfect Enemy Emerges

After a month of deconstruction, construction begins.

The chaos gets organized. The uncertainty gets structured. The rage gets focused.

A clear pattern emerges from the feed:

This group is responsible.
These people are the problem.
That ideology is destroying everything.

Not vague anymore. Specific. Named. Identifiable.

The person starts recognizing them everywhere. In news stories. In social media posts. In real life interactions. The pattern-matching brain, trained by a month of focused attention, now sees the enemy in places previously neutral.

Someone cuts them off in traffic — checks the bumper sticker, confirms the enemy.
A coworker disagrees in a meeting — notes their demographic markers, confirms the threat.
A news story about policy — scans for enemy involvement, finds confirmation.

The algorithm feeds this perfectly. Each recognition gets reinforced. Each confirmation gets amplified. The feed showing more examples, more evidence, more proof that the pattern is real.

Within weeks, the person's entire information environment has reorganized around a single axis: us versus them. Good versus evil. Truth-seers versus the deceived.

The enemy isn't abstract anymore. They have faces. Names. Characteristics. Behaviors. Patterns.

And they are everywhere.

Week Eight: You're One of the Few Who See

The isolation that began in fear now gets reframed as enlightenment.

"Most people are still asleep. You're awake."
"The masses are deceived. You see through it."
"They can't handle the truth. You're strong enough."

The loneliness gets converted to superiority. The disconnection becomes distinction. The social rejection becomes validation.

Of course they pulled away — they can't handle what I know.
Of course family is concerned — they're still blind.
Of course friends don't understand — they're not ready to see.

The communities the person has found online reinforce this constantly. Everyone in these spaces shares the same story: woke up, saw the truth, lost people who couldn't accept it, found real community here.

The pattern becomes identity.

Not just "I see this threat" — "I am someone who sees."
Not just "I believe this" — "I am awakened."
Not just "I oppose them" — "I am a warrior/guardian/defender."

The noun-declaration happens automatically. The frozen identity installs. The person becomes the pattern they're defending.

And frozen identities must be maintained. Protected. Performed consistently.

The person starts curating their online presence around the identity. Profile pictures change to symbols of the cause. Firmware update to signal alignment. Every post becomes performance of the awakened identity.

Offline, the withdrawal deepens. Why spend energy on people who can't see? Why maintain relationships with the deceived? The only meaningful connections are those who understand. Who share the knowledge. Who confirm the pattern.

The remaining social world shrinks to the forum, the group chat, the community of fellow seers.

Isolation is now complete.
But it doesn't feel like isolation anymore.
It feels like belonging to the only people who matter.

Week Twelve: The Righteous Path

The anger that redirected outward now gets sanctified.

"Your rage is justified."
"Your hatred is righteous."
"Your violence — if it comes to that — would be defensive."

The language shifts gradually. So gradually the person doesn't notice the escalation.

Week eight: "They're misguided."
Week nine: "They're actively harmful."
Week ten: "They're destroying everything."
Week eleven: "They're irredeemable."
Week twelve: "They're not even fully human."

Each step small enough to seem reasonable. Each progression justified by the previous. Each escalation feeling like logical conclusion rather than manufactured slide.

The dehumanization has begun.

Not through dramatic declaration. Through accumulated exposure. Through repeated messaging. Through gradual normalization of increasingly extreme characterizations.

"They don't think like us."
"They don't feel like us."
"They don't value what we value."
"They're fundamentally different."
"They're less than."
"They're other."
"They're parasites/cancer/virus/infestation."

The biological language isn't accidental. It's strategic. Because biological threats justify biological responses. Parasites get eliminated. Cancer gets removed. Viruses get destroyed.

The person consuming this language doesn't recognize it as dehumanization. Recognizes it as accuracy. "I'm not being hateful — I'm being honest. This is what they are. This is what the evidence shows."

The framework has locked completely. The enemy is fixed. The category is permanent.

And permanent categories demand permanent solutions.

Week Sixteen: Heroes Must Act

The final phase begins with historical reframing.

Every revolutionary gets lionized. Every resistance fighter gets celebrated. Every person who "stood up when it mattered" gets elevated to hero status.

The message underneath: "History remembers those who acted."

The content shifts from analysis to urgency:

"Time is running out."
"The window is closing."
"If we don't act now, we lose everything."
"The next generation will ask why we did nothing."

"Heroes are made in moments like this."

Manifestos appear. Not presented as calls to violence—presented as "statements of truth." Other people's documentation of their awakening, their understanding, their necessity of action.

Some from recent events. Some historical. All following identical pattern:

"I was blind, now I see."
"I tried everything else first."
"They left me no choice."
"This is defense, not offense."
"History will vindicate me."

The person reads these. Relates to them. Sees their own journey reflected. The awakening. The rejection by loved ones. The isolation. The rage. The clarity that violence might be necessary.

The comments sections fill with validation:

"Brave soul."
"Someone had to say it."
"More people need to read this."
"The truth they don't want spoken."

No one explicitly says "do violence." That would trigger platform moderation. Instead, the permission comes through implication. Through celebration of those who acted. Through normalization of extreme measures. Through constant reinforcement that heroism requires crossing lines.

The person experiencing this doesn't feel groomed. Feels prepared. Like finally understanding what must be done. Like accepting the burden that comes with seeing clearly.

The totalization is nearly complete.
The hopelessness is being cultivated.
The logic gate is being constructed.

But none of this is named. None of this is recognized. Just feels like natural progression. Logical development. Inevitable conclusion.

Sixteen weeks from lonely person seeking relief to radicalized individual considering violence.

Not through force. Through algorithm. Through careful sequencing. Through manufactured belonging. Through weaponized isolation.

The Invisible Transaction

Throughout this entire progression, someone has been making money.

The platform gets paid per minute of engagement. Rage engages longer than any other emotion. The angrier the user, the higher the advertising rates.

The content creators get paid per view. Extreme content performs better than moderate content. The algorithm rewards escalation.

The political operations get paid in attention and donations. Outrage converts to clicks. Clicks convert to email signups. Emails convert to donations. The angrier the base, the more reliable the funding.

The wellness merchants sell supplements to counter the cortisol. Security companies sell protection from the threats. Preparedness companies sell supplies for the coming collapse.

Everyone profits from the rage except the person experiencing it.

The isolated person at 3 AM doesn't know his attention is being auctioned. Doesn't recognize his isolation as inventory. Doesn't understand his rage as product being harvested and sold.

He thinks he's finding truth.
He's being farmed.

He thinks he's joining a movement.
He's becoming merchandise.

He thinks he's preparing to defend what matters.
He's being prepared to serve someone else's profit margin.

The merchants don't need him to succeed. They need him to stay engaged. Stay afraid. Stay angry. Stay isolated. Stay consuming content. Stay clicking. Stay watching. Stay radicalizing.

Because radicalization is profitable at every stage.

Your loneliness has shareholders.
Your rage has quarterly earnings reports.
Your hate is someone's revenue stream.

The Community of Shared Rage

But the person experiencing this doesn't feel exploited. Feels understood. For the first time in months—maybe years—feels like someone gets it.

The forum becomes home. The group chat becomes family. The fellow awakened become the only people who matter.

They share memes that outsiders wouldn't understand. Inside jokes about the enemy. Terminology that signals belonging. The language evolves into dialect. The identity solidifies into culture.

They celebrate each other's awakening anniversaries. Support each other through family rejection. Validate each other's rage. Reinforce each other's certainty.

When doubt arises—and sometimes it does—the community provides immediate correction:

"That's your old programming trying to pull you back."
"The enemy wants you to doubt yourself."
"Stay strong. You know the truth."
"We're here for you. We see what you see."

The mutual reinforcement creates closed loop. Every person's certainty supporting every other person's certainty. Little outside information penetrates. No contrary perspective gains traction.

The community has become echo chamber. But from inside, it feels like a truth chamber. The only space where reality gets acknowledged. Where the threat gets named. Where the necessary response gets discussed.

Bonding through shared enemy is powerful. Faster than bonding through shared values. More intense than bonding through shared interests. The rage creates intimacy. The hatred generates loyalty.

But it's toxic intimacy. Destructive loyalty.

The relationships aren't built on mutual growth — they're built on mutual confirmation of threat. Remove the enemy, the bonds dissolve. The community exists only in opposition.

This is why violence becomes necessary for some. Not despite the community — because of it. The identity requires the enemy. The belonging demands the opposition. The meaning depends on the fight.

Without the threat, there's no purpose. Without the enemy, there's no community. Without the rage, there's no identity.

So the threat must remain. The enemy must persist. The rage must continue.

Even if that means creating the violence that proves the necessity of the violence.

The Certainty Complete

The person who was drowning in uncertainty sixteen weeks ago now has absolute certainty.

About the threat: Real, urgent, existential.
About the enemy: Identified, organized, advancing.
About themselves: Awakened, chosen, responsible.
About the solution: Increasingly clear that normal measures won't work.

The rage isn't chaotic anymore. It's focused. Directed. Purposeful.

The worthlessness has converted to mission. The isolation has become strategic positioning. The suffering has transformed into meaningful struggle.

Every morning waking with purpose: monitor the threat, document the evidence, warn others, prepare for what's coming.

Every interaction filtered through the framework: ally or enemy, awakened or deceived, with us or against us.

Every piece of information evaluated by one criterion: does it confirm the pattern or contradict it?

The totalization is advancing. Not complete — but progressing. The entire identity structure organizing around the narrative. The whole meaning system depending on the enemy's reality.

Alternative futures are collapsing. Peaceful resolution seems impossible. The enemy can't be reasoned with (they're fundamentally different). Can't be converted (they're too far gone). Can't be avoided (they're everywhere).

The only question remaining: What happens when something you can't avoid, can't convert, and can't coexist with has to be addressed?

The logic is building toward a single conclusion.

The validation is coming from multiple sources: the community confirms it, the content reinforces it, the evidence accumulates, the pattern proves it.

At this point, the person can be understood as having entered the rage stage. Full rage. Target identified. Direction stabilized. Community bonded. Identity fixed. Certainty absolute.

Dehumanization progressing.

Most who reach this stage stay here. The rage becomes chronic. The hatred becomes identity. The certainty becomes permanent. But the violence never actualizes.

Why?

Because reaching the Rage stage doesn't mean automatic progression to Extremism.

Three factors must converge. Three thresholds must cross. Three conditions must align simultaneously during a pressure peak.

The next chapter maps those final thresholds — not to create fear, but to create recognition.

For anyone who sees elements of this progression in themselves: exits still exist, even here.
For anyone who sees this pattern in someone they care about: intervention points remain, even now.
For anyone who wants to understand why most people at this stage never cross into violence: the mechanisms that stop progression are identifiable and strengthable.

Even at the Rage stage, even with rage fully activated, even with direction stabilized and enemy identified —
the pathway continues only if the final convergence completes.

And that convergence is not inevitable.

It's rare.

The next chapter shows why.

And what stops it.

And what makes the difference between chronic rage and catastrophic action.

Not to frighten.
To illuminate.

To show that even at the edge, even at the Rage stage, even when everything feels inevitable —
choice remains.

If recognition arrives before the final threshold crosses.
If intervention happens before the three factors align.
If someone — anyone — is still reachable.

The merchants have led you here.

The algorithm has prepared you.
The community has encouraged you.

But they profit whether you act or not.
They win if you stay engaged.
They succeed if you remain isolated.

Your rage is their revenue.
Your hate is their product.
Your potential violence is their viral content waiting to happen.

They don't care about your cause.
They care about your clicks.

Follow the money away from the enemy they've given you.
Look at who's actually profiting from your suffering.
Notice who benefits from keeping you angry, isolated, and certain.

The enemy they've sold you might be real.
But so are the merchants who sold you the enemy.

And only one of those is actually extracting value from your pain.

Tomorrow we face the final threshold.

Tonight, there's still time to choose differently.

Chapter 27

EMERGENCY OVERRIDE

The Threshold

3:17 AM. A person sits alone in a room illuminated only by screen glow. The document is open. The plan is complete. The certainty is absolute.

The Totalization

Everything has aligned.

The narrative has become total. Not just something believed — something that is. The entire identity structure organized around it. Every thought filtered through it. Every relationship evaluated by it. Everyone who questioned it has been eliminated from the circle. Everyone who remains confirms it.

The totalization happened gradually. So gradually it was invisible. First cutting out people who "didn't understand." Then avoiding situations that might create doubt. Then consuming only information that validated the framework. Then bonding only with others who saw the same pattern.

Now the person exists inside a perfect closed system. Every input confirms. Every interaction validates. Every piece of information reinforces. No friction remains. No contrary perspective penetrates. No alternative reality exists.

The narrative isn't just believed anymore.
It's lived.
It's breathed.
It functions as reality.

And because it is total, questioning it would be self-annihilation. The framework has become the person. The person has become the framework. No separation remains.

The Hopelessness

The hopelessness is complete. Not depression — logical conclusion.

Every peaceful pathway has been examined and found blocked. Every normal channel has been tried and failed. Every alternative future has been considered and dismissed.

They won't stop on their own. Can't be reasoned with. Won't respond to appeals. Time won't improve things — time makes them worse. Every day they advance. Every week the window closes further. Every month brings closer to the point of no return.

Voting won't fix it — the system is rigged. Protesting won't change it—they ignore protests. Dialogue won't reach them — they don't argue in good faith. Waiting won't help — that's how they win.

The person has looked at every angle. Considered every option. Explored every possibility. The conclusion is unavoidable: No peaceful resolution exists.

The future has collapsed to two possibilities: Total defeat or dramatic action. Submission or resistance. Accepting the end or preventing it.

This feels like clear thinking. Like accurate assessment. Like finally accepting reality instead of clinging to false hope that things might somehow improve if everyone just keeps being nice and following rules and trusting the process.

The hopelessness doesn't feel emotional.
It feels mathematical.
It's feels certain.

The Permission

And the permission has arrived.

Started weeks ago. A manifesto read late at night. The logic was flawless. The moral framework clear. The historical precedent established. Violence wasn't transgression — it was imperative. Not something criminal but something heroic. Not evil but necessary.

The reasoning built piece by piece:

This is self-defense. They attacked first — culture, values, people, everything sacred. Just responding to aggression already initiated.

This is justice. They escaped accountability through corrupt systems. Someone must enforce what law won't.

This is protection. Future generations will suffer if no one acts now. Children will inherit dystopia if adults don't stop it.

This is love. For what's being destroyed. For who's being harmed. Real love protects. Real love fights. Real love makes hard choices.

The moral inversion completed. Violence became virtue. Destruction became creation. Killing became saving.

The community confirmed it. Not explicitly — no one said "do violence." But the celebration of those who acted. The elevation of historical resisters. The constant refrain that heroes are made in moments like this. The repeated messaging that time is running out and someone must act and history will vindicate.

The validation came from multiple sources. The ideology provided theological permission. The online community provided social permission. The manifestos provided philosophical permission. The constructed logic provided personal permission.

All converging. All aligning. All pointing toward the same conclusion.

The gate has opened.

Violence has transformed from unthinkable to necessary.
From transgression to imperative.
From evil to good.

The Convergence

These three factors — totalization, hopelessness, permission — have been building separately for months. Now they exist simultaneously. All three present. All three complete. All three reinforcing.

During a pressure peak. Late at night. Alone. Exhausted. The cortisol flooding. The sleep deprivation accumulating. The isolation absolute. The rage maximum.

This is the convergence. The threshold. The moment that statistically almost never happens despite millions experiencing rage, despite widespread radicalization, despite abundant validation.

Because all three factors must align simultaneously during maximum pressure. And usually something breaks the alignment. Someone reaches out. Something interrupts. A factor weakens before the others complete.

But not tonight.

Tonight all three hold.

The person sitting in screen glow has crossed into territory that most at Stage R never enter. The plan is made. The means are available. The justification is complete. The certainty is absolute.

What happens in the next three seconds determines everything.

The Interruption

The phone vibrates. Unexpected. Unfamiliar pattern.

The person almost ignores it. Focused. Committed. The plan requires execution. Distractions must be eliminated.

But the hand reaches automatically. Muscle memory. The screen illuminates.

A message from a number not saved. Wrong number probably. Spam likely.

"Hey, I know we haven't talked in forever, but I was thinking about you tonight. Hope you're doing okay."

A friend from before. From the time before the awakening. Before the cutting away. Before the totalization. Someone eliminated months ago for not understanding, for questioning, for being part of the problem.

The person stares at the message.

Three seconds pass.

In those three seconds, something shifts. Not dramatically. Not completely. Just slightly.

The totalization — which had been perfect, seamless, complete—develops a hairline crack. One person from outside the closed system has penetrated. One voice from before the narrative became everything has spoken.

The framework doesn't collapse. The certainty doesn't dissolve. The plan doesn't change.

But the totalization isn't quite total anymore.

Someone outside the system remembers them. Someone they cut out still thinks about them. Someone from before still cares.

The fingers hover over the screen.

Three seconds becomes six.

The crack widens slightly.

What if the friend knew what was being planned? Would they understand? Would they agree that violence is necessary? Would they support the action?

Or would they —

The thought doesn't complete. Can't complete. Because completing it means acknowledging doubt. And doubt means the certainty weakens. And weakened certainty means the unbearable uncertainty returns.

The ego defends. The framework reasserts. The logic rebuilds.

They don't understand. They can't see. They're still deceived. This message is distraction. Maybe even enemy tactic. The plan must proceed. The mission requires commitment. Heroes don't hesitate.

The phone gets placed face down. The document reopens. The certainty returns.

But not quite as completely as before.

The crack remains.

Path A: The Phone Call

In another timeline — or perhaps the same one a moment later—the fingers don't place the phone down. They type instead.

"Not doing great actually."

Send.

The response comes within seconds. "You there? Can I call?"

The person stares at the question. The plan requires focus. The mission demands commitment. Taking a call means delay. Delay means doubt. Doubt means failure.

But the fingers type anyway: "Yeah."

The phone rings. The person answers.

"Hey." The friend's voice. Real. Present. Immediate. Not text. Not curated. Not mediated. Just voice.

"Hey."

Silence for a moment. Then: "What's going on?"

The person doesn't know how to answer. Can't explain without revealing. Can't reveal without abandoning. Can't abandon without returning to unbearable uncertainty.

But the voice is there. Real person. Someone who knew them before. Someone outside the totalized system. Someone who might —

"I'm in trouble," the person hears themselves say.

Not planned. Not decided. The words just arrive.

"What kind of trouble?"

Another silence. Longer. The document still open on the screen. The plan still ready. The certainty still present but —

"I've been having thoughts. Bad thoughts. About hurting people."

The friend doesn't hang up. Doesn't judge. Doesn't panic. Just stays present. "Okay. Thank you for telling me. Are you safe right now?"

"I don't know."

"Are you planning to hurt yourself or someone else tonight?"

The question hangs. Honest answer means admission. Admission means intervention. Intervention means the plan fails. The mission aborts. The whole framework—

"Yes."

The word comes out. Can't be taken back. The totalization has cracked wider. The admission has created space. The isolation has been interrupted.

"Okay. I'm here. I'm not going anywhere. Can you tell me what's happening?"

And somehow—impossibly—the person starts talking. Not about the ideology. Not defending the framework. Not explaining the necessity. Just describing the pressure. The unbearable weight. The certainty that violence is the only solution. The hopelessness that nothing else will work. The totalization that makes questioning feel impossible.

The friend listens. Doesn't argue. Doesn't contradict. Doesn't try to logic away the framework. Just stays present.

"That sounds incredibly heavy. I can hear how much pain you're in."

Not "you're wrong." Not "that's crazy." Not "you need to stop." Just recognition of suffering.

The person talks for twenty minutes. Then forty. The plan still sits ready. The means still available. But the immediacy has shifted. The inevitability has paused.

"Will you do something for me?" the friend asks.

"What?"

"Will you call your local crisis line? They're trained for exactly this. I'll stay on the line with you until they answer."

The resistance rises immediately. "I'm not suicidal."

"I know. But you're in crisis. That's what the line is for. Not just suicide—crisis. What you're feeling, what you're planning—that's crisis. They can help."

The person doesn't want help yet. Wants action. Wants resolution. Wants the unbearable pressure to end through the only means that makes sense.

But the crack is widening. The totalization weakening. The isolation interrupted.

"Okay."

The friend stays on the line. The person dials. The crisis counselor answers. Another voice. Another human. Another interruption to the perfect closed system.

Three voices now. Three people. Three points of connection outside the totalized framework.

Not enough to solve everything. Not enough to eliminate the rage or resolve the worthlessness or fix the conditions that created this.

But enough to pause. Enough to interrupt. Enough to prevent the action that cannot be undone.

The person talks to the counselor for an hour. Then goes to the emergency room. Then gets admitted. Then begins treatment.

The plan never executes. The violence never actualizes. The permanence never happens.

Not because the person suddenly saw they were wrong. Not because the framework dissolved. Not because the worthlessness disappeared.

Because the isolation got interrupted. The totalization cracked. The three-factor convergence broke before the pressure peak reached critical.

Tomorrow exists. Uncertain. Difficult. Still carrying rage and pain and the framework that caused this.

But tomorrow exists.

Path B: The Silence

In another room—or perhaps the same room in a different moment—the phone doesn't ring. The message doesn't arrive. The interruption doesn't happen.

The three factors hold. The convergence completes. The pressure peaks without break.

The person acts.

What follows is not what the framework promised.

No clarity. No relief. No resolution. No meaning. No worth.

Just more chaos. More suffering. More worthlessness multiplied across more people.

The victims weren't what the ideology described. Weren't the one-dimensional enemy the framework created. Were humans. Complex. Finite. Carrying their own burdens. With families. Futures. Unfinished stories.

Gone now. Permanently. Because of action taken in moment of totalized certainty that felt absolutely true and turned out to be absolutely wrong.

The person — if they survive — sits in aftermath recognizing something the framework never prepared them for: The violence didn't reduce chaos. Didn't create meaning. Didn't establish worth.

Multiplied chaos. Destroyed meaning. Annihilated any possibility of worth.

The community that encouraged? Vanishes. Distances. "Lone wolf," they say. "Mental illness." "Not representative."

The movement that validated? Disappears. The content that radicalized gets memory-holed. The voices that gave permission go silent.

The ideology that promised vindication? Offers nothing. No divine intervention. No historical judgment. No future recognition. Just silence.

Alone. Completely. The isolation that drove the progression now absolute. The connection that might have prevented it unreachable. The tomorrow that existed before—gone.

The person isn't remembered as hero. Isn't vindicated by history. Isn't celebrated by movement.

Becomes cautionary tale. Case study. Example of what happens when someone breaks. Data point in research about radicalization.

The worthlessness that drove everything—the unbearable uncertainty about whether they mattered—has been answered with certainty: This didn't create worth. This destroyed it.

The violence that promised to matter through mattering dramatically has mattered in the worst possible way.

Not what the framework promised.
Not what the ideology guaranteed.
Not what the certainty suggested.

Just permanent harm. Irreversible damage. Multiplied suffering.

And the realization — arriving too late — that the totalization was false, the hopelessness was manufactured, the permission was lie, and the violence was exactly what the merchants needed to keep the system running.

One more tragedy to fuel the outrage economy. One more atrocity to radicalize others. One more cycle of violence begetting violence.

The person served the simulation perfectly.
Just not the way they thought.

The Pattern Across Time

Throughout history, the pattern repeats.

Different ideologies. Different enemies. Different justifications. Same mechanism.

A young man in first century Judea convinced that Roman occupation must be resisted violently. Totalization complete. Hopelessness absolute. Permission granted by zealot theology. Acts. Dies. Rome continues unchanged.

A woman in medieval France certain that heretics must be eliminated to save souls. Framework total. Hope for peaceful conversion gone. Church provides permission. Participates in violence. Realizes too late the humanity of those killed.

A teenager in 1960s America convinced that revolutionary violence will liberate the oppressed. Narrative consuming entire identity. All peaceful options seemingly exhausted. Ideology authorizing force. Plants bomb. Kills innocents. Revolution never comes.

A person in 2020s anywhere believing that [their specific enemy] must be stopped by any means necessary. Three factors converging. Pressure peaking. Violence actualizing. Same structural pattern. Same underlying mechanism. Same terrible math.

Different content. Identical structure.

The worthlessness driving it. The isolation enabling it. The totalization locking it. The hopelessness justifying it. The permission authorizing it.

And always — always — the aftermath revealing what the framework concealed: The violence didn't solve anything. Didn't create meaning. Didn't establish worth. Just multiplied the chaos it promised to eliminate.

But some — across all those centuries, across all those contexts — paused.

Felt the same pressure. Experienced the same totalization. Carried the same rage. Had the same access to permission.

But paused.

Three seconds. One interruption. A crack in the totalization. A moment of doubt. A flash of recognition. A connection that persisted.

And they chose differently.

Not because they were better people. Not because they had stronger morals. Not because they were less committed to their cause.

Because something interrupted the convergence before the pressure peak completed.

Someone reached out. Something broke the isolation. A memory surfaced. A sound interrupted. A thought intruded. A person stayed reachable.

The pattern broke. The progression paused. The violence didn't actualize.

Tomorrow existed.

The Worthlessness Recognition

A person sits in a therapist's office six months after choosing Path A. After the phone call. After the emergency room. After the hospitalization. After beginning treatment.

The rage hasn't disappeared. The framework hasn't dissolved. The certainty hasn't completely lifted.

But something has shifted.

The therapist asks a question: "Where did you first learn that your worth had to be proven?"

The person considers. "I don't know. Always? Isn't that how it works? You have to achieve things. Accomplish things. Matter through doing something that matters."

"What if that's not true?"

The person resists. "Then what determines worth?"

"What if worth doesn't need to be determined? What if it just is?"

The question hangs. Makes no sense at first. Violates every framework. Contradicts every metric the person has ever known.

Worth comes from productivity. From achievement. From status. From performance. From doing more than others. From being more than others. From mattering through measurable impact.

Doesn't it?

"The simulation — everything around you — runs on manufactured insufficiency," the therapist continues. "It needs you to feel worthless so you'll keep trying to prove worth through consumption, production, performance. The metrics are rigged. Designed to make you come up deficient. Always."

The person sits with this. "So the framework I built — the narrative about the enemy —"

"Gave you different metrics. A different way to establish worth. But same measurement system. Same fundamental lie that worth must be proven rather than recognized."

"But I almost —" The person stops. Can't finish.

"You almost tried to establish worth through violence. Through mattering dramatically. Through being remembered. Through proving you weren't nothing."

The silence extends.

"But it wouldn't have worked," the therapist says quietly. "The violence would have destroyed any possibility of worth. Would have confirmed the worthlessness rather than eliminating it."

The person knows this now. Has had six months to recognize it. To see what the framework concealed. To understand what the totalization prevented from being visible.

"The worthlessness was never true," the therapist continues. "But the isolation made it feel true. Made it impossible to reality-check. Made you carry unbearable weight alone until violence seemed like the only solution."

Another silence. Then: "So what now?"

"Now you learn to carry weight differently. Not alone. Not through proving worth. Through accepting that you already have it. Through connecting with others who are also finite, also struggling, also carrying more than they should carry alone."

The person doesn't fully believe this yet. The framework still whispers. The certainty still pulls. The rage still activates.

But the totalization has cracked enough to allow this conversation. The isolation has been interrupted enough to permit this connection. The worthlessness has been questioned enough to create space for alternative.

Not healed. Not solved. Not resolved.
But paused. Interrupted. Given time.

Tomorrow exists. And the day after. And the one after that.

Each one uncertain. Each one difficult. Each one requiring choice.

But each one possible.

The Exits Through Time

The exits exist at every stage. Real people. Real choices. Real interruptions that prevented violence.

A teenager at the Fear stage — fear locked in, narrative solidified — whose friend noticed the change and didn't let go. Kept showing up. Kept offering reality-checks. Kept providing diverse perspective until the Decision Point arrived and Path 1 became possible.

A young adult at the Isolation stage — deep in isolation, worthlessness settled — who saw a therapist's advertisement and called. One phone call. Treatment began. Connection interrupted the self-directed collapse.

A person at the Rage stage — full rage, direction stabilized, dehumanization progressing — who joined a mutual aid group to "help their community" and encountered actual humans whose complexity broke the one-dimensional enemy category.

Another at the Rage stage who started creating art to express the rage and found that creation metabolized what destruction promised to release.

Someone at the threshold — three factors converging, plan ready — whose cat jumped on the keyboard at the critical moment. Three seconds of interruption. Enough to pause. Enough to reconsider. Enough to choose differently.

The exits aren't dramatic. Aren't perfect. Aren't instant solutions.

Just interruptions. Pauses. Gaps in the totalization. Moments where connection penetrates isolation. Instances where reality-checking becomes possible. Seconds where a different choice can be made.

Real people finding real exits. Not because they were exceptional. Because something interrupted the progression before the convergence completed.

Because someone stayed reachable.
Because isolation got broken.
Because totalization cracked.

The pathway is real. The progression is predictable. The capacity for violence exists under sufficient pressure.

But the exits are equally real. Equally present. Equally available.

At every stage.
Even at the threshold.
Even at the edge.

Choice remains until the moment action executes.
And action can be interrupted. Paused. Prevented.

Through connection. Through intervention. Through anything that breaks the isolation long enough to create gap.

Tomorrow

The person who chose Path A wakes up in a different reality than the person who chose Path B.

Not perfect reality. Still carrying rage. Still holding framework. Still experiencing worthlessness. Still struggling with hopelessness.

But alive. Conscious. Present. Capable of choice.

Treatment continues. Therapy happens. The nervous system slowly recalibrates. The totalization gradually weakens. The isolation gets interrupted, inch by inch.

The framework doesn't dissolve overnight. The certainty doesn't vanish with one conversation. The rage doesn't resolve through single intervention.

But the trajectory changes. The pathway redirects. The momentum slows.

Each day another choice. Each moment another decision. Each interaction another opportunity for connection or isolation.

The simulation still operates. The merchants still profit. The algorithm still optimizes for engagement. The radicalization pipeline still functions.

But for this person — who paused, who called, who chose connection over destruction — the pipeline has been interrupted.

Not permanently. Not perfectly. The pressure could build again. The totalization could reassert. The convergence could realign.

But not today. Not tonight. Not in this moment.

Tomorrow exists.

And tomorrow only asks one question:
What happens when the unbearable weight gets shared?
When finite beings stop trying to be infinite.
When isolated humans return to refuge.
When the worthlessness lie gets rejected — not through individual strength, but through collective practice.

The simulation broke the design.
Empire weaponized isolation.
The marketplace extracted value from suffering.

But the design remains.
The architecture persists.

The ancient path waits.

For anyone who pauses long enough to see it.

PART VIII

Behind The Simulation

Revelation: What Was Always Real

Chapter 28

WHAT YOU SEE NOW

When Refuge Becomes Necessity

A PERSON FINISHES a book. Sets it down. Looks around.

The room is the same. The phone still glows on the nightstand. The notifications still accumulate. The morning will still arrive with its familiar weight.

Nothing has changed.

And everything has changed.

The feed still scrolls, but now the pattern is visible. The comparison still operates, but now the mechanism shows through. The anxiety still arrives, but now its architecture is exposed.

Seeing the simulation doesn't stop the simulation.
It just makes the simulation visible.

The Transparent Walls

Someone walks through a grocery store a week after recognizing the pattern. The fluorescent lights. The carefully engineered pathways. The product placement designed by people who studied which shelf heights trigger purchase.

Before, this was just shopping.

Now the layers show:
The music calibrated to slow walking speed.
The essential items placed at maximum distance from entrance.
The impulse products at eye level, the store brands hidden below.

Not conspiracy. Just optimization.
Systems doing what systems do.

The person still needs groceries. Still walks the engineered paths. Still responds to some of the triggers.

But something has shifted. The automatic has become visible. The invisible has become seen.

This is what it means to wake up inside the simulation: not escape, but recognition. Not freedom from the system, but clarity about how the system operates.

The walls don't disappear.
They become transparent.

What Seeing Changes

Seeing the pattern changes nothing external.

The algorithm still runs. The merchants still profit. The fear still circulates. The extraction continues whether witnessed or not.

But seeing changes the seer.

A person who recognizes the sales pitch responds differently than one who doesn't. Not immune — still susceptible, still targeted, still affected. But no longer automatic. No longer running code without knowing it's code.

The hand still reaches for the phone. But now there's a gap — microscopic, sometimes — between impulse and action. A moment where choice becomes possible.

That gap is everything.

Seeing changes nothing until seeing changes what you do.

The Three Movements

What remains after recognition?

Not more information. The book provided enough. Not more analysis. The patterns are clear. Not more critique. The simulation has been named.

What remains is movement. Three directions, each building on the last:

The first movement is internal. Clearing what blocks reception. Releasing what creates static. Preparing the self to receive what the simulation trained it to deflect. This is individual work — possible alone, necessary before everything else.

The second movement is relational. Learning to stay connected across difference. Discovering how to hold conversation without requiring agreement. Becoming someone who can remain present when others see differently. This is skill — practiced in whatever relationships already exist.

The third movement is rhythmic. Adopting patterns that sustain what the first two movements begin. Practices that work whether community exists nearby or not. Rhythms that create signal, making the practitioner visible to others walking the same direction.

Internal. Relational. Rhythmic.

Preparation. Skill. Practice.

The order matters. Each creates capacity for the next.

Not Emergency

Some arrive at this threshold in crisis. Breaking open. Desperate for anything that works.

Others arrive curious. Recognizing patterns. Wondering what comes next.

Both stand at the same door.

The journey ahead doesn't require emergency. Doesn't demand hitting bottom. Doesn't need catastrophe as credential.

Waking up is enough.
Seeing is sufficient qualification.

The only requirement is willingness to let seeing change something. To move from recognition to response. From pattern awareness to pattern interruption.

Not everyone who sees will move. Some will close the book and return to the feed. The simulation will welcome them back. It always does.

But for those who want more than seeing—
for those ready to let recognition reshape action—
the path exists.

Ancient. Tested. Available.

What the Simulation Said

The simulation had a story about reality:

You're behind. Run faster.
You're insufficient. Acquire more.
You're alone. Perform better.
Time is running out. Panic now.

This story generated specific behaviors. Scrolling. Comparing. Consuming. Competing. Each behavior fed the system that authored the story.

The loop was elegant. Self-sustaining. Nearly invisible.

Fear produced behavior.
Behavior produced profit.
Profit funded more fear.

The humans inside the loop experienced it as life. As normal. As the way things are.

What Reality Suggests

Reality offers different information:

There is no race — only walking.
There is no standard — only being.
There is no performance — only presence.
There is no scarcity of time — only this moment, which is sufficient.

These aren't affirmations. Not positive thinking. Not reframing.
They're observations. What remains when the sales pitch stops.

The simulation required urgency to function. Reality operates without it. The sun rises whether anyone panics or not. The seasons turn without optimization. The body breathes without productivity metrics.

The design predates the distortion.

Underneath every layer of simulation —
beneath Egypt, Greece, Rome, Algorithm —
the original architecture remains.

Instructions encoded before empire learned to override them.
Patterns that kept humans human across millennia of pressure.
Practices that worked not because they were commanded but because they matched reality.

Torah wasn't invented — it was given.
Instructions for how reality actually works, from the One who designed it.

The Threshold

This is the threshold moment.

Behind: everything the book revealed. The simulation's architecture. The fear merchants. The extraction systems. The violence that erupts when humans try to carry what they were never designed to carry alone.

Ahead: not escape, but engagement. Not transcendence, but practice. Not leaving the world, but moving through it differently.

The simulation continues. It will continue. No book ends it. No insight dissolves it. No awakening makes it disappear.

But within the simulation, another way of moving exists.

Those who practiced it left markers. Instructions. Warnings and invitations. They didn't escape their simulations — Egyptian, Babylonian, Greek, Roman. They walked through them. Stayed human inside them. Maintained something the systems couldn't fully capture.

The thread they held is still available.
Not as doctrine. As practice.
Not as belief required. As pattern that works.

Tomorrow

Tomorrow the phone will glow.
The feed will scroll.
The comparison will begin.

The simulation will offer its familiar story:
behind, insufficient, alone, running out of time.

And now, a different response is possible.

Not because the pressure disappears.
Because the one experiencing pressure has changed.

What follows shows how.

Seeing changes nothing until
seeing changes what you do

Chapter 29

THE INTERNAL WORK

The Restoration Protocol in Operation

A MAN SITS in a workshop on mindfulness. Corporate conference room. Fluorescent lights. Thirty employees learning to be present.

The instructor speaks about letting go. About acceptance. About releasing resistance.

The man nods. Takes notes. Uses the vocabulary correctly in the small group discussion.

Nothing changes.

Three weeks later, the same anxiety. The same patterns. The same reaching for phone, for distraction, for anything that numbs. The workshop becomes a memory, then a line on a self-improvement list, then forgotten entirely.

Not because the teaching was wrong.
Because the teaching couldn't land.

A woman reads about forgiveness. The book is compelling. The arguments are sound. She understands intellectually why holding resentment poisons the holder more than the target.

She decides to forgive.

The decision lasts until the next encounter with the person who wounded her. The body tightens. The anger surfaces. The forgiveness evaporates like morning fog.

Not because she didn't mean it.
Because meaning it wasn't enough.

Why Good Advice Fails

There's a reason good advice doesn't work.

The pathway between hearing and changing has requirements. Prerequisites the advice-givers rarely mention. Conditions that must exist before wisdom can travel from ear to action.

A person saturated with defended positions cannot receive new information. A system under pressure cannot integrate guidance. A nervous system in threat-response cannot access flexibility.

The teaching arrives.
The teaching deflects.
Nothing changes.

This isn't moral failure. It's architecture.

Guidance requires open pathway to reach formation.
Most pathways are blocked.

The Deflection Patterns

Watch how wisdom gets intercepted:

Someone hears a challenge to their certainty. Before the words finish, the response is forming. Not consideration—counter-argument. The challenge never reaches consideration. It gets processed as threat.

Someone receives feedback about their behavior. The feedback transforms mid-air into attack on identity. Defense mobilizes before understanding can form. The feedback bounces off.

Someone encounters a practice that might help. The mind immediately categorizes: too religious, too simple, too demanding, already tried something similar. The practice gets filed before it gets tested.

These aren't character flaws. They're protective mechanisms doing their job. The system learned to deflect because deflection once served survival.

But protection can become prison.

The same walls that keep threat out also keep guidance out. The same defenses that prevent harm also prevent growth. The same armor that protects the wound also prevents the wound from healing.

Deflection is not permanent identity. It's current structural state.

The question isn't "Am I a deflector?"
The question is "Am I deflecting right now?"

What Opens the Pathway

Two conditions allow guidance to land:

The first is disposition. Some people developed permeable defenses. They hear challenge without automatic counter-attack. They receive feedback without converting it to threat. Their pathway from perception to formation stayed open—through circumstance, through practice, through whatever confluence of factors shapes a receptive posture.

The second is desperation. Some people get broken open. Circumstance overwhelms the defenses. The armor cracks not through choice but through pressure exceeding capacity. What was protected becomes exposed. What was defended becomes permeable.

Both can receive what the defended cannot.

The first by habit.
The second by necessity.

If defenses remain intact—if deflection skills stay sharp—no protocol helps. Not because help is withheld. Because help cannot land where landing is prevented.

A woman arrives at a support group. Not because she felt ready. Because staying away finally cost more than showing up.

She doesn't want to be there. Doesn't want to need this. The defenses scream that this is weakness, that she should handle it alone, that admitting need means failure.

But the exhaustion is stronger than the pride.

She sits. She listens. She lets the words of others reach her without immediate deflection.

Something shifts.

Not transformation. Just opening. The pathway that had been sealed begins to unseal. Not through effort—through exhaustion of the effort to stay closed.

Desperation accomplished what decision couldn't.

The Return Sequence

A man sits in a chair he's sat in a thousand times. Same room. Same light. Same coffee table with the same ring stain he keeps meaning to sand out.

But today something is different. Not the room. Him.

The defenses are down. Not by choice — by exhaustion. The fight that sustained him for months, years, has finally cost more than it protects. The armor that kept everything out also kept everything in. And what was kept in has been building pressure until the structure itself began to crack.

He's not ready for wisdom. Not ready for a program. Not ready for someone to explain what he should do differently.

He's just — stopped. Sitting in the gap between who he was performing and who he might actually be. Not moving forward. Not retreating. Just present to the weight of everything he'd been outrunning.

This is where it begins.

Not with a decision. With a collapse of the effort to avoid the decision.

What Follows

What follows is a sequence. Not commandments — observations. What seems to work when people are ready to stop running and start moving.

The order matters. Steps skipped tend to reassert themselves. Stages rushed tend to collapse. The sequence respects how humans actually change — not how self-help books imagine they do.

This isn't theory. It's what the evidence shows. What recovery communities have observed for generations. What ancient wisdom encoded in practices long before anyone had a word for psychology.

Ten movements. Each one building on what precedes it. Each one impossible without what came before.

First: Stop the Internal War.

A person full of defended positions, stored grievances, and protective stances cannot receive anything new. The system is at capacity. Every input gets processed through existing filters. Every challenge converts to threat. Every invitation registers as manipulation.

The first movement isn't action. It's cessation of counter-action.

Stop fighting what is. Not acceptance as achievement — just temporary ceasefire. Let defenses drop enough to see what's actually happening rather than what the defended story says is happening.

This is the hardest step because it feels like surrender. The simulation taught that dropping defenses means death. That vigilance equals survival. That the moment you stop fighting, you lose.

But the war was with reality. And reality wasn't the enemy.

Nothing new enters while the war continues.

Second: Hold Position.

Once defenses lower enough to see clearly, the temptation is immediate: do something. Fix something. Move somewhere. The discomfort of stillness after years of frantic motion feels unbearable.

But the forces that created the defended state still operate. The feed still scrolls. The merchants still sell. The old patterns still pull. One notification, one trigger, one familiar voice — and the defenses snap back into place.

Holding position means staying at the threshold. Not advancing, not retreating. Maintaining the pause long enough for the pause to do its work.

A person who lowers defenses and immediately re-engages the chaos learns nothing. The gap between stopping and starting again is where the real seeing happens. It's uncomfortable. It's supposed to be.

The pause is not wasted time. The pause is where the architecture changes.

Third: Move Toward Stability.

Recovery requires proximity to something stable. Something that doesn't fluctuate with every notification. Something outside the system that created the saturation.

This might be a person. A place. A practice. A community. A recovery meeting resisted for months because it felt too religious, too structured, too much like admitting defeat. Anything that provides a reference point outside the spinning.

But proximity requires vulnerability. The defended self must become visible. The independent trajectory must be surrendered. Belonging must be accepted — not as weakness, but as design.

This is where the simulation's deepest lie gets tested. The lie that says: you should be able to handle this alone. That needing others means you're broken. That asking for help means you've failed.

The truth is the opposite. Isolated recovery isn't recovery — it's just a quieter version of the same imprisonment. The design is plural. Stability borrows from others until your own returns. This isn't losing agency. It's how agency actually works.

Isolation feels safer. Isolation increases disorder.

Healing happens in proximity.

Fourth: Release What Contaminates.

Toxicity held in compressed form — inputs, substances, habits that introduce noise — must release. Not through tighter grip. Through opening the hand.

This step is about what you're consuming. The doom-scrolling that feeds the anxiety. The substances that numb the feeling. The media diet that confirms the rage. The digital inputs that reliably generate chaos.

These aren't moral failings. They're contamination sources. They occupy space needed for something else. They keep the system saturated so the earlier steps can't hold.

A person who stops the internal war but keeps consuming the content that started the war will find the war restarting within hours. A person who moves toward stability but keeps ingesting what destabilizes will wonder why proximity isn't working.

Release often requires support, not resolve. White-knuckle abstinence is just another war. The hand opens when something else is offered to hold.

Cleansing isn't scrubbing. It's releasing.
Stop carrying what needs to leave.

Fifth: Simplify Until One Thing Remains.

The interior divided against itself cannot move. Competing loyalties. Contradictory commitments. Serving causes that pull in opposite directions. Maintaining identities that require different performances for different audiences.

This step is about what you're serving. Not what you're consuming — that was the previous step — but what you're giving your energy to. The obligations, the personas, the either/ors that consume energy without producing direction.

Simplification doesn't come from deciding harder. It comes from repeatedly yielding what doesn't belong. Letting go of the secondary until only the primary remains. Not addition. Subtraction repeated.

This is where people discover how much of their exhaustion comes not from doing too much but from doing contradictory things simultaneously. Performing confidence at work while dissolving at home. Presenting certainty online while drowning in doubt offline. Maintaining three different versions of self for three different audiences.

Each contradiction costs energy. Each unresolved either/or drains capacity. The simplification isn't about doing less — it's about stopping the internal fragmentation that makes everything harder than it needs to be.

Movement requires single direction.
A river that splits into a dozen channels loses the force to carve through stone.

Sixth: Feel What Was Avoided.

Beneath the defended positions and the distractions and the numbing lies something that was too painful to feel. The defenses exist for a reason. They protected against something real.

But protection extended past its usefulness becomes imprisonment.

The avoided feeling must be felt. Not forced — allowed. Not manufactured suffering — just cessation of the refusal to perceive what's already there.

This is where most programs fail. This is the step that gets skipped, medicated, rationalized, or rushed past. Because the feeling is uncomfortable. Because the instinct is to interpret rather than inhabit. Because the simulation taught that feelings are problems to be solved rather than experiences to be endured.

But the feeling doesn't skip. It waits. It will be felt now or felt later. The question isn't whether — it's when, and whether someone is present when it happens.

This is why isolation is so dangerous at this stage. Feelings that surface in solitude can overwhelm. The same feelings, surfacing in the presence of another human being, become survivable. Not because the other person fixes anything. Because witness changes the scale. Pain held alone is infinite. Pain witnessed is bounded.

The person sitting across the table doesn't need to say the right thing. Doesn't need to offer solutions. Doesn't need to understand completely. They need to stay. That's what presence does that advice cannot.

Stopping the anesthetic is not creating pain.
It's allowing pain that was always present to register.
And it registers differently when someone else is in the room.

Seventh: Name What Was Lost.

This is the step that addiction treatment, therapy programs, anger management courses, and self-help systems most consistently underestimate. And it's the step whose absence most reliably predicts relapse, recurrence, and collapse.

Beneath the defended positions, beneath the avoided feeling, lies loss. Real loss. Something that mattered, gone. Someone who mattered, absent. A version of self or life that will not return.

The father who left. The marriage that ended. The career that collapsed. The health that changed. The childhood that should have been different. The future that was promised and didn't arrive. The person you thought you were before the thing that happened.

Loss that isn't identified can't be grieved. And loss that isn't grieved doesn't resolve — it drives. It becomes the invisible engine behind the rage, the addiction, the depression, the frantic activity, the perfectionism, the numbness. Every behavior that baffles the person performing it — "Why do I keep doing this?" — often traces back to loss that was never named.

This is why addiction treatment so often fails. The substance is identified. The behavior is interrupted. The coping mechanism is removed. But the loss underneath — the thing the substance was managing — remains untouched. Unnamed. Unmourned. Still raw.

A person who stops drinking but never grieves what the drinking was covering will find another substance, another behavior, another numbing agent. Not because they lack willpower. Because the loss is still there, still demanding management, and the only tool that's been removed is the one that was managing it.

Mourning is specific. It requires naming. Not "I've experienced loss" — that's a category. But: "I lost my father's approval and I'm never getting it back." "I lost the person I was before the assault." "I lost twenty years to a career that didn't want me." "I lost the family I thought I was building."

The specificity matters because grief is specific. You can't mourn an abstraction. You can only mourn a particular absence. A particular face no longer at the table. A particular future that dissolved.

Unmourned loss stays raw. It doesn't heal — it festers. The energy of grief, unprocessed, becomes fuel for rage or despair. The person who cannot cry will eventually scream — or go silent in a way that's worse than screaming.

What is gone must be recognized as gone before movement toward what remains becomes possible.

Mourning is not wallowing. It's integration.
Naming loss is not dwelling. It's the door that allows you to stop dwelling.

Eighth: Let Pressure Release.

When internal pressure reaches capacity, it must go somewhere. This is physics, not weakness.

Tears are stored pressure leaving the system. The tightness in the chest, the lump in the throat, the burning behind the eyes — these are release valves. The body knows what the mind resists: that pressure unexpressed doesn't disappear. It accumulates.

The simulation taught that release is weakness. That composure equals strength. That holding it together is the goal. That the person who doesn't cry is stronger than the person who does.

The simulation lied.

What won't release safely will release destructively. The pressure that doesn't exit as tears exits as rage. Or collapse. Or violence against self or others. Or the slow internal corrosion that medicine calls chronic stress and the body calls dying slowly.

This step often follows the seventh naturally. Once loss is named and grief is allowed, the pressure has somewhere to go. The tears come not because they're forced but because they finally can. The body, given permission, knows what to do.

The permission often comes from witness. A person who has never cried in front of another human being discovers that the presence of someone who stays — who doesn't flinch, doesn't fix, doesn't look away — creates a container strong enough to hold what's been compressed for years.

Release happens when the container is stronger than the pressure. Community provides the container that solitude cannot.

Ninth: Stop the Scattering.

Energy dispersed into avoidance, distraction, pleasure-seeking, anything that prevents sustained presence — this energy must reconsolidate.

This step is about attention. Not what you're consuming (that was fourth) or what you're serving (that was fifth) — but where your awareness actually lives moment to moment.

The scattered self lacks capacity for sustained movement. Attention fragmented across dozens of inputs cannot focus on single direction. The constant checking, the reflexive scrolling, the inability to sit with silence for more than thirty seconds — these aren't character flaws. They're the attention patterns of a system that learned to scatter as a form of self-protection.

Scattering numbs. That's its function. If attention never rests on any one thing long enough to feel it, the painful things stay blurred. But so does everything else. The scattered person can't access joy any more than they can access grief. The numbing is comprehensive.

Reconsolidation isn't punishment — it's prerequisite. The person who has done the hard work of steps six, seven, and eight — who has felt what was avoided, named what was lost, let the pressure release — discovers that the scattering is no longer necessary. The thing it was protecting against has been processed. The attention can come home.

Rebuilding requires gathered resources.
Running and rebuilding cannot happen simultaneously.

Tenth: Now Flexibility Returns.

After the sequence — defenses lowered, position held, stability approached, contamination released, interior simplified, feelings felt, losses named and mourned, pressure discharged, attention gathered — something becomes possible that wasn't possible before.

Teachability.

Not smallness. Not self-deprecation. Not performed humility that collapses at the first challenge.

Actual flexibility. The capacity to receive feedback without collapse. To change direction when evidence arrives. To admit uncertainty without identity crisis. To hear a challenging idea and let it reach consideration instead of converting it to threat.

This is what the workshop couldn't produce. What the forgiveness book couldn't generate. What all the good advice couldn't accomplish. What the simulation said was weakness and the ancient design says is strength.

Humility isn't the starting point.
It's what becomes possible after everything else has been done.

And this is what the simulation could never simulate — because this can't be performed. It can't be optimized. It can't be achieved through individual effort or purchased through any program.

It's what happens when the layers come off in the right order. When the design is respected rather than overridden. When the sequence that was always there — encoded in ancient practice, confirmed by modern evidence, available to anyone willing to stop running long enough to begin — is finally followed.

The simulation built the layers. Empire enforced them. The marketplace profited from them.

The design removes them. One at a time. In order. Together.

Not back to Eden. Not to perfection. Not to certainty.

Back to the flexibility that was there before the first framework froze it. Back to the human the simulation was built to prevent.

What Happens When Steps Get Skipped

A man attends a corporate workshop on emotional intelligence. The instructor is compelling. The concepts make sense. He decides to be more open, more flexible, more receptive.

The decision lasts until the next meeting where his idea gets challenged. Counter-argument forming before the sentence finishes. Defense mobilizing. Challenge deflected. The workshop might as well have never happened.

Not because the teaching was wrong. Because the teaching couldn't land.

A woman reads about forgiveness. The arguments are sound. She understands intellectually why holding resentment poisons the holder more than the target. She decides to forgive.

The decision lasts until the next encounter with the person who wounded her. The body tightens. The anger surfaces. The forgiveness evaporates like morning fog.

Not because she didn't mean it. Because meaning it wasn't enough.

A teenager starts meditating. Downloads the app. Does the breathing exercises. Feels calmer for twenty minutes. Returns to the same anxious patterns by lunch.

Not because mindfulness doesn't work. Because mindfulness installed on top of unprocessed grief, unnamed loss, and unreleased pressure is decoration on a crumbling foundation.

The "humble" person explodes in rage. The "forgiving" person discovers the resentment intact. The "mindful" person returns to the same anxious patterns.

Not because they failed morally.
Because they skipped structurally.

The nervous system has order of operations. The psyche has prerequisites. Trying to install flexibility on a foundation of rigidity doesn't produce a flexible person. It produces a rigid person with flexible vocabulary.

The work cannot be skipped.
It can only be done or avoided.

What This Enables

A man who completed the sequence sits in the same corporate workshop. Different year, different topic. The instructor says something that challenges his current thinking.

The old response would have been immediate: counter-argument forming before the sentence finished. Defense mobilizing. Challenge deflected.

Instead, a pause. The words land. Consideration happens. The challenge reaches formation.

"Huh. I hadn't thought of it that way."

Not performance. Actual reception. The pathway stayed open.

A woman encounters the person who wounded her. The body still tightens — some responses are permanent. But beneath the tightening, something different.

The grief was felt. The loss was named. The pressure was released.

The wound is still a wound. But it's a wound that has been tended rather than defended. Acknowledged rather than armored.

Forgiveness becomes possible — not as decision, but as consequence. The natural result of a system that processed what needed processing.

The Weight of Solitude

Some of this work can happen alone.

Defenses can lower in solitude. Position can be held without witness. Contamination can be released. The interior can simplify. Attention can gather.

But steps six through eight — feeling what was avoided, naming what was lost, letting pressure release — these are where solitude becomes dangerous and community becomes design.

Pain surfacing in isolation can overwhelm. Grief named to an empty room can echo until it becomes unbearable. Pressure releasing without a container can flood rather than flow.

The sequence works because it reflects design. And the design is plural.

A person isolated by geography or circumstance can begin the work. Can make real progress through the early steps. Can prepare the ground.

But the deepest layers — the loss that was never named, the grief that was never witnessed, the pressure that was never held by anyone — these almost always require another human being in the room. Not fixing. Not advising. Just staying.

This is why recovery communities exist. Why therapy works when it works. Why the ancient practices were never solitary — they were communal. The design knew what the simulation denies: that some weight only moves when someone else helps carry it.

The work can start alone.
The deepest work rarely finishes alone.

The Promise

When resistance stops, something arrives.

Not reward for good behavior. Not transaction for obedience. Just natural consequence of removing interference.

Some name it grace. Others name it flow, alignment, finally getting out of my own way.

The name matters less than the experience: when the pathway opens, what was always flowing can finally reach its destination.

Guidance arrives because guidance was always arriving.
The work doesn't earn this. The work removes what was blocking it.
Stop deflecting what was always coming toward you, and it arrives.

Tomorrow

The person who chose Path A wakes up in a different reality than the person who chose Path B.

Not perfect reality. Still carrying remnants of the framework. Still feeling the old pull. Still living in a world where the simulation operates, the merchants profit, and the algorithm optimizes.

But alive. Conscious. Present. Capable of choice.

The trajectory has changed. The pathway has redirected. The momentum has slowed enough for something other than reaction to become possible.

Not permanently. Not perfectly. The pressure could build again. The totalization could reassert. The convergence could realign.

But not today. Not tonight. Not in this moment.

Tomorrow exists.

And tomorrow asks only one question:

What happens when the unbearable weight gets shared?

When finite beings stop trying to be infinite.
When isolated humans return to refuge.
When the worthlessness lie gets rejected — not through individual strength, but through collective practice.

The simulation broke the design.
Empire weaponized isolation.
The marketplace extracted value from suffering.

But the design remains.
The architecture persists.
The ancient path waits.

For anyone who pauses long enough to see it.

Chapter 30

STAYING CONNECTED ACROSS DIFFERENCE

Walking the Ancient Path Together

TWO FRIENDS SIT across a table. Coffee between them. Years of history beneath them.

One mentions a political figure. The other's face changes. Micro-expressions cascade: surprise, then judgment, then the slight withdrawal that precedes argument.

"I can't believe you actually support —"

"I didn't say I support, I said —"

"But you just —"

"You're not listening to what I actually —"

Twenty minutes later, one leaves. The other stays, staring at cold coffee. Something has torn. Not the friendship exactly — but the ease of it. The assumption that they could say anything.

They'll talk again. But differently now. Certain topics will be avoided. Certain thoughts will stay internal. The connection survives, but narrower. More careful. Less alive.

This is what the simulation taught:
Disagreement threatens belonging.

Watch how it operates:

A family gathers for a holiday. Within an hour, the conversation drifts toward contested territory. Someone states a position. Someone else's body tenses. A third person tries to change the subject. A fourth pushes back.

Voices rise. Faces flush. The meal continues in silence, or erupts into argument, or fragments into separate rooms.

Afterward, the post-mortems: "I can't believe he said that." "She's been brainwashed." "We just can't talk about anything real anymore."

The family stays connected — technically. But whole regions of thought become no-fly zones. Relationship continues within shrinking boundaries.

Each boundary creates pressure.
Pressure accumulates.
Eventually, some families stop gathering at all.

A person scrolls through contacts. Dozens of names. Maybe hundreds.

How many could they call right now — not for small talk, but for actual conversation about something that matters? How many would stay on the line if disagreement emerged? How many relationships could survive one of them saying, "I see this completely differently than you"?

The scroll continues. The number shrinks.

The simulation didn't just isolate people physically.
It made connection conditional upon agreement.

The Equation That Breaks Everything

The training installed an equation:

Disagreement = Threat to Belonging

Once this equation runs, certain outcomes become inevitable:

Agreement becomes performance. People say what maintains connection rather than what they actually think. Authenticity decreases. Relationships become mutual performance of acceptable positions.

Beliefs become identity. If disagreement threatens belonging, then beliefs must be defended like self. Challenges to ideas feel like attacks on existence. Flexibility becomes impossible.

Tribes form around positions. People sort into groups where agreement is guaranteed. Echo chambers aren't accidents — they're refuge from the exhaustion of conditional belonging.

Opponents become enemies. Those who disagree aren't just wrong — they're threats. The same protective mechanisms that guard against physical danger activate against ideological difference.

Conversation becomes combat. Every exchange carries stakes. Every discussion risks rupture. The goal shifts from understanding to winning, from exploring to defending.

This is the water everyone swims in.
The training so complete it feels like nature.

But it's not nature. It's installation.

And what was installed can be uninstalled.

When the Equation Breaks

What if disagreement didn't threaten belonging?
Not agreement — disagreement. Actual difference. Real divergence in how two people see the same reality.

What if that divergence could exist inside connection rather than threatening it?
Some relationships operate this way. Not many. But enough to prove it's possible.

A grandfather and grandson sit on a porch. Their political views share almost nothing. Their news sources don't overlap. Their predictions about the future contradict entirely.

They've been talking for three hours.

Not arguing. Talking. The grandson explains what he sees. The grandfather listens, asks questions, pushes back, tells stories from decades the grandson never lived. Neither convinces the other. Neither tries to.

At the end, the grandfather says: "I still think you're wrong about most of this. But I understand better why you see it that way."

The grandson drives home, thinking. Not converted — but loosened. Some certainty softened into question. Some assumption revealed as assumption rather than fact.

The connection isn't despite the disagreement.
The connection contains the disagreement.

When the equation breaks, something different becomes possible:

Curiosity replaces defense. Ideas can be examined rather than protected. Thinking becomes possible again.

Identity separates from belief. You can be wrong about something without being diminished. Error becomes information rather than exposure.

Connection deepens through difference. Agreement requires nothing. Staying present through difference requires everything.

Opponents become people. Those who see differently aren't threats — they're access to reality you haven't encountered yet.

This isn't a different formula. It's a different capacity. And capacity requires practice.

The Skill

This is skill, not sentiment.

The warm feeling of "I should be more open-minded" accomplishes nothing. The vague intention to "really listen" collapses under pressure. Good wishes don't survive contact with someone who sees the world as genuinely threatening your deepest values.

Skill survives what sentiment cannot.

The skill has components:

The pause before response.

Not agreement. Not disagreement. Just pause.

The training installed immediate reaction: hear position, generate counter-position, deliver counter-position. The sequence happens faster than conscious thought.

The skill interrupts the sequence. Hear position. Pause. Let the position exist in awareness without immediate evaluation. Notice what happens in the body. Then — only then — respond.

The pause is not passive. It's the most active thing possible: refusing the automatic.

The question that isn't attack.

"Help me understand why you see it that way."

Not "How can you possibly believe that?" Not "Don't you realize that's wrong?" Not the rhetorical questions that are really statements with question marks.

Actual curiosity. The recognition that this person, with their history and their wounds and their particular path through life, arrived at this position through some process. What was the process?

Curiosity about the path isn't agreement with the destination.

The admission that costs nothing and changes everything.

"I might be wrong about parts of this."

Not "I'm wrong." Not abandoning position. Just acknowledging what's true for every finite being who's ever held a belief: certainty is not available to humans. Not about politics. Not about religion. Not about what's happening in the world or what should happen next.

The simulation required certainty. Reality doesn't provide it.

Admitting uncertainty isn't weakness. It's accuracy.

And accuracy, spoken aloud, changes the room. The other person's defenses — raised against the attack they expected — lose their target. The conversation shifts register. Something else becomes possible.

The capacity to stay when staying is uncomfortable.

The moment disagreement surfaces, every instinct says: leave. Change the subject. End the conversation. Exit the relationship if necessary.

The skill is staying.

Not staying to win. Not staying to convince. Staying to remain in connection with another human who sees differently. Staying because the connection matters more than the agreement. Staying because leaving confirms the equation the simulation installed.

What Staying Accomplishes

A woman notices her brother changing. His social media darker. His references more extreme. The online communities he mentions sound like pipelines she's read about.

She wants to argue. To send counterarguments. To debate him back to reason.

Instead, she stays.

Texts that aren't about politics. Calls that ask about his life, his work, his actual day. Visits that don't mention the algorithm-fed ideology he's absorbing.

He knows she disagrees. She hasn't hidden it. But she hasn't made the disagreement the condition of connection.

Six months later, he's still in the ideology. But he's also still talking to her. Still has one voice outside the closed system. Still reachable.

She didn't pull him out. She kept a door open.

When the ideology eventually fails him — when it promises what it can't deliver, when the certainty cracks — she'll still be there. Not saying "I told you so." Just present. Still connected.

The connection she maintained is the crack in his totalization.
Not argument. Presence.

A man holds political views his entire social circle considers repugnant. He knows this. He's been told — publicly, repeatedly, with increasing volume.

One friend stays.

They argue sometimes. Vigorously. The friend doesn't pretend to agree, doesn't soften his challenges, doesn't perform neutrality he doesn't feel.

But he also doesn't leave.

"I think you're wrong about this. I think it's causing harm. And I'm not going anywhere."

The man has many people telling him he's right — online, in communities organized around agreement. He has many people telling him he's evil — also online, in communities organized around opposition.

He has one person telling him he's wrong *and* staying.
That one person has more influence than all the others combined.

Not through superior argument. Through maintained relationship.

The Reversal

Here's what the simulation hid:

Certainty doesn't strengthen connection. It prevents it.

The person who knows they're right has nothing to learn from the person who's wrong. The conversation is already over before it starts. One will teach; one will learn. One will win; one will lose.

But two people who hold their views without certainty — who know they might be wrong, who've been wrong before, who understand that human perception is limited and human reasoning is flawed — these people can actually meet.

Not in agreement. In shared uncertainty.

"I think I see something you don't see. What do you see that I might be missing?"

This isn't relativism. It's humility.

The views aren't equal—one might actually be more accurate than the other. But the viewers are equal: finite, limited, capable of error, in need of other perspectives to see what they cannot see alone.

Certainty isolates.
Uncertainty connects.

Only the simulation requires certainty.

Where to Practice

This skill doesn't require a polarized Thanksgiving dinner to develop.

It develops in small moments:

Someone at work holds a view that triggers the automatic reaction. Instead of internal dismissal or external argument — pause. Curiosity. "How did you come to see it that way?"

Someone online posts something that generates immediate counter-response. Instead of the comment already forming — pause. Recognition that this is a person, with a path, who arrived at this place somehow. Perhaps say nothing. Perhaps ask a question. Perhaps simply refuse the combat.

Someone close — friend, family, partner — expresses something that feels wrong. Instead of correction — pause. Exploration. "Tell me more about that."

Each small practice builds capacity for larger ones.

The skill that can stay present when a family member shares a conspiracy theory is the skill that can stay present when a stranger expresses a worldview that seems dangerous.

Same skill. Different scale.

The Limit

This isn't instruction to maintain connection with everyone in all circumstances.

Some connections are unsafe. Some relationships require distance. Some people have demonstrated through action — not just belief — that proximity causes harm.

The skill is discernment, not dissolution of all boundaries.

But most of the relationships that fractured over the last decade didn't fracture because of genuine danger. They fractured because the simulation trained everyone to experience disagreement as danger.

Uncle with different politics: probably not actual danger.
Coworker with different religion: probably not actual danger.
Friend whose life went a different direction: probably not actual danger.

Felt like danger. Activated the same responses as danger. Generated the same impulse to flee or fight.
But feeling isn't fact. Training isn't truth.

The skill discerns between actual threat and simulated threat — and stays present through the simulated ones.

What This Creates

A person who can stay connected across difference becomes something rare:

A bridge.

Not a bridge that pretends both sides are equal. Not a bridge that has no position. The bridge knows what it thinks. The bridge has convictions, values, beliefs.

But the bridge also has relationships on multiple sides. The bridge can translate: "Here's what they're actually trying to say." The bridge can humanize: "They're not evil; here's what's driving that position." The bridge can connect: "You two should actually talk."

The simulation profits from division. Every severed connection reduces the friction that prevents extremism. Every lost relationship removes a reality-check that might interrupt radicalization.

The bridge restores friction. Maintains reality-checks. Keeps doors open that the simulation wants closed.

This is not neutrality. It's something more active.
Neutrality avoids conflict. This posture endures it.

Refusing to let disagreement accomplish the isolation that makes everything worse.

The Posture

Internal work cleared the interference.
This chapter describes the posture that becomes possible after clearing.

A posture of held uncertainty. Of genuine curiosity. Of staying when staying is hard.

Not because disagreement doesn't matter — it does. Not because all views are equal — they're not. Not because conflict should be avoided — sometimes it shouldn't.

But because connection maintained across difference is the opposite of what the simulation wants.

And what the simulation wants is usually a good map of what to refuse.

"I might be wrong about parts of this. What do you see?"

That sentence, spoken genuinely, changes almost any conversation.

Try it once. Watch what happens.

The room shifts. The defenses lower — not just theirs, but yours. Something becomes possible that wasn't possible in the combat frame.

Not agreement. Not conversion.
Contact.
Two finite beings, uncertain about everything, staying in the room with each other.

That's the skill.
That's the practice.
That's what makes everything else possible.

The person who doesn't need to win can stay in the room.

Chapter 31

THE RHYTHM THAT HOLDS

Accumulated Disorder Needs Release

FRIDAY, 6:47 PM. A woman sets her phone face-down on the kitchen counter.

Not dramatically. Just a small motion—screen to wood—that marks a boundary.

The week doesn't vanish. The emails remain unread. The anxieties haven't resolved. Everything that demanded attention five minutes ago still exists.

But something has shifted.

She lights candles. Not for anyone watching. The apartment is empty. Just flame meeting wick, light spreading across surfaces that spent the week unseen.

Then she sits.

Not to meditate. Not to optimize. Not to accomplish the sitting. Just to sit with what remains when the producing stops.

The first twenty minutes are uncomfortable. The phantom notifications. The urge to check. The restlessness of a nervous system trained for constant input suddenly receiving none.

Then the apartment starts to exist.

The quality of the light. The sounds from the street. The accumulated week beginning to discharge through attention itself.

She eats dinner she prepared earlier—food made by hands rather than delivered by app. Later, a book. Physical pages. Later still, sleep. Earlier than weeknights. Deeper.

Saturday morning arrives differently. Not with alarm. Not with immediate inventory of what's behind. The hours stretch without agenda. She walks. Calls a friend—actual voice. In the afternoon, a neighbor knocks unexpectedly. They sit on the balcony. Talk. Watch the light change.

None of this is productive. None of it optimizes anything.

All of it is different activity.

Twenty-four hours later, the phone turns over. The world's demands resume. But something has reset. The weight is the same, but the capacity to carry it has restored.

This is Sabbath. Not religion. Not rule. A technology older than the anxieties it was designed to address.

She didn't have to understand it. She just had to keep it.

The Physics

Here is what the simulation never mentions:

Every system accumulates disorder. This isn't philosophy. It's thermodynamics.

The human nervous system is not exempt.

Seven days of inputs—notifications, comparisons, performances, demands—build pressure. The body absorbs it. Stores it. Compresses it. By day six, the compression approaches capacity.

Without release, day seven's inputs overflow into irritability, anxiety, hypervigilance. The system designed for rhythmic discharge begins operating in chronic overload.

This happens whether anyone believes it happens. The physics don't require faith.

The ancient word is *Shabbat*.

Not "rest" as English speakers understand it. Something more precise:

The weekly stabilization of what exists by ceasing the labor that transforms and beginning the activity that restores.

Not stopping. Switching.

From production to restoration. From reshaping to holding. From transformation to stabilization.

The simulation taught that rest means collapse on the couch, numb with entertainment, recover enough to resume production Monday.

That's not Sabbath. That's maintenance of the extraction schedule. Sabbath is different activity. The kind of doing that prevents collapse. Not absence of motion—redirection of motion.

What It Actually Does

Five functions. Each necessary.

Cessation of transformative pressure. Six days of pushing, producing, reshaping. Sabbath stops the push. Not because work is wrong—but pushing without pause accumulates into pathology. The woman who sets her phone down isn't earning rest. She's preventing collapse.

Active stabilization of relationships. The simulation fragments. Atomizes. Sabbath gathers. The ancient practice wasn't solitary retreat—it was eating together, being present together. The neighbor who knocked wasn't accident. The rhythm creates conditions for connection.

Sabbath is inherently plural. Designed for we, not just me. The person practicing alone is practicing half of it—sustaining themselves until the others appear.

Healing and restoration. Sabbath isn't about doing nothing. It's about doing what heals. This is what Jesus demonstrated, healing on Sabbath despite religious objection. Not violating Sabbath—fulfilling it. The religious leaders saw rule-breaking. Jesus saw function-completion.

Memorial and reflection. The doom cycle operates through generalization. "Nothing ever works." "I always fail." The lies are unfalsifiable because they're stated abstractly.

Sabbath memorial interrupts with specifics. Once per week: *What actually happened these seven days?*

"Monday I couldn't function until noon. Tuesday was manageable. Wednesday I had a conversation that felt real. Thursday the weight returned. Friday I made dinner with my hands. Saturday I'm here, noting this."

Fifty-two entries of "this actually happened" cannot coexist with "nothing ever changes."

This isn't journaling as self-improvement. It's memorial. Stones of remembrance. Evidence against the lie.

Reconnection with Source. Twenty-four hours of existing without performing. Being without producing. Presence without audience.

For those who locate this in relationship with the divine—Sabbath becomes that walk. For those who don't—the reconnection still occurs. The physics operate regardless of the theology.

What Jesus Actually Did

If Sabbath is essential, why did Jesus seem to break it?

Look closer. On Sabbath, Jesus healed. He restored. He lifted burdens. He refused to let human-made fences choke life.

He performed the exact function of Sabbath.

The religious leaders saw transgression because they'd converted Sabbath into prohibition list. They'd frozen the rhythm into rules.

He embodied its function while transgressing their interpretation.

"The Sabbath was made for man, not man for the Sabbath."

This isn't abolition. It's clarification.

For those who follow him: he didn't release you from Sabbath. He demonstrated what Sabbath is for.

For those who don't: the pattern still describes what works. Healing is Sabbath. Restoration is Sabbath. The function operates whether you name its source or not.

Why This Prevents Violence

Return to the pattern this book has traced: Uncertainty. Narrative. Fear. Isolation. Rage. Violence.

The pattern doesn't require monsters. It requires accumulation without discharge.

Each day's pressure adds to the previous. Without regular discharge, the pressure builds toward threshold. Small provocations trigger large responses. The system becomes volatile.

Sabbath is the weekly off-ramp.

This isn't metaphor. It's mechanism.

Fifty-two times per year, the pattern gets interrupted. Fifty-two times per year, the accumulation discharges. Fifty-two times per year, the threshold stays unreached.

How to Begin

Sabbath requires four things: a time, a boundary, a different activity, repetition.

A time.
The original rhythm: Friday sunset to Saturday sunset. Not arbitrary—coordinated. The power wasn't just in the rest. It was in the shared rest. When everyone stops together, the pressure to continue disappears. Community becomes possible because everyone is available.

This is what's been lost.

When shops closed on Sundays—even if the wrong biblical day—the collective synchronization still functioned. You couldn't work even if you wanted to. The rhythm was enforced by shared practice, not individual willpower.

Now everyone chooses their own day. Or no day. The person practicing Sabbath swims against a current that never stops.

This is honest: Sabbath practiced alone, on a day you chose yourself, is not the full design. It's sustaining — but partial. The rhythm wants community. Wants shared time.

If you have community that shares the rhythm — practice with them, on their day. The specific shared day is the point. The collective synchronization is the mechanism. Choosing your own day is better than nothing, but it's a different practice.

If you don't have this yet, practice anyway. The partial is better than nothing. But know what you're missing. The design is plural. The rhythm wants we.

What stabilizes the system isn't rest alone — it's rest that arrives on schedule.

A boundary.
The phone turns face-down. The laptop closes. The boundary is physical before it's psychological. The device that connects to the simulation gets placed out of reach.

The first few weeks feel like withdrawal. The difficulty is information—it reveals how captured you've been.

Stay with it. What felt unbearable at week one becomes unremarkable by week six.

A different activity.
Not nothing. Different something.

Things that heal: walking, making, gathering, tending. Things that connect: eating together, talking without screens. Things that memorialize: reflecting on what actually happened, noting them specifically.

Repetition.
One Sabbath accomplishes little. Fifty accomplish everything.

Not willpower holding it in place—architecture. The week shapes itself around the coming rest. The system stabilizes because stability has become reliable.

This Week

This Friday evening, try it.

Set the phone face-down. Sit with what remains when the producing stops. Notice the discomfort. Notice it passing.

Eat something you made. Walk somewhere without destination. Sleep when tired.

At some point, take ten minutes: What actually happened this week? Be specific.

Saturday evening, let it close. Notice how Monday feels.

Try it again the following week. And again.

The ancient path isn't ancient because it's traditional. It's ancient because it's structural.

The nervous system needs what the nervous system needs.

Sabbath isn't stopping. It's switching—from transformation to stabilization, from production to restoration, from reshaping to holding.

Practices That Work Alone (And Make You Findable)

Maintaining the Pattern in Isolation

A WOMAN LIVES in a town with no one who sees what she sees.

She looked. Tried the churches — found performance. Tried the meetups — found networking. Tried the online communities — found more simulation dressed as alternative.

No weekly circle. No Wednesday night gathering. No community of people practicing what she's recognized.

She's alone in this. For now. Maybe for a while.

The question becomes: What does she do with what she sees?

She could wait. Many do. Wait for the right community to appear. The right people to arrive. The right conditions to align.

Waiting feels reasonable. Responsible, even. Why practice alone what's meant for together?

But waiting has a cost. The seeing fades without practice to anchor it. The capacity built through internal work erodes without rhythm to maintain it. The skill of staying connected atrophies without regular use.

A person who waits for perfect conditions often finds themselves back in the simulation before conditions arrive.

She decides not to wait.

Not because she has answers. Because she has recognition—and recognition requires response.

The practices she adopts aren't invented. They're patterns that worked for people in situations worse than hers. Rhythms that kept humans human through exile, persecution, displacement.

If the patterns worked in Babylon, they can work in a small town with no community.

She begins.

A man tries the usual solutions. Meditation apps. Weekend getaways when he can afford them. The occasional digital detox that lasts until Monday morning.

Nothing holds. The pressure rebuilds faster than the solutions release it.

Then he tries something different. Not reduction of inputs — complete cessation. Not occasional break — predictable rhythm. Not when he feels like it — whether he feels like it or not.

Twenty-four hours. Phone off. Work stopped. Screens dark.

The first few weeks feel like withdrawal. The phantom vibrations. The reaching for absent device. The anxiety of what might be happening without his attention.

But around week three, something shifts.

The nervous system learns: this is coming. Every seven days, release happens. The compression doesn't need to reach critical because discharge is scheduled.

Sabbath isn't religious observance. It's scheduled entropy release.

The man doesn't call it Sabbath. Calls it his "offline day." The name doesn't matter. The rhythm does.

Six days of accumulation. One day of release.
The pattern works because it matches design — not because anyone believes in the design.

The woman in the small town adopts the same pattern. Friday evening to Saturday evening—the original rhythm, though she doesn't know why that particular timing.

She discovers the why through practice: it creates a hinge in the week. The pressure of Monday through Friday releases. Saturday evening through Sunday becomes genuinely restful rather than anxious anticipation of Monday.

The pattern works alone.

No community required. No one watching. No accountability partner.

Just body responding to rhythm the way bodies do.

Morning Orientation

A person wakes. Before full consciousness, before intention, before choice— the first orientation happens.

This moment matters more than most realize.

The mind waking from sleep is malleable. Undefended. The first inputs shape the trajectory of hours that follow. What enters in those initial moments becomes the lens for the day.

Two options exist. Not as moral achievement—as gravitational direction.

Gratitude or grievance.

The feed offers grievance. Scroll for thirty seconds: here's what's wrong, what's threatening, what you're behind on, what others have that you lack. Grievance arrives effortlessly. The simulation serves it like breakfast.

Gratitude requires intention. Not forced positivity—just inventory. What exists. What functions. What remains. The body that woke. The breath that continued through sleep. The fact of another day when many don't receive one.

This isn't optimism. It's orientation.

The woman in the small town experiments. One week of phone-first mornings. One week of gratitude-first mornings. Not journaling—just inventory. Internal noting of what exists before engaging what demands.

The difference is measurable. Not in mood exactly—in capacity. The gratitude-first days hold more. Absorb more. Respond rather than react more.

The practice takes two minutes. No equipment required. No community to validate.

Morning orientation works alone.

A man keeps a note by his bed. Three words: "What exists today?"

Not affirmations. Not goals. Just the question.

He answers it before anything else. Before the phone. Before the worry. Before the day's demands load into consciousness.

Some mornings the answer is minimal: "Coffee. Sunlight. This breath."
Some mornings more arrives: "That project I'm building. The friend I'm meeting. The fact that I get to try again."

The practice doesn't eliminate difficulty. It establishes ground before difficulty arrives.

What enters first shapes what follows.

Creating Over Consuming

The simulation offers infinite consumption. Endless scroll. Bottomless content. Always something to watch, read, react to.

Consumption leaves no trace. Hours pass. Nothing remains. The consumer is slightly more depleted than before, slightly less capable of production.

Creation reverses the flow.

A person who makes something — anything — exists differently than a person who only takes in. The maker has externalized something internal. Has proof of their own agency. Has added rather than subtracted.

This doesn't require talent. Doesn't require audience. Doesn't require quality.

Bread baked and eaten by the baker alone is still creation.
Words written and read by no one are still creation.
Garden tended for private satisfaction is still creation.

The practice is direction of energy: outward rather than inward. Making rather than taking.

The woman starts small. One meal per week made from ingredients rather than packages. Not performance — practice. The hands working. The attention focused. The result consumed with awareness of its origin.

Something shifts. The meal isn't just food. It's evidence. She can make things. She can transform raw material into something that sustains.

The simulation said she was consumer. The bread says otherwise.

A man stops watching other people live.

Not entirely — he still sees movies, reads books, enjoys art. But the hours of passive observation of strangers' curated lives—that stops.

The hours reclaimed become hours of making. Nothing significant at first. Fixing things around the house. Learning an instrument badly. Writing thoughts no one will read.

The content of the making matters less than the direction of it.

Energy moving outward rebuilds something that energy moving inward depletes.

Creating works best alone — before audience becomes motive, before performance contaminates practice.

Presence at Meals

A person eats three times a day, more or less. That's twenty-one opportunities per week for practice.

Most meals happen in absence. Screen playing. Mind elsewhere. Food entering body without registration.

The practice is simple: one meal per day with nothing else. No screen. No reading. No distraction.

Just food. Just eating. Just the experience of sustenance entering body.

The woman tries it. Lunch alone at her kitchen table. No phone. No background noise. Just the sandwich and the eating.

The first few minutes are uncomfortable. The silence feels wrong. The absence of input creates restlessness.

Then the food starts to exist. Textures register. Flavors arrive. The act of eating becomes actual rather than automatic.

Twelve minutes. That's all. Twelve minutes of presence in a day of absence.

But those twelve minutes create reference point. This is what presence feels like. This is what the body notices when noticing is allowed.

The practice extends. Not forced—just noticed. Other moments begin to register. The walk to the car. The shower. The spaces between tasks.

Presence practiced in small moments becomes available in larger ones.

A man realizes he hasn't tasted his coffee in months. Drinks it every morning. Never tastes it.

He starts there. One cup. Full attention.

The coffee is different than he remembered. Better in some ways. More bitter in others. Actual rather than assumed.

He's been living in assumptions. Eating assumed food. Drinking assumed coffee. Experiencing assumed life.

The meal practice interrupts assumption with actuality.

This works alone. Perhaps only works alone at first—before returning to meals with others, now capable of presence that wasn't possible before.

The Signal

Here's what the woman didn't expect:

The practices make her visible.

Not through announcement. Not through evangelism. Through divergence.

She leaves work on Friday afternoon while others continue. Someone notices. "Hot date?" "No, just unplugging for the day." "Every Friday?" "Every Friday."

A conversation starts. Not about religion or philosophy. About rhythm. About why. About what it's like.

The practice created signal. The signal created connection.

She brings lunch from home. Real food, obviously prepared. A coworker comments. "You made that?" "This morning." "That looks amazing."

Another conversation. About making versus buying. About time and attention. About what's possible when consumption isn't default.

The practice created signal. The signal created contact.

The man mentions his offline day to a neighbor. Not preaching — just explaining why he can't be reached on Saturdays.

The neighbor's face changes. "I've been thinking about trying something like that. Does it actually work?"

A relationship shifts. Not from strangers to friends — but from neighbors to people who might practice something together.

The practice created signal. The signal created possibility.

This is how scattered people find each other.

Not through organization. Not through announcement. Not through recruitment.

Through visible practice.

The practices that sustain you in isolation are the same practices that make you findable to others. The rhythm that releases your entropy is the rhythm that identifies you to others keeping the same rhythm.

You don't hide a light under a basket. Not because hiding is wrong — because hiding prevents the light from doing what light does.

Private practice sustains you.
Public practice makes you findable.

Both are necessary.

What to Look For

If seeking others, certain patterns indicate refuge architecture:

Predictable rhythm. Communities that gather consistently — same time, same place, week after week. Not events but patterns. The consistency itself signals something about what they're building.

Shared burden. Groups where need is spoken and met. Mutual aid networks. Recovery communities. Religious gatherings where people actually know each other's struggles. Not performance of community — actual interdependence.

Diversity held together. Spaces where people disagree but don't leave. Where difference exists within belonging. Where homogeneity hasn't been mistaken for health.

Presence over content. Gatherings where showing up matters more than what's said. Where bodies in proximity do work that words can't accomplish. Where the container matters as much as what's contained.

These exist. Not everywhere — but more places than the simulation suggests.

Recovery meetings. Religious communities that haven't calcified. Neighborhood groups organized around mutual care. Maker spaces. Community gardens. Choirs and bands and teams that practice together.

Different names. Different contexts. Same architecture.

The question isn't whether refuge exists.
The question is whether you're findable to it — and it to you.

Beginning

The woman in the small town has no community. Not yet. Maybe not for years.

But she has practice. She has rhythm. She has visible divergence that creates signal.

She's becoming findable.

And in the meantime, the practices work. The entropy releases. The mornings orient toward gratitude. The meals arrive with presence. The creating continues.

Not waiting for conditions to align.
Not postponing practice until community appears.
Practicing now. Here. Alone if necessary.

Because the practices work alone.
They work because reality works that way — not because community validates them.

And because, eventually, practice creates conditions for contact.

Tomorrow

Tomorrow the choice arrives again.

Sabbath or grind.
Gratitude or grievance.
Creating or consuming.
Presence or absence.

No one watches. No one scores. No community holds accountability.

Just the question: What kind of life are you building? And will others who are building the same be able to find you?

The practices are available.
The rhythm is offered.
The signal is possible.

Begin.

Chapter 33

WHEN REFUGE APPEARS

Recognizing and Joining Real Community

A MAN WALKS into a room he almost didn't enter.

Wednesday evening. Community center basement. Fluorescent lights humming. Folding chairs arranged in a circle. Coffee that's been sitting too long.

He'd driven past twice before. Sat in the parking lot once, then left. The resistance was physical — body refusing to cross threshold into visible need.

Tonight the loneliness outweighed the resistance.

He sits. Doesn't speak. Watches.

People arrive. They know each other — that's obvious from how they move, how they greet, the shorthand of established relationship. An insider's space. He's outside it.

The meeting starts. Someone shares. Not performance — actual disclosure. Struggle spoken without shame. Failure named without collapse.

Others listen. No one fixes. No one advises. Just witnesses.

Something in the room is different than anything he's experienced. He can't name it yet. Just knows: this is not the simulation.

A woman finds a different room. Saturday morning. Back of a bookstore. Eight people discussing a text none of them fully understands.

She came for the ideas. She stays for something else.

The discussion is rigorous — people disagree, push back, challenge interpretations. But no one leaves. No one sulks. The disagreement doesn't threaten the container.

After an hour, the formal discussion ends. No one moves. Conversations continue in clusters. Someone asks about her week. Actually asks — not as performance, but as interest.

She'd forgotten this was possible. People staying. People caring. Connection that didn't require agreement or performance or careful management of presentation.

She returns the next Saturday. And the next.

Recognition

Refuge doesn't announce itself.

No sign says "Here is what you're looking for." No neon marks the threshold between simulation and alternative. The rooms look ordinary. The people look ordinary. From outside, nothing distinguishes these gatherings from any other.

The recognition happens from inside.

Something in the room works differently. The usual rules—perform, compete, protect—don't apply. The weight everyone carries becomes visible and shared. The defenses that exhaust themselves in every other space can lower here.

Not paradise. Not perfection. Just refuge.

A space where humans can be human without the simulation's constant interference.

The man attends for three months before he speaks. Just shows up. Sits in the circle. Listens. Absorbs the pattern.

No one pressures. No one asks why he's silent. The space holds him without demanding performance.

When he finally speaks, it's not eloquent. Halting words about what brought him here. The loneliness. The sense that the life he'd built was hollow. The fear that he'd die without anyone really knowing him.

The circle receives it. No gasps. No advice. Just recognition — others nodding, others who'd said similar things, others who know.

He drives home different than he arrived. Not fixed. Not solved. Just slightly less alone than he's been in years.

The unbearable has become slightly more bearable.

Through sharing.

The Architecture

Refuge has structure. Not rules imposed — architecture discovered. Patterns that work, proven through repetition across centuries and contexts.

Safety.
A man says something in the group he's never said out loud. The room doesn't flinch. No one reaches for advice. No one changes the subject. The silence that follows isn't empty — it's holding.

He comes back the next week. Says something harder. The room holds again. This is safety — not safety from challenge, but safety from annihilation. The knowledge that speaking truth won't result in exile. That failure won't mean expulsion. That the relationship will survive the revelation.

This safety isn't automatic. It builds through consistency. Same time, same place, same people showing up regardless of what was said last week. The nervous system learns what the mind takes longer to trust: this space holds.

Difference.

Two people in the group see the world differently. Not politely differently — fundamentally. One is certain about things the other questions. One processes through talk; the other through silence.

The friction is uncomfortable. The impulse is to sort — find people who agree, shed the ones who don't. Build a room where everyone nods.

But a room where everyone nods is a room where no one grows. Agreement feels safer. Agreement produces brittleness. When the first real challenge arrives, the group that practiced only agreement shatters — because it never learned to hold tension.

Real refuge includes people you disagree with — and the disagreement doesn't destroy the container.

Stability.

The first argument in a new community often destroys it. Someone says something. Someone takes offense. The rupture feels fatal. People leave.

The twentieth argument in an established community strengthens it. Rupture happens — repair follows. Rupture again — repair again. Each cycle builds trust that conflict won't be terminal. The scar tissue becomes the strongest part of the bond.

This can't be rushed. Stability develops through repeated repair, not through the absence of conflict. The community that has never fought is the community that hasn't been tested. The community that has fought and survived knows something the untested community doesn't: we can hold this.

Rhythm.

Weekly. Not monthly. Not occasional. Not "when we can make it work."
Six days of accumulation — inputs, pressures, the simulation's daily download. Then processing. Six days of noise. Then digestion.
Monthly gatherings allow too much buildup between processings. By the time the group meets, too much has happened to address. The backlog overwhelms the container. People arrive already saturated and the gathering becomes another source of pressure rather than relief.

Weekly rhythm keeps current. Metabolizes in real time. Prevents the accumulation that fragments communities. The pattern itself does work that intention alone cannot accomplish.

The woman notices the bookstore group has all four elements. Not because they planned it — because what works gets repeated.

The safety developed through months of showing up. The diversity exists naturally — different ages, backgrounds, perspectives. The stability built through small conflicts survived. The rhythm holds at weekly.

No one designed this. They just kept meeting until meeting became architecture.

What Happens Inside

A man shares something he's never told anyone. The group holds it. Doesn't fix. Doesn't advise. Just witnesses.

Weeks later, he realizes: the secret lost its power. Not because he processed it alone — because he processed it witnessed. The shame that required hiding can't survive being seen without rejection.

This is what refuge does that solitude cannot.

The isolation compounds shame. The witness dissolves it.

A woman brings a crisis to the group. Not the managed version — the real one. Marriage ending. Career collapsing. Everything she built coming apart.

The group doesn't rescue her. Can't. The crisis is hers to navigate.

But they do something else. They stay. They check in between meetings. They show up at her door with food she didn't ask for. They sit with her when the waves hit.

The crisis doesn't become smaller. But she doesn't face it alone.

Weight that would crush an individual barely strains a collective.

Testing Together

The man brings a belief to the group. Political. Strongly held. He's never examined it — just absorbed it.

Someone pushes back. Not attacking — questioning. "Help me understand why you see it that way."

His first instinct is defense. This feels like threat. But he's been in the group long enough to know: this isn't threat to belonging. This is testing of belief.

The conversation continues for an hour. His position shifts. Not reversed — nuanced. The certainty softens into something more like conviction-with-humility.

"I still think I'm mostly right about this. But I understand better why reasonable people disagree."

Afterward, he shares a meal with the person who challenged him. The relationship didn't fracture. It deepened.

This is what refuge enables: testing what isolation prevents.

Alone, beliefs calcify. Unchallenged, certainty hardens. Without friction, frameworks become prisons.

Together, beliefs stay flexible. Challenged safely, certainty becomes appropriate confidence. With friction that doesn't destroy, frameworks remain tools rather than identities.

The Grief

Six months into the group, the woman breaks.

Not crisis this time. Just grief. The accumulated losses she'd been outrunning finally catching up. Parents long dead. Dreams long abandoned. Versions of herself she'll never become.

She thought she was past this. Thought the losses were processed.

They weren't. They were stored.

The group holds the grief. No one tries to stop it. No platitudes about silver linings. No rushing toward resolution.

Just presence while the waves move through.

It takes weeks. Some meetings she can barely speak. Others she's functional again. The processing doesn't follow schedule.

The group waits. Stays present. Keeps showing up.

And eventually, the grief integrates. Becomes part of her rather than weight she's carrying. The losses are still real — but they're mourned now rather than defended against.

She couldn't have done this alone.

Not because she's weak. Because humans weren't designed to mourn alone. Grief is communal work. The witness is part of the processing.

Refuge provides the witness.

Becoming Refuge

Here's what isn't obvious from outside:

Sometimes you become refuge before you find it.

A man has no community. No weekly circle. No group that practices what he's recognized. He's practiced alone for two years. Findable, but not yet found.

Then a coworker breaks.

Not dramatically — quietly. The performance slipping. The exhaustion showing through. The careful management of presentation starting to fail.

The man recognizes it. He's been there. Knows what the early stages look like.

He doesn't try to fix it. Doesn't advise. Just stays. Keeps showing up. Asks real questions. Listens without agenda.

The coworker starts talking. Then keeps talking. The isolation cracks. Someone finally sees.

The man didn't find refuge. He became it.

One person. No structure. No weekly meeting. Just presence offered to someone drowning.

This is also how refuge works.

Not always circles and meetings and architecture. Sometimes just one human staying present for another.

A woman notices her neighbor struggling. The signs are subtle — but she's learned to see them. The withdrawal. The lights off too early. The car that doesn't move for days.

She brings food. Not as project — as presence. Sits on the porch. Doesn't push. Just available.

The neighbor starts talking. Then crying. Then talking more.

No community existed for this neighbor. But refuge arrived anyway — in the form of one person who noticed and stayed.

You may find refuge.
You may become refuge.
Often, you'll do both—at different times, for different people.

The design doesn't require buildings and programs. It requires humans willing to see each other and stay.

The Wait

Some reading this will recognize the room immediately. The community exists. The people gather. Walking in is all that's required — and all that's been missing.

Walk in.

Don't overthink it. Don't wait until you're ready. Don't audit the community for perfection before committing. The man who resisted a recovery meeting for two years — too religious, too structured — eventually walked in because loneliness outweighed resistance. He arrived carrying two years of solitary practice. The community was better for it. The waiting wasn't wasted. But the walking in was what changed everything.

If the room exists, enter it.

Others will read this and know: the room doesn't exist yet. The geography is wrong. The options are limited. The visible communities are calcified or captured by simulation logic wearing religious clothing.
This is real. It can't be fixed by pretending otherwise.

But waiting doesn't mean passive. And alone doesn't mean unproductive.

While you wait: the practices continue. The becoming-findable proceeds. And something else begins — you start becoming refuge for whoever crosses your path. The coworker who's struggling. The neighbor whose lights stay off too long. The person in your life who needs someone to stay and not flinch.

You may find refuge.
You may become refuge first.
Often, the second leads to the first.

The timeline varies. What doesn't vary: practicing alone builds the capacity that community will eventually need. No one who practices alone is wasting time.

What Refuge Actually Looks Like

One more thing, because the simulation has one final trick: the fantasy of perfect community.

The communities that function still have conflict. Still have people who annoy each other. Still have failures of care and lapses of attention and moments when the whole thing feels like too much work.

Some meetings are terrible. Some weeks no one has capacity for anyone else. Some seasons the whole group barely holds together.

This isn't failure. This is human.

The fantasy of perfect community is itself a simulation — one that prevents people from accepting actual community with all its friction. The person who waits for the perfect room will wait forever. The person who walks into the imperfect room and stays discovers something the fantasy never delivers: repair is stronger than perfection. The scar tissue becomes the strongest part of the bond.

Refuge works not because the people are perfect but because the architecture holds imperfect people together long enough for the rhythm to do its work.

Show up anyway.
Stay anyway.
Keep practicing even when the practice feels pointless.

The rhythm holds what individuals cannot.
The architecture carries what personalities can't.
Find community if you can.
Become community while you wait.
And when refuge appears — imperfect, frustrating, human — walk in.

You were never meant to carry this alone.

Walking Home

You wake up.

Not exhausted this time—just awake.

The phone still glows on the nightstand. The notifications still accumulate. The constructed reality still hums around you, doing what it was designed to do.

But something has shifted.

You can see it now.

The feed scrolls—but you recognize the pattern. The anxiety arrives—but you know its architecture. The urgency screams—but you hear the merchant behind the voice.

The simulation is still running.
You're just not running its code anymore.

This is what waking up actually feels like.

Not transcendence. Not escape. Not sudden perfection or permanent peace.

Just... seeing.

The false layer becomes transparent. The profitable story reveals itself as story. The prison shows its edges—and edges can be walked through.

You're still here. Still paying rent. Still dealing with the same systems, the same pressures, the same people.

But you move differently now.
Less frantic. More present. Like you're not in the same race everyone else is running.
Because you're not.

You've found the exit the Introduction promised. It was exactly where it said it would be—waiting beneath the noise, preserved by those who remember, available to those who seek.

And now you understand: the exit isn't a door you walk through once.

It's a direction you keep walking.

Two questions echo across every human life. The same questions that followed the first humans out of the garden. The same questions that pursued every generation since.

Where are you?

The honest answer, now:

Here. Present to what's real. Seeing through the construction. Practicing what works when everything else fails.

Not arrived — oriented. Not finished — begun. Not escaped — returning.

You know your location now. Not geographically — internally. The coordinates are different. The map has been redrawn.

You're walking toward what's true, away from what's always been false.

That's enough. That's everything.

Where is your brother?

This question prevents the first from becoming private enlightenment.

Your brother is everywhere. The barista performing for rent. The driver terrified of being late. The neighbor whose lights stay off too long. The family member absorbed in ideology. The stranger on the screen, reduced to category.

Each one carrying weight. Each one inside their own simulation. Each one potentially reachable — if someone stays present long enough.

They're walking too. Somewhere. Maybe nearby, maybe distant. Maybe visible, maybe not yet.
But walking. Also capable of waking. Also returning, even if they don't know it yet.

And maybe —eventually— keeping the same rhythm. Because the design is plural. The day wants we, not just me. The full practice waits for others to share it.

You're becoming what you needed when you were lost: someone who stops, who sees, who stays. Someone who holds the door.

Even if you're the only one you know who sees this.
Especially then.

Remember what the Introduction promised?

That friend who deleted everything and seems... lighter.
That professor who laughs at what everyone else fears.
That neighbor who has people over every Friday night—actual people, actual food, actual laughter that carries through the walls.

They do know a secret.

You're one of them now.

Not because you're special. Because you're awake enough to see the pattern and willing enough to stop running it.

Others are walking too. You may not see them yet. They may be years away from crossing your path. But they exist.

In every generation, some have seen through. Some have practiced the design. Some have kept the thread intact across impossible conditions.

The remnant persists. Scattered but real. The thread continues. Thin but unbroken.

You'll find them. Or they'll find you. Or you'll recognize each other in the way you move — less anxious, more present, carrying weight but not carrying it alone.

And when you do, you'll understand: this was never about individual awakening. It was always about walking each other home.

This book ends.
Your walk continues.

The simulation will still be there tomorrow. The merchants will still be selling. The algorithms will still be optimizing. The fear will still be circulating.

But you'll move through it differently.
Seeing doesn't make the simulation stop. It makes you stop mistaking it for reality.

The gap between impulse and action has widened. Choice has become possible where only reaction existed before. That gap is everything.

The practices work. The rhythm holds. The weight distributes when finally shared.

Six days of accumulation. One day of release. This isn't metaphor—it's how you stay human inside systems designed to make you otherwise. The rhythm that held others in Babylon will hold you now. Not because you believe it should. Because the nervous system needs what the nervous system needs.

And each week, the memorial: What actually happened these seven days? The specifics that break the lie. The evidence that accumulates until "nothing ever changes" can no longer survive what you've recorded.

Fifty-two weeks from now, you'll have fifty-two witnesses against the doom. That's not hope. That's architecture.

Truth is what remains when frameworks fall away. And it's been there all along — waiting beneath the noise, preserved by those who remember, available to those who seek.

You found it.

Not because this book gave it to you.
Because it was always yours — just buried under layers of empire, beneath generations of fear, behind centuries of extraction.

Now you've remembered.

The Presence that walked in the garden still walks. Still asks. Still waits for response.

Where are you?

Walking home.

Where is your brother?

Walking too.

The door you found? Keep it open.
The path you're on? Others will join you.
The weight you're carrying? It was never meant to be carried alone.

Walk humbly — you don't have all the answers and weren't meant to.
Walk faithfully — the practices work whether you feel them working or not.
Walk together — even when together means trusting that others walk unseen.

The exit was always here.
Now you've finally seen it.

Welcome home.